Charles A... *Reece*

TRAVELS WIT

Where the search began.
Alice and Charles at Aberdare Cemetery, spring 1999.

This book is dedicated to no other than

Alice

Edited by Bourke A. Le Carpentier

Overleaf: Where the search began. *Photography by Wayne Hankins*

We had been camping in our caravan at the Country Park and had gone to the Old Cemetery to meet Wayne Hankins who was going to photograph Mother Shepherd's grave which had been restored again. Wayne, at the last, suggested a photograph of ourselves. It was twenty years since we had begun our search there. What a lot had happened since.

The cemeteries of the South Wales Valleys are huge, even reflecting that half of the people left their stricken mining villages and towns following the terrible slump in coal following World War I. It is the death and injuries which was the true cost of coal over the preceding 100 years. When life was so cheap and death was the grim reaper met with every day when a man went down into the depths of the earth with just a lamp, pick and a shovel. The hope of eternity took hold as the last hope in the Revivals of John Wesley in the 18th Century and later the 1859 and 1904 Welsh 'Awakenings'. The masses of graves, like those of the battlefields are a silent reminder of the faith of those in another and better world to come.

ISBN 0 9513092 1 8

Printed by A McLay & Co Ltd
Longwood Drive
Forest Farm
Cardiff CF4 7ZB

TRAVELS WITH ALICE

Contents

Travels With Alice

The author: Charles Aaron Preece is a retired probation officer with 25 years' experience in London Prisons, Magistrates and Crown Courts. His business life changed after discovering the interest of his great-grandmother in prisoners and their families. A Salvationist for over 40 years, following a wonderful experience of conversion during the 1955 Billy Graham Crusade in Glasgow, Charles was on Aircrew duties with the R.A.F. during the Second World War, is married to Alice who has accompanied and supported him on most of his research. They have three daughters, six grandchildren and four great-grandchildren.

Any further information can be obtained from Charles A. Preece, 43 Ulleswater Road, Southgate, London, N14 7BL. Tel 020 8886 0573, 020 882 1021, Mobile 077 10 287 708.

With acknowledgments to South Wales Argus

Alice served with the NATIONAL FIRE SERVICE on 24-hour Watch (Control) Room Duty during World War II and as a telephone operator, at a large North London Station. With two colleagues she was responsible for sounding the alarm bells which brought the firemen sliding down the pole from their canteen three stories up. They would race for their appliances pulling on their jackets as they went. Calls would come in from the street fire alarms, the Police, Air Raid Protection Wardens and members of the Public. The Ambulance Service also had to be alerted. On her rest days she cycled to her home where she cared for her father. After the War, Alice was awarded the Defence Medal.

Acknowledgements

It is not easy at the end of ten years research to make proper tribute to all those who have helped me. In such a personal work as this I would not wish anyone to feel that they had not been remembered. Individual letters of appreciation will be written when the book comes to be sent out.

Alice in her Welsh Costume

FOREWORD

I HAVE NOT found it easy to write this book. When I was preparing my previous book, the story of my great-grandmother, Pamela (Mother) Shepherd, it was her story and I only had to relate it. One of my probation colleagues, it was, however who said about the present book, "but it's not your story". This book is more our story but it came about because of her. Without her being, I do not know what I would have been. I have tried to live out, I feel in some measure, what she might have done in different days. I feel that her influence has been very real. She was above all else a "Jesus only" woman and Christ has shone out of her life.

Pamela Shepherd's great key to the hearts of her people was her ordinariness. You can't be more ordinary, more down to earth than a washerwoman and a rag-sorter. Yet Psalm 68:13 says

"Though ye have lien among the pots yet shall ye be as the wings of a dove covered with silver and her feathers with yellow gold."

Through trying to write about her, I caught something of that vision and it lead me to places of which I had never dreamed.

My hope is that my plain account will lead other plain men and women to place their hand in that of the Almighty, that they may realise the wonders that the Lord has in store for them.

The ten years which went into the preparation, the research, the practical outworking of Woman of the Valleys was shared with my wife Alice who unstintingly supported and encouraged me to write what she too felt was a record of a wonderful experience.

Southgate, London, March Millennium Year 2000.

Dinas Mountain behind St Mary's church where Dick Penderyn, Martyr of South Wales, is buried.

Aberfan. The price of coal. Just some of the children's graves.

Chapter 1

MAN ON A MOUNTAIN

A CHILL WIND WHISTLED around me on Dinas Mountain, high above my hometown of Port Talbot, in South Wales. It was a bleak January day in 1957, a few days after Christmas. From somewhere, came the melancholy bleating of sheep. Hundreds of feet below me, the grey streets of little terraced houses were squeezed together between the distant, sombre sea, the docks and the foot of the mountain. Port Talbot was a steel town, which never seemed to sleep. It throbbed with life and industry, pulsating without ceasing. From time to time, the night skies blazed like fiery Northern Lights when the furnaces were opened and the molten metal cascaded into the darkness. Far away was the crash of a mechanical hammer, thumping methodically. There were hisses and clangs, the rumble of lorries unloading, all the noise of a huge steelworks, dominating everything.

"I've had to come away from that dynamo of life, that tumult of mind-shattering heaviness to ask myself some questions," I told myself. I hardly wanted to start thinking. That great earth-shaking hammer seemed to have flattened me. Rattling furiously along its narrow band of steel, an express train hurtled over the rails towards London, 200 miles away. Tomorrow morning, my wife, three daughters and an unborn child would be on that train. We had only enough money for a fortnight, no place of our own in which to stay and no certainty of a job when we got there. Twenty years earlier, like Dick Whittington, as a boy of 16, I had gone on that express because there was no work in the town for a school-leaving teenager and not much money for my parents to keep a growing lad and three little ones as well. Sooner or later, we youngsters all had to go from the Wales of impoverishment, of long dole-queues of shabby men, to find a job, any kind of job, somewhere, anywhere. Now I was a man of 36.

I got up from the broken wall on which I was sitting and made my way to the very top of the mountain. On the summit, there was a triangulation pillar, used for survey purposes. It was a plain, concrete obelisk about four feet high, nothing special, just a level stand, I supposed, for surveying instruments. "Was there not an urgent, burning need to take a look back on my recent life, to obtain some new bearings myself, to map out the future, as obscure as the valleys of Glamorgan up there in the mists?" I was not sure whether I was thinking or talking aloud to myself. The small grey column could perhaps be some kind of altar, perhaps, in my confusion. I thought that I would kneel there for a moment and ask for some kind of guidance for the uncertain days which lay ahead. "God help me," I thought. "I'm desperate."

Upward from the dull depths of the town, like some kind of sweet incense floated "Onward Christian Soldiers" being played by an unseen Salvation Army Band. "Strange" I reflected. "Of course, it's Sunday afternoon." I remembered my great-grandmother Shepherd who had died up there in the Valleys, in Aberdare, 25 years previously. She had been someone important in The Salvation Army but I did not know much more than that. "Now where was I? How did I come to be in this unbelievable situation?" Like the slow playback of a film, the high points of the past two years came into focus, one by one, like magic lantern slides, conjured up without effort by the vivid imprints into my mind. "Similar to Scrooge", I smiled wryly.

The first picture was a drizzling, dark March evening in 1955, outside the red sandstone Kelvin Hall in Glasgow. I was in a queue of mostly middle-aged women; it seemed, waiting a long time to get in to hear the evangelist Billy Graham. The whole city was turning out to hear him. I had felt curious. I also felt rather self-conscious, being the only man around there. A newsboy glanced at me, in an odd way, I thought, then went along the line calling out 'Crusade Special!' There was a low hum of conversation from the women. I wished my wife had been there with me. I would not have felt so conspicuous. Alice had wanted me to go to Haringey Arena when the preacher had been in London, near where we were living then, the previous year.

"I don't want to hear a red-hot gospeller from America telling us how to live" I had retorted. The truth had been that I was somehow afraid of what I might hear about myself - moral failure, man of the world. Now it was different. The business, which I had built up over seven years, was on the point of collapsing. On the face of it, that night, I had a splendid new job as a well-paid representative for a Manchester firm, an expense account, good hotel accommodation, a new car, nothing to worry about. But something within me was shaken. The self-confidence, which had driven me successfully ahead over the years, was strangely gone. There was a puzzling emptiness inside me. I had wandered into a church a few weeks before, to hear a minister say in a broad Scots accent "He that humbleth himself shall be exalted and he that exalteth himself shall be abased". I do not know what else the man said. I could not get those words out of my mind. I felt as though I had been found guilty and sentenced in some court of law.

I certainly felt I had been brought low. I tightened my heavy fawn Crombie greatcoat around me in the raw dampness of the night. I felt a curious sense of anticipation, of expectancy, of something going to happen.

Then I did not mind being the only man in a queue of women. The main auditorium was full by the time we got in and I found myself in an annexe of some kind where apparently a circus was normally staged. It was painted up, in part, still like a circus, with garish boxes. With the buzz of 5,000 people around me and only a blank, closed-circuit television screen to look at, I wondered what I was going to get out of this peculiar place. Then a song, which I did not know, 'Trust and Obey' was announced and the atmosphere suddenly changed. The organ music was lively and the singing seemed enthusiastic and homely. I began to feel more relaxed and to enjoy a new kind of experience far removed from the 'churchy' kind of meeting which I had expected.

I can remember very little of what followed. There was a moment, I recall, when Billy Graham held up his Bible in one hand, and followed it with his eyes and recited:

"-EYE HATH NOT SEEN, NOR EAR HEARD, NEITHER HAVE ENTERED INTO THE HEART OF MAN, THOSE THINGS WHICH GOD HATH PREPARED FOR THOSE THAT LOVE HIM." "This man really believes what he is saying," I told myself. Part of my critical business instinct was looking for the 'catch' part in all this. He seemed genuine, different, simple. I could not remember hearing a man talking like this before.

Towards the end of the address, he said people should come forward if they felt that God was speaking to them. There was a curious thumping of my heart. I could feel my pulse racing. It was an emotion I had never known before. I found myself lifted out of my seat and next thing; I was standing down at the front, by the screen, alone.

I spoke to a man who seemed to be some kind of official. "I am answering the call". I did not know what else to say. He pointed towards a doorway and I walked into a large room, full of empty chairs. I paused, then a line of people started filtering in from the main hall and so I joined them and sat down.

A young man wearing a red blazer with a Bible College badge, who appeared to be some kind of student, sat down beside me and began to talk. Then he asked me to pray. I could not remember ever having done so since I was a child, except to recite from the Book of Common Prayer, but when I tried, it seemed to come naturally enough, in a clumsy way. I admitted the sinfulness and unworthiness of my life as best I could, which burdened my mind, and then asked God for "The peace which passeth all understanding." A dimly remembered phrase from my distant Sunday-School days.

My young counsellor seemed to have some difficulty with me after that. I did not feel so religious about it all somehow. In fact, I felt somewhat

3

in a daze altogether. Unnoticed by me, my young friend, had, put up his arm, indicating that he needed some help himself and this signal brought an elderly clergyman along. He calmly heard me relate how such expressions as 'The Blood of the Lamb' did not mean very much to me and how indeed I simply could not understand most of what was being said.

His strong Scottish voice was measured and sure. "Do you feel that something has happened to you tonight?" he asked quietly. "Oh yes", I replied. "Hold on to that then " he told me "and don't worry about what you don't understand". That was all and I left.

Outside the Kelvin Hall, I instinctively brought out my silver cigarette case and Ronson lighter, my inseparable lifestyle equipment. I had been several hours without a smoke. I would never have lasted that long in the usual way. I was hopelessly dependent upon cigarettes. Without them, even when I tried, I soon became reduced to a tense, nervous man whose hands trembled and whose brain seemed to stop functioning. I did not seem to be able to think straight. Only a deep intake of nicotine would calm me down. Life without the prospect of a cigarette was just a grey horror, a kind of hell of nerve jangling, near-explosion from normality, ready to erupt without the sedation of tobacco.

I had been smoking for the past 20 years and then more heavily and dependently since that first crash in the RAF during the war when I lay awake all night, in the hut, smoking continuously. Before that night, it had just

Hooked on cigarettes. The Author. Coastal Command, 86 Squadron, North Coates.

seemed a harmless, pleasurable habit. Afterwards, my nervous system seemed to have locked on to cigarettes in a sinister, addictive way. I remembered that first flight, the day, after the 'prang'. As we took off, I had felt as weak as water in the gun turret and suddenly realised what flying could mean. There were years of it ahead, if I survived that long. No wonder I had become unwittingly hooked on a substance which brought some kind of relief from intolerable stress.

Now I stared at the cigarettes in my opened case. I had gone for them automatically but it burst in on my mind that I simply had no desire to smoke. "I had not consciously prayed for help in there," I thought, as I stood on the pavement, a curious figure of a man who must have looked as though he was transfixed. It seemed as if God had read my mind anyway. There was no sense of need, no tension, just a great feeling of peace within me. It did not make sense. It was unbelievable. I was dumbfounded. My mind was reeling as I put the cigarette case back in my pocket, got on a clanging Glasgow tram and went wonderingly back to the hotel.

The next morning the porter brought my usual pot of tea. After a sip, without thinking I reached for my cigarettes, handy as always, on the bedside locker. But I realised that I did not feel like a smoke. I lay back on my pillow. This was incredible. I always had a fag first thing in the morning. Apart from the time when I had been ill in hospital with meningitis, in Cairo, during the war, I had been smoking since I was 16. My mind flew back to the Kelvin Hall last night. What on earth had happened there? I gave up trying to figure it out.

Only one thing was certain, I seemed to have lost my craving for cigarettes. I used to carry a box of 50 around with me in those days. When I was out on my business calls that day it was quickly observed that I was offering my cigarettes as usual but not smoking myself and so the questions soon came. I could only tell people that since I had been to the Kelvin Hall the night before, I just did not want to smoke. "It was a miracle." I said. I seemed to have been cured. A few days ago, I would have gone crazy without a cigarette.

Talking about Billy Graham somehow did not seem like talking religion. I felt I simply had to know more about what was going on in the Crusade meetings but how to get inside was the problem, with the barrier of those endless hours of long queues being the only way to get in. I remembered that the minister in the Church of Scotland at Broom which I had started attending had said that stewards were required. So, next night, I went along, and walked purposefully to an entrance marked "Stewards". A man sitting at a makeshift table hardly looked up as he handed me a badge. I was in. I could not believe it. For a few weeks after that, I helped with the collections, showed people to their seats, gave out songbooks and once helped to carry out an old lady who had fainted!

So this had been my 'conversion', I thought as the time went by and I still did not want to smoke. It was the religious experience I had wondered about, yet when the moment had come it had seemed so natural. I had gone to see Mr. James Christie the old minister at Broom, shortly afterwards to tell him of my Kelvin Hall experience.

I felt that I was doing God a good turn, somehow. The dear man dropped to his knees in his study in the manse, to thank God for what had happened to me. A sense of awe came over me. I felt cut down to size and the only place for me, too, was on my knees. I wondered what was happening to me.

Some days later, Mr. Campbell, the Baptist minister who had told me to "just hold on to the bits which I did understand", invited me to speak at his church about my new life. When I found myself on a platform, my legs shook. What did I have to say after all? Only that I had stopped smoking somehow and felt at peace with myself in a marvellous new way. Hardly a sermon! And it would not take long to say that little piece, I thought.

The people started to sing a hymn which I hadn't heard before, 'Send The Light' and the surging lilt of the music carried me away so that I could hardly stop talking, once I had started. After I had spoken, a young man came up to me with a kind of bright light in his eyes. I had gone quietly to a corner of the church to think about something which Mr. Campbell had prayed for me: "AS FAR AS THE EAST IS FROM THE WEST, SO FAR HATH HE REMOVED OUR SINS FROM US, TO REMEMBER THEM NO MORE." The young chap wanted to talk. I took him to Mr. Campbell. I felt curiously elated - in fact, an older man mentioned something about being careful not to get carried away by my feelings. It was shortly after this, that my new-found exhilaration was suddenly brought down to earth.

I had flown down to Lancashire to the works. My new boss (whom I shall call Henry) was a man I had known for several years. The agency I had developed with him had been successful and profitable and we had become good business colleagues on first names terms. I had stayed with him and his wife in their private house. Then a major investment I had made with a friend, manufacturing a new kind of road-roller in the contractors' side of my business had failed when the Korean War broke out and we ran into critical production problems for vital parts. To prevent the complete collapse of my business, I suggested that I should go to Scotland for him, a territory in which he was interested.

The matter of settling in Scotland, involved selling our house in

London and finding a property near Glasgow where I was to establish an office. I did so, in the form of a new but unfinished bungalow standing in two thirds of an acre of ground, in the suburb of Whitecraigs, a choice residential area. Henry sent me a cheque for £2,000, which I needed as a bridging loan with a "good luck" note. My intention was to gradually realise the sale of my stock and repay those who had invested in my firm. With my working capital gone, I could not continue to run my business although there should be sufficient assets to repay the shareholders. I had no creditors as such. It seemed a good solution to an unfortunate situation. It was a bitter pill, however. I had been proud of my little business, which I had built up from nothing over seven years, and of being my own boss.

I could see that it would not be quite the same again. Now, however, my whole world had become new and my smoking problem had vanished. I felt ready for anything in the business world. My thrill of the Glasgow meetings which were indeed, something everybody was talking about in Scotland, was naturally the subject of much of my conversation. In Manchester, then, I tried to let Henry know about my new-found faith. We were both heavy smokers and in his office, he pushed his desktop box of cigarettes across to me in the usual way.

"Thanks, Henry, but I've been able to stop smoking - an amazing thing has happened to me, at the Kelvin Hall... It was a Billy Graham Crusade meeting" I began to explain. There was a heavy silence. The reaction surprised me. Most people shrugged or grinned when I had to say that I was not smoking any more. After what seemed a long time Henry said "Charles, I hope you won't take this religious matter too far. One of my competitors down here even holds a midday meeting in his works." Suddenly, I felt a cloud come down between us. He drew heavily on his cigarette. I had already told him previously that I had decided to stop drinking for a while, as it seemed to affect me sometimes.

The two attributes of a salesman were to mix easily with clients and not to stick out too much like a sore thumb. Indeed, these two aspects of communication were considered very necessary. Now Henry saw that I had abandoned both. I returned to Scotland with a premonition that things had gone terribly wrong. In the event, after speaking to Mr. Christie, Henry accepted my undertaking not to jeopardise, as he seemed to see it, my business potential with religious talk. Although feeling that I had been restrained, I settled down to a solid stint for the next two years, determined to show that I was a good salesman as well as a Christian.

Everything seemed to go so well. The two older girls, Margaret and Christine, went to a local private school as we were some distance from State schools. They wore smart brown uniforms of which they were proud. Little Pauline, our ray of sunshine was too young for school but looked forward to it eagerly and not to be outdone in this exciting new life adopted as her uniform a nurse's outfit, (a Christmas present,) which she wore daily while awaiting her own schooldays. Another proud part of her wardrobe was one of her sisters' ties with broad horizontal stripes, which was carefully knotted by Alice daily as an indication of her scholastic plans. In the meantime, Pauline loved tracking purposefully into Glasgow with Alice, sometimes in the snow, to look fondly at the big green-and white toadstool and camp equipment in the Guide shop. Alice who had never even been a Brownie took training to become a Guide Captain in answer to a call for a leader from our Church of Scotland at Broom. Alice was very proud of the fact that her Guide Company produced the ultimate standard in several Queen's Guides, one of whom was later to be Christine.

We had fun at home while I ranged far and wide over Scotland, somehow managing to get back each Thursday evening for a Christian Endeavour meeting for the children. The ground around the house enabled us to have a tent erected, a campfire, and 'Sausage Sizzles'. Between us, we had quite a youth programme going. Through the Christian Endeavour, we linked up with a beautiful holiday home called Ardeneden in the lovely Kyles of Bute. From a vantage point on a hillside, high over the estuary of the Clyde, a retired sea captain had said to me proudly, "Man, I've voyaged the world but there's never such a view as this". Bonny, bonny Argyle. So we sailed down the Clyde on the 'Waverley' one of the famous paddle steamers, with the rolling green banks on either side, lilting accordionists playing on the decks until we arrived at Tighnabruaich pier and smelt the seaweed-strewn rocks, 'the tangle of the Isles'. Later, we formed a gospel choir, with a tambourine as our only musical accompaniment and entertained the steamers which brought our holiday guests, then marched away to the house which revelled in its parties, charades and outings.

There was the magic of the sunsets behind the islands, the silver sands of the hidden, unspoilt beaches, the freshness, the forest walks, the tumbling streams, the gaiety of it all. I remember 12 year old Margaret confidently at the wheel of a fishing boat out in the Kyles and realised that she was growing up. All the teenagers had a record catch which we took back and fried after a singsong in the hold. If this was revival, it was a taste of heaven, a bit of Eden itself. Everyone seemed to be our friend. Life was full, even exhausting but felt like one long holiday through the summer months looking after the stream of visitors. There was a sense of purpose which we had not known before. Ardeneden cast a spell over all who came and there were many romances to its credit.

We were asked to be house parents at a Children's Special Service Mission at Crail, a little fishing harbour on the Fife Coast, near St. Andrews, and were thrilled to be part of the team of brilliant young University students who prepared lively meetings on the beach. There was singing all the time: on the cliff walks, down at the harbour square, at the railway station when we farewelled some of the group, and in the house where we all lived as one happy family. For the four children we had with us, it was a thrilling experience and another dimension of Christian life. It was all so wonderful in the warm after-glow of the Crusade which had set Scotland alight.

Our big white bungalow was next to a farm, on high ground looking out over the twinkling lights of Glasgow by night, and by day, the Campsie Fells, north of the city and sometimes, when it was clear, Ben Lomond. There was a rippling burn at the bottom of the long garden where a stand of trees sounded like the sea when the winds blew the branches and rustled the leaves. Alice's Dad came from London and started digging for a vegetable garden. We planted scores of Douglas firs and masses of Livingstone daisies on our rockery. Our little estate began to take shape. We had mostly large, well-kept houses and gardens around us and soon made friends with our neighbours, who had brought us flowers when we first moved in.

We tried to start our days by reading the little Bagster-family book of Bible readings, 'Daily Light' when we had had our breakfast. Grace usually consisted of one of the choruses we'd learnt on the Beach Mission. If we ever forgot, which happened sometimes when, as new Christians all, we were in too much of a hurry for Alice's porridge, we had a strict overseer in Pauline, a 3-year old tot in a highchair who, a spoon upright in each hand would sternly order "Say Grace!"

At home in Kelvin, we had fun around the roaring open fire in our 30 foot long lounge. The family visited us from London and Wales, and admired our spacious Scottish home although by now we were on a rather tight budget, with the increasing costs of installing ourselves.

Mr. Christie, that lovely, level-headed man who had come out of retirement in England to take charge of our new, little local church had once led a prayer group in our home. We had sung "The Lord's My Shepherd" because we didn't have enough song books and everybody knew it. After playing the piano, Mr. Christie had spoken to us then had fallen to his knees in the middle of us all, laughing and weeping at the same time "I've been overcome by my own message" he smiled through his tears. Of such stuff was 'Kelvin'.

Pauline's main Christmas present one year was a metal red-and-white rocking-horse named 'Foxhunter' which Alice ordered from a catalogue. I remember Alice riding it by way of demonstration while we all stood around cheering. It remained a trusted family member until it rode into the nursery of the Salvation Army Hoxton Goodwill Centre in London where I am sure it found a worthy stable.

There was a tolerance in Scotland born out of the old covenanting days, I found, so long as one was open and clear about one's religious convictions. What businessmen did not like was humbug. A man had his right to his own views. They thought, even if these seemed mighty strange to them. I came to love Scotland and its democratic ways, its rugged independence. I heard Billy Graham say once that next to his own country and home town, he would like to live in Glasgow. Perhaps he was just being kind, I thought, but I felt the same way. It was a rough and tough city in many ways but it had a beating heart and a warmth of its very own. "It's the friendliest place in the world", a stranger said to me in the street, "but you have to make the first move". I found that it was true. As a stranger to the city, there was an initial reserve, which evaporated on the instant once the ice was broken. It was a lesson I tried to take with me for the rest of my life.

One day, I came across a man who related how he could go into the City Hall, put his head around the door of the office of the First Citizen of Glasgow, the Provost, whom he had known and say "Hello, Bobbie - how are you? I wouldn't go in to bother him, mind - he's a busy man now but it's great to be able to do that, isn't it?" said the man.

Around this time, too, there was a City-wide campaign to stamp out T.B. in the United Kingdom. At strategic points in the streets, mobile X-ray units were stationed and there were queues at every one. The reward for spending some time in being checked was a little yellow badge with the slogan 'A SPLIT SECOND TO SAVE A LIFE'. The campaign was a marvellous success.

Glasgow seemed to be a fantastic place for wonderful happenings. It was a new world to me in many ways. The very trees seemed greener   as Spring came to Scotland to match the Springtime in my heart. Now I felt like a bird let out of a cage. I flung myself into this new world of purpose, of vital, warm relationships with people.

I had been given my own moment of truth, even before the Crusade. Shortly before the Kelvin Hall experience I had decided I was not going to drink for six months. I did not consider that I had an alcohol problem and hardly knew what an alcoholic was, except that such were the destitute men who sometimes begged for money on the side of Glasgow's River Clyde. I had been drinking since a youth but could never remember being drunk although I knew about occasional hangovers and had felt bad about some of my behaviour after I had been drinking. I told myself that I always knew when to stop. However, this belief had been rudely shattered.

I had been entertaining a group of salesmen in the bar of my hotel and having a cold at the time, someone suggested a "Whisky Mac", a mixture of whisky and ginger wine. I was anxious that night. I wanted to get these men to cooperate with me in my sales drive in Glasgow. I had to get results, orders to send back to Manchester, to prove to Henry what I could do. The drinks came fast. I certainly had many more than ever before. It was not until my friends suggested moving on to a club on board a ship on the Clyde, and I had to send a porter up to my room, for my big coat, that I realised I was hardly in control of my limbs. Yet I was perfectly conscious of what was happening. It was if something had taken control of me physically and I was powerless.

Out in the bitter night, by the rough, cobbled side of the river, I got out of the car and the cold cut into me. "Go ahead on your own," I told the men. "I'm not feeling too good. Leave me here in the car for a bit." After some hesitation, they left me. I got out of the car again and sunk to my knees on the snowy ground. My head seemed to be on fire. I scooped the crisp snow off the stones and held it to my burning forehead. "What a sight, I must be!" I thought. "I'm glad my wife isn't here to see me. Not much of a successful man, like this, Crombie coat and all".

Then I was conscious that out of the night a woman had appeared, with a little girl holding her hand. She stood silently for a moment, looking down at me, then asked in a strong Glasgow accent, "Are ye all reet then?" "No, I'm not all right" I thought to myself, "I'm all wrong." However, I managed to gasp "Thank you Missus. I'll be all right in a minute." And she went, with the little girl looking back at me, kneeling on the ground.

My mates returned soon afterwards. They knew that I was in trouble and took me back to the hotel. The next morning, I had the worst headache I had ever known. It seemed to last for two days. It was a frightening experience. It was something more than 'one over the eight.' There had been no railing by the river. Just a quayside. And the black water below. Supposing I had stumbled into the Clyde, that night. I had been helplessly incapable, literally paralysed with alcohol, plain drunk. In my full-length, heavy greatcoat, I would have sunk like a stone, with no one to hear on that dark, deserted, icy corner of the Glasgow waterfront. I felt I was the biggest failure of all. I decided then, that I had better not drink for a while. There had been one or two other occasions of late when I seemed to have lost control, when somehow I couldn't stop. At the same time, I could not see it working out. Drinking with customers was part of the warp and weft of my work as a salesman. I would never do business without drinking. Then came the acid test.

Angus Cameron (not his real name) was the boss of a transport concern on the Scottish Border. I told a fellow salesman that I was going to call on him. "You'd better get down there early", he shot at me. "That man drinks a bottle of whisky before lunch". Accordingly, I set out from home at 6 a.m. and at 9 o'clock was knocking at his office door.

"You Glasgow fellows get up in the morning" he grunted. "You'll be wanting to talk about those trailers, I suppose. Come on then, let's take a walk down to the yard," and he closed the office door behind him. A woman was outside her cottage as we passed and he stopped to enquire, in a friendly way, about her husband who was off work. He seemed a good sort of man. I liked his open way of speaking. He was a pretty important employer too. "Let's go and have a drink" he said. "But the pubs aren't open yet!" I answered quickly. My hopes of getting on with the business, beginning to fade. "That's all right " he replied, "I know the landlord of a place around the corner."

Like a lamb being led to the slaughter, I followed him to the back door of a small back-street pub where a stocky, tough little Scot opened up in response to Cameron's quiet knock, and let us silently into his only bar. It was not much of a place. Drinking was the only business that went on there. The chairs were still piled on the tables from the night before and a smell of stale smoke hung heavily in the dusty air. The Landlord had been sweeping out.

He put away his broom and, without a word, went behind the counter, brought out a bottle of whisky and poured Cameron a tumbler, best part full. Then he turned to me and in a broad Lowland accent said matter-of-factly, "What will ye have?"

My heart sank. If I refused, I would offend Cameron. I could say goodbye to the business for which I'd come a hundred miles. Also to all the future prospects with him and the other bosses, used to settling their business ritually over the whisky bottle. I would be committing commercial suicide in refusing. This was what Henry had feared. Yet, if I went back on my intention, I'd be regarding myself as a man of straw.

It seemed an eternity while I stood there at the bar. I was aware that the little Scot and Cameron were looking at me curiously. At last, hovering on saying "Just a half..." I found my voice. I just about choked "If you don't mind, Mr. Cameron, I've decided not to drink for a while." It sounded very lame, even to me and I stood there miserably.

Cameron put down his glass, looked at the landlord and in an astonished voice demanded "Did you ever hear of a man coming into a pub to do business and then not wanting to drink?"

I wondered what the little man would say. He couldn't afford to upset his best customer, either. The publican looked steadily at his patron. "Mr. Cameron ... if he doesn't want to drink, he's none the worse a man for that," he said. Then turning to me asked, "What would you like then?"

"A lemonade, please," I gasped gratefully. So, it was the publican in a plain little Scots pub who started me on the road to freedom from, what for me anyway, was something which had so damaged my life. It was a humbling thought that I was to keep in mind for the next 40 years of total abstinence. As for Angus Cameron, hard-drinking man that he may have been, he too helped to launch me on that road and for that I was ever grateful. He swallowed his whisky and said, "You are a strange one. You've come a long way though, so I'd better give you an order. Let's go back to the office." There he doubled the business for which I'd hoped.

I drove back to Glasgow in a very sober and reflective mood. I would need to be frank and forthright about my decision not to drink. If I had told Cameron at the beginning, I might not have found myself in the pub situation at all. Also normally, I would not have had much time for the everyday kind of man who ran that little pub. Yet without his plucky view of someone he didn't even know and perhaps didn't agree with, I would have been overwhelmed. I'd met with another kind of Robbie Burns: 'A man's a man for aw that...' And that good fellow, Angus Cameron -. Was there any way of helping him? His business was bound to suffer in the end. He couldn't keep on drinking at that rate. What a pity.

One of the ministers who counselled me at the Kelvin Hall was a tall, broad-shouldered Scot, the Rev. John McIntyre, a soft, Gaelic-speaking Highlander of the United Free Church of Scotland - the "Wee Free" as it was popularly called. It had chosen to remain independent from the State Church of Scotland at a time when they had had to decide whether to exist without State support or not. It had meant something at the time when the Covenanters had gone out into the moors, churchless and penniless but with consciences clear of the abuses of the time. It seemed drastic to me, from what I understood, but I recognised an uncompromising holding to the truth as they saw it. Their simple unwavering faith was something I was to experience when I was invited to stay with John and his family as their guests at the Manse in Falkirk, an industrial town about an hour's drive from Glasgow.

Living in a hotel, I missed my family at weekends in particular, so I was pleased to accept the MacIntyres's hospitality. Also, I wondered how these Christian folk lived behind the scenes, as it were. I felt I wanted to know more. The focal point of their home seemed to be their handicapped daughter Sybil, who was about 15 at the time. She sat all day, paralysed, in her chair

13

except when John carried her up to bed at night,   on   his   back. Everything had to be done for her. She could not speak but her bright eyes were alive with intelligence and light. Sybil could have been in a home for permanently, incurable handicapped children but the McIntyres felt that God had given Sybil to them to be loved and cared for and not put aside in this way. It was an extraordinary example of Christian belief in action. My own life, in the world of commerce, seemed very shallow in comparison.

The next revelation was what happened after breakfast. Grace before meals I had known since a child in the little Welsh village of Pontrhydyfen where I was born. I think we were only about 5 or 6 at the time when, with my cousins we had sat around the little cottage table and chanted:

> *"Be present at our table Lord,*
> *Be here and everywhere adored,*
> *These mercies bless and grant that we*
> *May feast in Paradise with Thee."*

The grace never varied. It seemed to be the only one we knew but it was something significant to our young minds. Over all the years between, it had not been part of our life. This particular first morning, after the children had gone to school, John read the scriptures. Then, he and Mrs. McIntyre, just got down on their knees in the kitchen and began to pray. This seemed peculiar. However, my mind did fly back to an occasion when I had been home on leave while in the RAF. Our parish priest at the time, Rev. Dewi Morgan, later to become very well known as the Rector of St. Brides, Fleet Street in London, had suggested a word of prayer before he left. No one had ever prayed like that in our home before. We thought that we were Christians. We even said Grace sometimes. But there had come this moment when there seemed to be a Presence in our little Welsh kitchen, with the big coal fire and the shining brass fender.

Even so, I was a bit nonplussed. I don't think that I had knelt down except in church, or since as a small child, my mother had taught me a little bedtime prayer:

> *"Gentle Jesus, meek and mild,*
> *Look upon a little child.*
> *Pity my simplicity,*
> *Suffer me to come to Thee."*

There I had remained ever since as far as uttered words went, a child in the unseen world of prayer, except for that moment in the Kelvin Hall. As a teenager I had been confirmed in the Church in Wales which seemed a more or less automatic procedure at the time, when my wayward heart had been prepared as best as could be done, I believe, by our Vicar, for full acceptance into the Church. Now it seemed only good manners to join these kind people in what was their way of starting the day. They were just talking to God about everyday matters. Not reading from the Prayer Book, but speaking in a very natural sort of way as though He was with us there in the room. Mrs. McIntyre was a former District Nurse and John knew how to repair cars and had driven coaches full of tourists for his father, in the Highlands before going into the ministry. Had they not been such practical, down-to-earth folk, I would have thought it weird.

As it was, I felt I was experiencing a new dimension of life and thought. It seemed like the Kelvin Hall had come right back into our lives again. I felt that I should be rushing out on my calls, as I intended working from the Manse, but it was still early in the day for visiting so instead I prayed as best I could, with the McIntyres over practical details of work. When I did go out, I certainly felt stronger. More purposeful somehow.

So two years passed happily by. Then a sense of unease came to me in my work. One day, Henry took me off an important assignment which I had developed because it was feared that as I was not drinking, I might not be able to cope with the top-level management concerned. I felt I could not ignore these signs of increasing personal disapproval, notwithstanding the business I was obtaining. Then an opportunity arose to take the management of the Christian holiday home Ardeneden where we had spent such happy times. In those days I was used to making quick decisions for the family. My wife and children were away from the house, helping at the home at the time and it was not too easy to contact them, as I should have done. I sent in a letter of resignation. I realised my mistake when Alice returned home and told me that she did not altogether feel like going into that kind of work. I flew down to Manchester to tell Henry that I would like to withdraw my resignation as I had been mistaken, and to try to arrive at a better understanding with him for the future.

I remember that uneasy meeting in his office and his question. "Are you sure that you have not been mistaken altogether in your thinking?" "No, not altogether but only in this particular matter." "If you want to go full-time into Christian work, I wouldn't want to stop you." "It doesn't seem to be the way ahead, just now." The matter seemed to rest there and I returned to Glasgow after phoning Alice to tell her that I would be continuing with Henry. But a few days later while I was working in the garden, on Saturday morning, a telephone call came through from Manchester. It was short. My resignation stood and I owed Henry £2000. No doubt I was a puzzle to my former friend and after 40 years and wondering whether he is still alive, I would not hold those events against him. In my zeal for my new faith, I was probably unwise in persisting in my expression where it seemed to be unwelcome and perhaps misunderstood, and for not appreciating that it must have cast doubt on my interest in my work. There were faults in my communication on a personal level, I realised. It was a pity. However, my most important Scots customer whom I had come to know, learning of my difficulties, advised me not to sell my house while a suitable post was being worked out for me to take up in his employ, so the plight was not as hopeless as it could have been. Suddenly, however, I felt that the business world was not where I should be any more.

My errors of judgement were a pity. There was a conflict in my mind, however I strived. Were these factors a sign in themselves that it was time for a major change? Something to which I was afraid to face? Was I being muzzled by the considerations of business? Was I perhaps wanting my own way in seeking to talk freely about Christ 'in season and out of season'? I felt very confused and uncertain. Being a Christian was not the clear-cut matter it had seemed at the beginning. Why didn't God make it more plain, I wondered? I loved my wife but we were not seeing eye-to-eye any more. I thought that Alice had felt I had let them down, that I had been carried away by all the Crusade fervour and that now things were going wrong and turning to ashes in our mouths.

My brother in South Wales had a milk round and needed help just at that time. Alice felt like leaving Scotland too and we had a sense of our work there having been done. I decided to place our new bungalow, which had been bought to establish myself for the business purposes, on the market, instructing my solicitors to repay Henry the balance of the loan out of the eventual proceeds which should more than cover it. All our money had gone into the big bungalow as the costs had been much more than we had anticipated. We then put our furniture into store and returned to Port-Talbot, while we were considering the next step and waiting for the house to be sold.

I wondered whether I could study part-time at the Bible College of Wales in Swansea, part-time in preparation for a new career in some kind of full-time Christian work. I felt tired and in need of a break to think about things in a new situation. I told the good business man who was ready to employ me, given a little time, that I was going to work with my brother on a milk round. "I hope the housewives will give you a crust," he said wryly. It didn't make sense to him that I was turning my back on the commercial world. I just felt that I somehow had to be free of its constraints.

South Wales, however, seemed a different place to the one I had known as a boy of 16. The work on the milk round was friendly and to begin with, I felt very fit as a result of the manual work in the fresh-air. There was no pressure to be selling. My family was supportive. We were ourselves divided in family accommodation however. There was no money forthcoming from the sale of Kelvin to enable us to buy our own home in Wales. The days were long. I did not have enough time to study as well.

After a while I found myself becoming tired with the 4.30 a.m. starts, seven days a week. The Bible College reminded me plainly that my first duty was to provide for my family so life seemed to mean picking up the bits of my business experience again and just getting on with it. Efforts to find full time Christian work were fruitless. There was still no other work in the town. Alice was now expecting our fourth child.

My brother's immediate need was over and London with its wider prospects made us think that we should retrace our steps - but for what, we did not know. I wrote to former business friends telling them that I was coming back and would be looking for work.

The only comfort I could find at this time was to read in the Crusade magazine that when William and Catherine Booth had themselves returned to London from their itinerant preaching engagements, they "did not have a sixpence to call their own." I had never realised that they had been so poor.

Catherine Booth. "Without sixpence to call her own". 'The Army Mother', Pamela Shepherd's inspiration.

Apart from a few weeks' money, we were broke too, but I didn't want my family to know how terribly wrong things had gone financially. I was now being pressed for settlement of accounts for which I did not consider myself responsible. The house would have to be sold, it seemed, on a falling property market for much less than it had cost us. I felt broken too as far as pride and self-sufficiency went. What a lesson it was for the work which God had indeed prepared for me in the days which lay ahead.

I got up from my knees on the mountain top. I felt calmer now. Down in the town, the few belongings which we could take with us on the train had to be packed. "Come by all means" my wife's sister Lilian had replied when Alice wrote to ask if she could put us up for awhile in London until I could find a job and we could sort ourselves out. There might not be enough blankets, however, she had said, and so we filled camping kitbags with these and the next morning my brother took us all down to the train. Back in London we had a warm welcome from Alice's father and sister, in the family home. While waiting to hear from my business friends regarding possible work, I decided to sign on at the Labour Exchange. I had never done this before and it was an unbelievable experience. Mercifully, we had somewhere to live but our money was almost gone. The Exchange people were unable to make any payment for a few weeks as technically I had left my job on the milk round. I was advised to apply for Public Assistance to augment the 'dole' on which, they said kindly, it would not be possible for us to live. It seemed the last straw. All this time we were waiting on the sale of the house in Scotland, in which the last of our money was tied up. The market however seemed impossible in terms of a buyer.

One day, when I was going around for advertised vacancies in the City, I found myself passing the door of a voluntary agency concerned with mental health. On impulse, I went in and asked if I could see one of their workers. A woman of my own age appeared. I related what had happened to me since the Kelvin Hall days. I asked her plainly whether she thought I had become seriously unbalanced. I told her that I was feeling almost overwhelmed by the impoverishment which had suddenly fallen on us. I had determined not to reveal to my family how nearly destitute we had become. I felt that the Lord knew and that was enough.

The woman had listened to me without comment all the while. Now she said simply, "Considering all that's happened to you, I think you've come through it very well." It was a comfort, at least, to know that this trained person had not told me that I was mad or needed some kind of treatment. Then I consulted the Rev. Dewi Morgan, who was by now a well-known writer with a very successful Fleet Street ministry in London. I thought highly of our former curate. He had turned his hand to anything in his younger days. He took me into the Chapel at Church House, Westminster where he now worked and showed me a small box which contained some relics of a former missionary in the South Seas. "Genuine martyr's relics" said Dewi, "but you do not have to make a martyr of yourself too, Charles." Then he went on to tell me how the Spirit of God had driven Jesus out into the Wilderness. "I think this is how it is with you now. Ultimately you will find an outlet. Just get on with life in the meantime and remember your family responsibilities." It was good advice.

A painful experience was with another old friend, my bank manager for many years. He had helped me to build up my little business from nothing. Now it was a case of nothing again, ten years later. My story of how everything had gone, arising out of my Kelvin Hall experience only elicited an angry silence, then he burst out bitterly: "You have denuded yourself of all but the bare necessities of life. You had no right to do it." He was angry with me. I felt very sad.

Like my family, he was thinking that I had either gone out of my mind or else had become some kind of religious crank. I could see that I could have made my break with commercial life without so much hardship to the family. I felt very sorry about this. I had not meant it to be so. I had followed my own ideas of what I thought the Lord wanted me to do instead of waiting more, and being patient. I had thought the road ahead would be clearer somehow. I had a lot to learn. "Make plain my path before me, 0 Lord, because of my enemies," I prayed. I wondered if David had felt like that when he was a fugitive from Saul in the desert hills of Judea.

So, I went around filling in endless application forms at what seemed spurious, slave-market job shops with hundreds of cards of vacancies in their windows but nothing definite once you went inside, only a requirement to complete time-consuming histories for their own gain. All that the Exchange offered was a commission-only job selling encyclopaedias but this was no immediate solution. I needed a wage of some kind and quickly. Then a letter arrived from my business friend who had been away from his office, asking me to come and see him. This led to a job in his contractors' plant yard, helping his manager. I was taught a lot in that factory situation where I rubbed shoulders with a good-hearted bunch of mechanics and drivers. I even had my first article "Witness in a Workshop", published in 'Crusade', a Christian magazine. I started evening classes at London Bible College.

Then our baby arrived, a little boy whom we called Alan, who looked just like Alice. He was born at home but there were some breathing problems and Alan was taken to hospital. A phone call came for me one night at College and I was called out of class. A doctor was at the other end of the line: "This is the North Middlesex Hospital. I am afraid we have some bad news for you, Mr. Preece. Your little boy is dead. We believe it is congenital heart disease. We would like to do a post mortem. I'm sorry to have to tell you this."

I had to go home and break the news to poor Alice who was still in bed recovering from the birth. I could only take her hand and say, in Job's words, "The Lord gave, the Lord hath taken away. Blessed be the name of the Lord." She sobbed.

A long time afterwards, I came across a gentler interpretation. That "the Lord does not take away. He receives." If Alice had not stood by me, I don't think that I could have lasted out. "I'm the only one you have left," she had said. The only one who had not abandoned me and my strange new belief. And it was true. It was all something of a mystery to her, as her own Christian experience had been very different to mine. She was just waiting faithfully until what must have seemed to her, my brain-storm had passed. We received a letter from our old minister, Mr. Christie in Scotland, to whom I had written telling him of our loss. "You now have a family foothold in Heaven. Part of you is already there", he replied, adding, "You are privileged to suffer with Jesus." Why did one have to suffer, I wondered? What was the point? At least Heaven was that much nearer and more real, with our three-day-old son there, waiting for us.

Shortly after this blow, the feeling grew within me that the key to our future had something to do with my great-grandmother Shepherd of Aberdare, who had been almost 94 when she died n 1930. I knew 'Grandma Shepherd' as we always called her at home, had been well-known as a Salvationist, many years ago but our family had since become members of the Church in Wales as there hadn't been any Salvation Army hall in the village where they lived. My mother spoke of her with something like awe. "When you were a little boy, Grandma Shepherd prayed for the devil to be taken out of you," Mam told me once. But no one seemed to be able to tell me very much about her. I had only been nine years old when Grandma Shepherd had died and my memory of her was of seeing a lady who seemed older than anyone I ever knew, who sat without saying anything in an armchair in her little kitchen.

She seemed to like to eat the cereal named Force. There was a funny little doll like a man, called "Sunny Jim". My Aunt Polly who looked after her, told me a rhyme: "High o'er the Fence leaps Sunny Jim. Force is the food that raises him." To my boyish mind, there was some kind of strange power around her which I had never felt anywhere else. Eighteen months later came another letter out of the blue. It was from a London manufacturing firm that had been recommended to contact me by the director who had been going to

HUGUENOT HERITAGE 1685-1985

Alice Comes from Huguenot forebears, the French Protestants who have sought refuge in Britain since the time of Elizabeth I in varying numbers according to the extent of persecution at the time. They were mostly highly skilled in the crafts and professions of the day, silk weavers, gold and silversmiths, agriculturalists, law, medicines and the sciences. Described sometimes as 'The Cream of France'. Their story, eradicated largely from French official history even as the Nazis later burnt Jewish books, is kept alive by the Huguenot Society of London and a 1685-1985 HUGUENOT HERITAGE Tercentenary Commemoration was held very successfully.

A beautiful example of the Huguenot Cross in the form of a ladies necklace, this one belonging to a daughter of Alice and great-great grand daughter of Mother Shepherd.

HUGUENOT CROSSES

(From *La Croix Huguenote,* by Pierre Bourguet)

The region of origin of the design for the cross, according to M. Allier (quoted by M. Bourguet) was the region near the Mus(e de Desert. The cross can be made in gold, silver, or any other metal, or in wood or porcelain. It is sometimes called "Le croix cevenole". It was in great demand at the beginning of the 20th century in the old Protestant regions as a sign of recognition between the heretics (Calvinists) of France and other countries, especially of Holland.

The design is the Maltese cross, the insignia of the Knights of St John of Jerusalem; the cross of Languedoc is very similar.

The insignia of the order of St Esprit founded in 1578 by Henri III was a Maltese cross with a dove in the centre. In many protestant regions of France there existed an ornament called Saint Esprit which was a dove with outstretched wings.

The first Huguenot cross, in the second half of the XVII century was a Maltese cross with a small drop (ampoule) suspended from it. Some of the early crosses were made at Lyon, others in the Cevennes. The cross with the suspended dove was created about 1688 by Maystre, a jeweller of N(mes. The old and classic symbol of the St Esprit regained its former importance because the jeweller of N(mes combined the dove with the cross as a protestant symbol, one which had been invoked by protestant priests dying for their faith in earlier times.

Chapter 2

TREASURE TROVE IN ABERDARE

ONE WEEKEND, ALICE and I drove to South Wales and, with my mother, we made our way up the Neath Valley to Aberdare to see friends who had faithfully looked after the grave ever since Grandma Shepherd had passed over, more than 25 years before. These good people gave me her Bible which they had treasured for all this time. They also suggested that I went to see their local historian, Mr. W. W. Price, the respected former headmaster of Llwydcoed School, which was reputed to be the first school at Aberdare where people wore the Welsh costume. I found the venerable old scholar in his book-lined study and he quickly from his archives put his hand on a newspaper cutting about Grandma Shepherd. It was from the 'Merthyr Express', dated 21st November 1925, when I was only four years old. The article was one of a series, called 'Women at the Wheel'.

This was a treasure trove indeed. The first public account which I had ever seen, written by someone who had sat and listened to the story of her life told when she was nearly 90. I read avidly of Police Court Mission work - that would be the Probation Service now - and of her concern for men who had been in prison. Something clicked in my mind. If that was what Grandma Shepherd had done in Aberdare, perhaps that was what I should do in London. I now knew why I had had this strange compulsion to journey there.

The dear old man, proud of his records and the honorary degree that the University College of Wales bestowed upon him for his skill and learning in keeping them, had something else for me though. He smiled with the serenity of his years and said, "Yes, I remember your great-grandmother ... Once I was speaking in the open-air, outside the park gates. There I was, up on my stand - Socialist, I was - when 'Mother Shepherd' as we all knew her of course, went by. 'Never mind about all that!' she called out, smiling, 'tell them about Jesus!' "

The old headmaster was thinking back perhaps half a century, but to him it seemed as fresh as though it had been yesterday. I felt sure that I was on the right trail. My feelings were soon to be put to the test.

Just after I had taken up my new job, I learnt that John, one of the drivers whom I had known in the factory, had been committed to Pentonville

Prison for stealing. I thought I would try to see him. The high grey walls of the prison reared above my head like some impenetrable fortress. The great doors were locked fast.

I had never been to a prison before. I knocked at a small door set in the large ones and wondered what would happen. There was a rattle of keys and the solid sound of the door being opened. A burly officer appeared and I explained that I would like to see one of the prisoners, as a firm I knew was prepared to give him a job on release. I was told to come inside to a waiting room. A welfare officer was called, who asked me to come back a week later, when he would arrange for me to see my prisoner friend.

I subsequently saw John. He told me that he had got drunk during his dinner break and, back on the job of driving a roller at some factory premises, had come across a lot of pens which had apparently been thrown out on a heap. Thinking they were defective, he had picked up a lot of them. His problem was that he had not asked if he could do so and he was later found in possession of them. Also, it was not the first time John had been in trouble. So he ended up with three months in prison. It was a mindless kind of offence, the like of which I was to hear so much in the future.

When John was released, a few days before Christmas, the company were as good as their word, although they had never seen him. Moreover, the director concerned, gave him a warm word of welcome and urged John to forget the past which, as far as they were concerned, didn't exist any more. He was to start after the holidays.

Then someone with far from unblemished record himself recognised John after his interview and complained to the management that their clothes would not be safe with an ex-prisoner around. The director phoned me to say they were very sorry but it couldn't be done after all. I had the sad experience of going, with him to John's home, to tell my friend so. The balloons were decorating the little Council house, the Christmas tree was lit up in the window and all the youngsters were getting ready for the festivities when we called. We asked John to step outside a moment and we told him what had happened. "What a Christmas present," I thought. I suddenly felt very angry and began to realise what a family man with a number of children was up against when trying to re-establish himself in life. Then a few days later, the blow fell on me.

The managing director of the new firm I had been working for since the beginning of the year, some eight months, sent for me and told me that while they had nothing against me, they had been refused a fidelity bond on me. They would have to give me a month's notice.

I told the director that I was dumbfounded. I said I didn't know exactly what a fidelity bond was anyway, as I had never been asked to provide one in my life. There certainly had been no mention of any such requirement when they had written and offered me a job, on recommendation from a major customer. I was told it was company policy that all their staff were fidelity bonded. They could not tell me why their insurers would not grant a bond. It was a confidential matter where reasons were never given. I said I couldn't think of any reason why I should be refused a bond. My company had been properly disposed of through my accountants in agreement with my shareholders. I had even disclaimed my own financial interest in order to provide the best settlements. I had never been in trouble in my life.

The director agreed that if I could obtain a bond, they would reconsider employing me. So I went off, puzzled, to consult an insurance broker. Fortunately, commission from my sales work was sufficient to keep me going, this time for three months, while my broker dealt with the business, telling me that it could probably take some time.

The months passed and I busied myself with writing. Then I was told there were difficulties. I could not obtain any positive information, only hints in this specialised, secretive even, form of insurance. Belonging to the Salvation Army was mentioned vaguely, carrying large sums of cash, problems in Scotland, difficulties with an employer...

To be judged so critically by men who had never met me, nor heard what I had to say, seemed a travesty of justice. I was effectively being debarred from any responsible employment, as though I had a criminal record. It seemed incredible. To be blacklisted without a word being said. This seemed to be a world which I didn't know existed. I thought grimly of the old tag:

> *"One man's word is no man's word*
> *Justice needs that both be heard."*

This became a turning point in my life. Previously I had simply felt sympathetic to men coming out of prison with huge problems in getting on their feet again. Now, I positively identified myself with them. I knew what it felt like to be put down by faceless forces in a world which did not know the whole story by any means. I threw myself into seven months of hectic voluntary work, meeting men at the prison gate at Pentonville and trying to acquire training as an Associate of the Blackfriars Settlement.

Then came the opportunity to become a welfare officer with the Royal London Discharged Prisoners' Aid Society. I confided my difficulties to the Rev. Fraser Thompson, a Methodist Minister who was then the Secretary, and who helpfully steered me through the interview formalities.

The salary was a very low one. "You are not overpaid," said an Inland Revenue official whom I consulted once. The other officers at the time were older, retired men with pensions of various kinds. The society was a voluntary agency with some State support. To make the income livable, I began to work in what little spare time there was for the Salvation Army Assurance Society as a part-time agent. There was a certain irony insomuch that the Society needed a collector's bond to cover itself against the loss of money which I would be carrying. I was assured by my Superintendent that there would not be any trouble over this and, in fact, the insurers providing the cover turned out to be the same company which had refused the fidelity bond earlier.

My first appointment attached me to Wandsworth Prison where one of my duties was to examine, on the night before their release the following morning, the clothing of the men who were being discharged and to make replacements where needed and as far as our limited funds allowed.

I was so raw, so far away from this terrible part of our society, a level of poverty which I had hardly known to exist. This grim job soon reduced me to tearless desperation. I quickly discovered why it was so unpopular with the prison staff and relegated to a voluntary agency. We were generally viewed as misguided 'do-gooders' anyway and, in those days, barely tolerated by the official system.

Judging by their so-called 'property', I rapidly concluded that at least half the men in prison must have been in quite poor, even destitute circumstances when they had been arrested. My mind flew back to the workhouse times of Charles Dickens, the horrors of the starving outcasts of his day. The myth of criminals being successful men was, for me, soon dispelled forever. I had never met with the prisoners as they were only names and numbers. About 10 per cent possessed clothing only fit for a scarecrow. Their shoes were broken or their boots had great holes; socks were awful cobwebs and shirts were ragged. Vest and pants were mostly non-existent. I never saw a handkerchief ever. The items which could not be washed, such as crumpled, concertina-like sacks of trousers, ancient jackets with torn linings and cuffs, often had burn marks and shouted to the skies of the means of those who had been draped in them.

Sometimes there would be an ex-Army greatcoat but any overcoat was the exception, even in the depth of winter or pouring rain. All of this terrible, awful-to-handle collection would never have been accepted for a jumble sale and would moreover, be smelling to high heaven of a strong insecticide.

The men who came into prison, following their arrest, wearing these indescribable rags were, in fact, known to the prison reception officers as 'copperkits'. When they were received from the bombsites, the derelict back-street houses and park benches of South London, what they were wearing was gingerly dropped into a copper tub. A powerful disinfectant, ethyl formate, was poured in and a lid placed on top while the drastic fumigation process went on. After some time in this witches' cauldron, the still dirty contents, regarded as unwashable, were stuffed into kit bags from which they eventually emerged, distorted and disheveled, if deloused, with a biting, acrid odour which could be inhaled many yards away. The lepers of old could hardly have smelt more foul. I couldn't help saying to one of the prison officers that if I had had to change, on release, from the warm and decent prison battle dress into these loathsome rags and then go out ignominiously through the gate, I would want to get drunk myself, at the first pub I came to. It seemed indescribably degrading.

"These are not men, they are animals" an officer had retorted, adding "You ought to be here yourself, first thing in the mornings, when they go out and then you would see". said another officer "And when they come in, the fleas just jump off them and run about on the floor". It was a miserable job, dealing with men in that condition, but it was a challenge to me too. What sort of men were these 'copperkits'? Going to the gate, early in the morning at 7.30 when they were discharged and sober, would enable me to find out.

In those days, too, as the list of names of those going out, was called by the officer at the gate, he would stand half in the way with his clip board so that the men, one by one as their names were read out, would have to stoop to get past him, in a final act of humiliation, it seemed to me. I wondered whether it was necessary.

There did seem however to be a moment of profound truth, of impact on a man's mind, at the gate. There he stood, sober and in his right mind, the first time perhaps for many years, to be met on release and perhaps ready for someone to show him a new way.

About this time when wondering whether to attempt this unpromising work, I was sitting one Sunday evening in the Salvation Army hall at the Archway. There were two stained glass windows at the back of what had been a chapel. One bore the words of William Booth, "Go for souls" and the other, "Go for the worst". It seemed a word to me from the Founder himself.

My day started with the alarm set for 5.45 a.m. and then a breathless hour's drive from Palmers Green in North London, where we lived, over the Thames to Wandsworth Prison. Those quiet hours in the early morning when London was just beginning to stir, winter and summer, for the next two years, brought strange encounters. I soon found out that nearly half the men I met had served honourably during the Second World War and very few of them had ever been arrested for more than being drunk and disorderly. None were serious criminals. I discovered an ex-Guardsman who had had seven toes amputated in Lambeth Hospital, after being frostbitten through sleeping out in the terrible winter of 1963. There was an ex-sergeant-major, still erect and commanding in his bearing after 23 years excellent service. He had never been in trouble until he left the Army. Now his face once cruelly slashed had a long scar from chin to crown, after some drunken fight.

Another was a seaman who had voyaged the world, fought in convoy actions and been torpedoed. A fellow sailor, when returning intoxicated to his ship, had lain for hours in a stupor across the railway sidings at the docks. In the darkness, a shunting wagon had taken off both his legs. Now like Douglas Bader (who once came to Wandsworth to talk to the men) he had learnt to walk without a stick. His was the sad world of prison, however, incarcerated too in his alcoholism without as well as within the walls. All that 'Tin-Legs' could not do was to walk backwards up the iron stairs onto the landings. No 'Reach for the Sky' for him.

There were other men, skilled at their trades, haunted by the memories of people who bad died in public-house brawls. No one on the hard-pressed prison welfare staff, in those days, ever saw them on their short, endlessly revolving-door sentences. They were the 'seven-day drunks' not regarded as real alcoholics anyway but contemptuously as 'Wet Brains' who were beyond recovery, due to their brain damage.

I had a little Ford 5 cwt. van at the time. I found that I could squeeze seven men into the back and off we would go to an unpretentious Italian cafe near the Discharged Prisoners' Aid Society office, by Blackfriars Bridge. The proprietor didn't bat an eyelid when I turned up with my motley crew in the cold mornings and ordered steaming cups of tea and wonderfully-smelling bacon sandwiches. There was a curious tradition among the men of refusing the prison breakfasts on the last day of their sentence but they accepted a mug of tea. So the 'breakfasts' went down well. Afterwards, they were invited to come back to the office when it opened at 9 a.m. if they wanted help, but most silently faded away into the strange underworld whence they had come.

One morning, when the blue van seemed even more packed than ever, its thin sides literally bulging, a wag in the back found the breath to say, "Gor blimey, Guv, if the law stops us, we'll say we are on our way to do a bank job and you are the 'Brains'!" I am sure that particular morning when the lads piled out in a back street, near the cafe, on a freezing, sunless corner between two warehouses, we would have looked very suspicious. More so when I dug out my collection of thin, second-hand macs and tried to fit out my merry band.

Once, a little man who in between sentences, seemed to earn a living as a busker, produced a tin whistle from his pocket and regaled us all the way with a non-stop repertoire of the classics - it didn't seem possible. Another jovial character had been a choir-boy in Dublin Cathedral. He sang us every word of 'Ave Maria', in Latin, in a beautiful treble voice. One sad and silent former schoolmaster was deaf after being blown up in the Western Desert. He was a graduate of a Scottish university. Pathos and absurdity were all mixed up in those early-morning adventures from the prison gate. The men had nowhere to go. No families. Nothing. Only the handouts which we could offer.

Could anything be done with men such as these? Were they too far-gone in their alcoholism? Was it indeed as hopeless as everyone was telling me? A waste of time bothering with them? That was the hardest part of it all, the pitying, if not disparaging attitudes to the work with what were commonly regarded as the dregs of our prisons. I knew so little anyway. No one seemed to be able to tell me either. Only my own spiritual experience of change kept me going when the 500 or so stage army of drunks from the London prisons began to besiege our office as the word went around that we were trying to do something for them.

I remember looking out of the window of the office one grey morning, with a desperate prayer in my heart: "Lord, give me some sign if I am right or not to go on with this." Then along came Fred, rejoicing in the name of 'Manchester' and known all over the South London bombsites. Fred called his particular group who spent their time around the Elephant and Castle neighbourhood 'The Twilight Brigade' when they were not in prison, that is. Many of them indeed were living in the twilight of their lives at this time, and were not to live very much longer.

Everybody liked Fred. He was a tall, pleasant-looking man with a friendly manner who never had a hard word for anyone. There was a sad, defeated air about him, a gentle melancholy which he seemed unable to shake off. Fred's wife had died and he had lost contact with his son and daughter whom he had last known in Manchester a number of years before.

From time to time, Fred would be irresistibly drawn back to Manchester, hence his nickname. He said it was to look for his children. Invariably, he failed to find them and this led him back to the bottle of the awful-smelling surgical spirits which they were all reduced to drinking. A medicine-sized bottle at that time could be purchased for today's equivalent of, I suppose, about 30p, something like the price of a can of lemonade, except that it was the strength of half-a-bottle of whisky. It was toxic, of course, and its taste and smell were made the more poisonous to discourage it being drunk. The homeless alcoholics simply added orange squash and the resultant deadly cocktail was known as 'jake'.

One day Fred, whom I had been meeting quite regularly at the prison gate, turned up at the office after one of his fruitless Manchester searches. He was penniless and had no plans in life for anything at all. A Salvation Army hostel within walking distance, was the only place where a man in his condition could obtain a bed. The next day Fred agreed to see a local doctor, who, in his own time, held a clinic for drunks, near our own office. In between the interviews, a dear, middle-aged receptionist lady just sat and talked to the applicants and fortified them with coffee from a kettle which was permanently on the boil. Fred took the pills which were meant to keep him from being able to drink, and went back to the hostel saying that he would come and see me the next day. To my surprise, he did so. Fred told me that it was pretty wild in the place after 'Lights Out' when fights started among the drunks, but to my amazement, as he had previously seemed so hopeless, he wasn't drinking. When, day after day, Fred turned up sober and I contrived to find him odd jobs which enabled me to give him a few shillings in the old currency and his bed vouchers, what had seemed absolutely impossible a cause, suddenly appeared to offer some hope.

About this time, a psychiatrist from the Maudsley Hospital gave a lecture to local social workers and suggested that cases could be referred to him at the Out-patients Department. This was the first chink of light from the Health Service. Before all this, we felt a sense of horror when these terrible-looking creatures literally came tapping their way in. To ask them into a private office seemed utterly out of the question, so they were seen, or rather contained, in a sort of closed-in box, with a counter. They often had infected wounds from camp-fire burns, were bleary-eyed and mostly inarticulate.

A prison governor, around this time, out of his long experience, referred to them as "shells of men - ghosts of humanity, sunk in complete mental apathy whose dereliction is tragic". But what could we do? None of us knew. And then when Fred responded, even to our very basic efforts, he seemed to point the way for the vagabond hordes behind him. It was a visiting psychiatrist to the prison who also gave us a clue when he spoke of "the catalytic effect of someone who cares".

Fred did subsequently relapse following another disappointing search in Manchester, but on the strength of his efforts I was able to get him into St. Francis Hospital, to be dried out. I remember visiting Fred later. He was sedated, cleaned and shaven in a spotless, hospital bed and looking distinguished even. He came across to me as a different man, a regular patient. I had never imagined him in a normal situation, only as a fearful character in scarecrow clothes.

I suddenly felt challenged to compare my attitude of hardly having time for such an outcast, with the hospital's medical care and attention, as if he was entitled to all the service of an ordinary citizen, in an emergency situation, as indeed he was. I reasoned that if the doctors had not thought he was sick, they would not have admitted him. Our care should be on the same level. If he could survive in the tough hostel situation we ought to try to give him a proper chance in the world outside prison.

There was a small group of committed Christians in my own Wood Green locality, in North London, who would assist if I could find some kind of meeting point to which the men now being hospitalised and found accommodation could come. One Saturday night, while, as a Salvationist, I was selling 'War Crys' in a local pub, The Kings Head, I asked the friendly landlord, on impulse, if he had a room to let which wouldn't be too dear. We didn't have a penny to spare at this time.

"What do you want it for?" he naturally enquired. "A sort of club for alcoholics," I offered, hesitantly. "You've got a nerve!" he replied. "Are you out of your mind wanting to bring men like that to a PUB?"

"I want somewhere neutral," I said. "If I asked them to come to a room in a church, they wouldn't come, but a pub is just the sort of place to which they are used."

"All right!" he responded, shaking his head a little, "Come with me and I'll show you what I could let you have". It was a bare room over a bar.

"How much will it be?" I enquired, diffidently. "Just for Friday nights - pay night..." I added. "You should have asked me that to begin with!" he quipped, then with a grin, "Nothing. You Salvationists would worm your way into anyone's heart". So Bob Starling launched us out, the second publican to play a vital part in my life.

The word was sent around the prison gates: "IF YOU CAN'T STOP DRINKING, COME TO THE KINGS ARMS, WOOD GREEN". It was so simple. The novelty of the message brought, men to see what on earth it was all about. There was a flight of stairs at the back of the pub which led to our room so the men did not have to go through the pub itself. The clubroom equipment consisted on the opening night of a collection of mugs, a plastic bucket for washing up, a primus stove for tea-making and a dozen ham rolls from the bar.

About twelve men turned up from contacts at the gate. A committee from among the men unanimously elected Fred as Chairman. The whole thing went like clockwork. Everybody said they would come the following Friday. In the event, only Fred, Laurie, one of the principal volunteers, and myself turned up. "Where's the Committee?" Fred demanded. "Back in gaol", I had to say.

However, incredibly the meetings in The Kings Arms went on. We shared the upper floor of the pub with a girls' dancing class, a pigeon fanciers' club and a West Indian Gospel Assembly. It was like a market place with the substantial background of cooing of pigeons, the tinkling piano with strident dancing instructions and exultant bursts of "When the Saints Go Marching In". I don't know who were the more bewildered, our men or our workers. When we found a busker who played the accordion we were really in business and our drunks were laughing more than they had done in years - and all on tea or lemonade.

The meetings which followed were ever-changing, uncertain, perplexing, sometimes turbulent, but a steady stream of men from prison and derelicts from the road found their way up the stairs, until the landlord changed. He was upset by some mentally-ill man who didn't even belong to us and so we had our marching orders and were on the road again. We had to find somewhere else and went to see our local M.P., Mrs. Joyce Butler, resulting in the Wood Green Council giving us the use, rent-free, of a disused ironmonger's shop, in property due for demolition and re-development and fortunately, just a few doors away from our first-love, The Kings Arms.

Our volunteer workers were of high calibre, with many of professional standing. Nevertheless, we were untrained however and inexperienced amateurs without any guidance in this kind of work. (One ultimately became a Justice of the Peace.) We were not withstanding about to show what could be done. Then came another break. The nearby Friern Hospital (the old Colney Hatch Mental Asylum) became interested in studying the homeless type of alcoholic and were prepared to take our men, straight from prison, until we could find them local lodgings. This gave us a tremendous fillip. It meant that we could get them away from the awful 'skippers', as they called their dens in empty, condemned houses. If mentally ill, what were these men doing in prison anyway and being treated as criminals?

The name 'WAYFARERS' was suggested for our enterprise by one of the men from Tooting Bec Hospital and so it was. What happened then could fill a book and perhaps some day it will be written (See the Appendix). The small shop, with its bright neon lights in the gay, ruby-curtained windows with attractive floral decorations and posters, shone like a lighthouse in the Wood Green High Road, and to see what had once been only a name in our minds now boldly painted on the fascia made the previous two years' work and struggle seem worthwhile.

The incredibly easy access to Wayfarers took people by surprise. A door opened straight off the pavement - it had been a shop after all - just like going into someone's lounge. One night, in fact, a man from the pigeon club at The Kings Arms came in by mistake and looked around. "Sorry, mates - I thought this was a pub by the sound of it!" A chirpy character retorted, "We've got everything else here, Cock, except the beer!"

It was strange that the birdman had thought it was a pub. "Maybe, in time, Wayfarers could become as much of a British institution," said one of the volunteers. "There were British Restaurants during the War. How about British Wayfarers?" "The idea is the thing!" another added. " 'British Wayfarers'... 'Her Majesty's' could give the country the greatest saving in penal institutions since Elizabeth Fry made England think of what was happening in its prisons", said one of the women. "Every Magistrates Court should have a sign 'This way to Wayfarer House'." came a further voice from the volunteer group. Ideas ran riot that evening.

We had some distinguished visitors. One was an eminent American social administrator who was very encouraging in his remarks. "You folks have certainly got this project off the ground." "It's your idea," I told him, "based on your research." (See Appendix III: 'Skid Row in American Cities') "But you've put it into practice", he replied.

Another guest was the consultant psychiatrist to whose encouragement and practical medical help the whole work owed much. "England could do with a thousand Wayfarer Houses", was his verdict.

Into our life at this time came Penny. One morning as soon as the office opened, a youngster of 17 presented himself. Sitting down at my desk, he put his hand inside his battered jacket and like some street urchin conjurer produced a tiny, silky, black kitten, beautifully marked with a white bib and four white paws. Laughingly, as though he didn't have a care in the world, he said "I've come out of the 'Ville' with her. We just walked out of the gate. 'Big Escape!'

"What happened?" I asked. "Well, the word went round the 'Nick' that the 'Cat Man' was coming - you know, every now and again they think that there are too many cats wandering around so they send for a man to come and take them away. When the lads hear about it, they hide the cats everywhere. In the ovens, if they're out - all sorts of places where they won't think of looking, you'd be surprised. Got a drop of milk for 'er, Guv? She ain't had no breakfast either. I'll have to go and look for somewhere to live then."

After hungrily lapping up the saucer of milk, she was walking about over my desk as though she owned it all. "What about the kitten - she seems a bit restless?" "Could I leave her with you until I find a place?"

All the lad had was a small brown-paper parcel containing his 'property', his sole possessions in the world. It was cold and I found an ex-naval coat for him. It was somewhat large but all I had. I wondered how on earth he would fare in looking for a roof over his head, especially with a kitten to care for.

"All right, I'll keep her for a day or two - come back as soon as you've found a place," I told him, wondering what I was letting myself in for. During the week 'Penny from Pentonville came with me to work in the Discharged Prisoners' Aid Society office, making friends with all those other inmates who had also just come out. She had a habit of crawling over my back and on to my shoulder as I drove the van, and I felt like Long John Silver with his parrot, but otherwise she was a real little lady. I never saw the youngster again.

We were living with my father-in-law at the time and felt much as though we were homeless too, after the loss of Kelvin, our lovely house in Scotland. Grandpa was a keen gardener and had a life long feud with the cat tribe whom he averred darkly were somehow responsible for ruining his best plants. When Penny was not at the office with me, we frantically hid her, much as in her former days at Pentonville, every time Grandpa's footsteps were heard approaching along the passage to the kitchen where she was shut in.

Her charmed life could not continue indefinitely, however. One day she was caught red-handed, like some of her former cell-mates, sitting on the floor as large as life, right beside Grandpa's armchair. I think the old gentleman had known all the time that something was going on and her friendly ways and good behaviour won her a reprieve.

The story of the 'escapee' being harboured by the Discharged Prisoners' Aid Society found its way up to the Prison Commissioners of that day, who thought it was very funny. We had Penny twelve years before her time came. Never was a former inmate at large from the 'Ville' for so long. She served the cause well, too. She was always a poignant reminder of the homeless men coming out of prison with nothing but their pitiful 'property'.

Alice took on the job of trying to find lodgings in Wood Green for the 'Wayfarers' coming to us. It meant frankly telling friendly, unsuspecting landladies who had never had any prisoners as lodgers, yet alone homeless alcoholics, that they had nothing to fear as we were responsible and would be supportive to them. It speaks for our men that they never caused any trouble. When the pressures of their new lives became too much for them, they just disappeared. Their landladies came to us looking for them. They often said they had been nice men and that they could come back.

Into the old ironmonger's shop, which by this time, had been converted into a homely 'parlour on the pavement', there came one night a journalist by the name of Kenneth Martin who had been told of our existence and thought that there might be a story. Ken later brought with him a brilliant young photographer, Michael Hardy, who had done work for 'Paris Match', the famous French picture paper. They spent some time with us, resulting in an article which appeared in the 'Weekend Telegraph' of 25th February 1966, giving a graphic account of what had now become widely known as 'Wayfarer House'. I was told that 2,000,000 copies of this prestigious supplement to the Telegraph were being published. It seemed breathtaking that our effort was being made known to this extent, even internationally.

The Salvation Army 'War Cry' followed suit with a back-page article by a young reporter Trevor Howes, later to become a Major and Editor-in-Chief of the U.K. Territory publications. The feature used some of Michael Hardy's splendid photographs, and was entitled "WHERE CAN A MAN GO?" Many thousands of this account went out too.

BBC Wales had 'phoned, immediately on publication, asking for an interview as they had picked up the Welsh connection. I referred them, according to procedure, to my Head Office but I didn't hear any more. The 'Telegraph' article had described me as 'a Billy Graham convert', which of course, was quite true, but my Head Office had fears that this 'religious angle' would upset the London County Council who had funded my work, now based on the hospital in Wandsworth Prison. I don't believe that it ever did, especially as subsequently I was later invited to give evidence, both written and verbal, before a Parliamentary Select Committee charged with the task of producing a Blue Paper, 'Habitual Drunken Offenders'. (See Appendix).

It was a pity that the script had only been read over the phone to our Secretary at the time, and some corrections made, instead of being submitted in writing, but journalists often work in a hurried way. The price of publicity can also involve a certain amount of risk in presentation. The Press would term this 'journalistic freedom'. However, hundreds of men of a kind never previously dealt with on such positive lines were being befriended and this was now becoming known.

Anyway, I tried to divert the focus of the endeavour from myself to the little band of community volunteers whose tremendous efforts kept Wayfarer House open six nights a week. All this was on a shoe-string budget which was all that could be provided by the Royal London Discharged Prisoners' Aid Society which employed me. The voluntary Society was financially stretched to the full. It had been a heroic struggle for many years to bring its work to the point which it had now attained and I had been grateful for its support. (See Appendix)

These citizen-volunteers, who had never been in trouble or in a courtroom in their lives, found that by coming out into the no-man's land of a room over a pub, a great gulf into another world had, in a small way, been overcome. So, 'Wayfarers' all, drunks and volunteers alike, we ate our sandwiches, drank lemonade and gallons of tea, endlessly played the 'Joystrings' records which were popular at the time, to 'mop up' the tensions, talked ceaselessly, washed up in a plastic bucket like campers, and prayed wordlessly that something would come of our endeavours.

Men were coaxed into hospital, found lodgings, cleaned up in their rooms when they had lapsed. Landlords and landladies were appeased, doctors' appointments made and kept. Workers went chasing after them on bombsites when they disappeared, which was the worst that happened. They were met at prison gates, brought home to meals. Doorbells were rung in the middle of the night, home telephones never seemed to stop demanding attention from folk in trouble. Drunks landed on us, harmlessly but gloriously 'tight'. Jobs were found, jobs were lost. Tools were procured on credit for a time from the noble-minded firm of Tyzack, and their new owners vanished with the instruments of their trades. My old RAF aircrew director friend Alf Flowerday had the debts quashed. Years afterwards, one man at least, a bricklayer, made good and was last heard of as a stalwart in Alcoholics Anonymous. It was a galaxy of events, a maelstrom of activity, and I wondered how much longer we could all keep it up.

In the meantime, Fred was doing well as a deputy manager of a hostel for alcoholics in Oxford. A great vision came to him one night of the work he had to do in this field (his own story is told in the Appendix) and this led at last to him being re-united with his son and the daughter whom he had long sought in Manchester. She wanted to take the first plane back from Canada, where she was now living, when she discovered that her father was still alive.

There was also Archie who, unaided by any of us, had gone on to become a playwright, BBC broadcaster, and author of several books, and who gamely, with Vi, his staunch wife, compiled filmstrips of their lives, to be used with the prison groups.

I recall Moira, whom Friern Hospital had cured of T.B. She was a refined Irishwoman, beautifully-spoken, coming from a well-to-do 'County' family with a background of horse-and-hounds and a 16 h.p. Austin - a big car in those days. But Moira hadn't slept in a bed for seven years, it was said, until we got her into hospital. Desperate family trouble had broken her marriage. She had come penniless to London and had ended up on the streets, like Nelson's Lady Hamilton, a homeless alcoholic. Until she was 35, she told me, she had never touched alcohol. She had cooked for the boys on their campfires like some backwoods Florence Nightingale.

Michael's face comes before me too. I remember taking him down to St. Francis Hospital in the little van. He sang non-stop in his melodious Irish voice. He might have been going to his wedding. Eventually he found work. He said it was at Battersea Dogs' Home. He went on to explain "It's a kind of 'Spike' for dogs". (Reception centre for the homeless and a former workhouse). Everybody knew what 'the Spike' was. The end of the road. Over thirty years later, we still see Michael from time to time. He comes to have something to eat with us but mostly just to talk. 'Higher Power' is an expression much in his vocabulary and A.A. is his way of life. After a good stint as a hospital porter, Michael qualified for a council flat on retirement and has a wonderful flair for saving up and going to holiday camps at home and even travelling abroad. A long way from the 'spike' and still full of laughs. We drifted into a new kind of terminology - in fact Alice complained once that I was "beginning to talk like the men". It was their way of communicating and as we found ourselves identifying with them, it was all too easy to pick up their language.

One man was known as 'Little Ginger' - surnames were seldom used - and I wondered why whenever I saw him as he was always as black as night from the smoke of bombsite fires. Then I interviewed him while he was having the compulsory bath on reception into Wandsworth Prison and realised that under the grime he was indeed a glorious ginger.

Another character who rejoiced in the nom-de-guerre of 'Steal-a-Horse' following being found riding, in Aldgate, under the influence and with reckless abandon, a policeman's mount which he had inexplicably managed to purloin.

Just a simple country lad was 'Little Peter' whose troubles started outside a shop when someone just asked him to hold a parcel for them ... and then the police arrived.

Chris the Ulsterman knew all the names of the books of the Bible by heart and would recite them effortlessly. George was a dapper former Army sergeant who always contrived to look as though he was going on parade but was as homeless as the rest. And even more hopeless with his apparently incurable alcoholism which defied every effort made, in view of his background.

'The Twins', two men in their thirties, were inseparable and went everywhere together, including prison.

'Big Henry' was a soft-spoken Orkney Islander and former ship's bosun who marched around the wealthy London suburbs as a drain-cleaning expert, an imposing set of bamboo rods on his shoulder and in his pocket a bottle of disinfectant which he distributed liberally around the manhole covers on completion of his work. "They like to see it", he confided once when seeking to borrow the price of such a bottle to provide visible evidence of a job well done and calling for generous remuneration. This was how genial Henry supported a substantial alcohol problem in between manipulating his equipment in an impressive manner.

'Big Jim' came from Liverpool and thus was also known as 'Scouse'. "I'm so full of pills for my problems that if you shook me, I'd rattle", he told me once with a wry grin. He was frighteningly able to collapse at any moment. Another Jim was a skilled painter who had a beautiful crystal rosary which had been his mother's. He had somehow been able to hold on to this, when there was little else of value in his possession.

Eddie had married the nurse who looked after him and had become a changed man, on fire with his Christian conviction. Accompanied by his caring wife, he had sought me out many years afterwards, just turning up out of the blue on the doorstep one Sunday afternoon.

Andy, a tough steel scaffolder had arrived at the house with a car after a peculiar psychiatrist had told him that car ownership was only a pipe-dream. "I am sick and tired of being sick and tired," he had told me in prison when I asked him why he wanted to stop drinking. This forthright man became known to his building gang as the 'Coca Cola Boy' as this was his favourite tipple when the rest of the boys were on something stronger - not that anyone would want to argue with Andy, anyway.

Then there was 'Big John', the ex-Japanese prisoner-of-war veteran and expert organiser who became my right-hand man and married Elizabeth, our volunteer cook after establishing himself as a haulage driver and buying a house. One day John turned up at Brixton Prison where my office was just outside the gate, with a large lorry fitted with a hydraulic grab. It was a very valuable outfit worth a good few thousands of pounds. "Pack up this welfare stuff and get into muck, Charlie. There's money in it!" he advised. Poor John did not live so long after to enjoy it, but I'm sure that be died happy. Les had a spare artificial leg in his 'property' and I carried this for him on my shoulder out of Wandsworth Prison one morning. He was to die of cancer in Pentonville Prison Hospital only a little later but two of our ladies visited him to the end. He had no one else.

As our volunteers said in a meeting one evening, "A few months ago, we would have been paralysed at the sight of a homeless drunk. Now, we are coping as though we'd been doing it all our lives." "What's happened to them would have flattened most of us." "Their sense of humour is incredible. We've had some laughs." "Their personalities kept us going." "Never mind

selectivity - 'Whosoever will may come,' I reckon."
"If you want a motto, how about 'Let the handicraft of your work be your prayer'?"

WORMWOOD SCRUBS

One day, I found myself sitting in a cell in Wormwood Scrubs where I had been sent as a welfare officer after Wayfarers had closed down when I had taken up my appointment with the Inner London Probation Service and was waiting to see a man who had applied for an interview. The room was a former cell, bare but for a plain table and two tubular chairs. It was as impersonal as a railway waiting room. I put my papers on the grey table and went to the heavily barred window. Looking out, all that could be seen was a concrete yard and a brick wall, black with the grime of all the years since Victoria was on the throne.

The feeling swept over me, "I'm glad to be here." I smiled to myself at the strange thought. How could it be? There could hardly be a more bleak place in human existence. Not a spot of comfort or colour. Nothing but a mass of grey heaviness which oppressed the spirit like a physical dead weight. Yet, perhaps I would give a little light to a part of it for someone. I could only do it in a place like this. I sat down and tried to look as cheerful as I could for the man who was coming.

The harsh shouting of commands in the prison hall outside the heavy door, the tramp of feet, the echoing of voices in the high-domed, four-storey building, the restless movement of the human bee-hive of the building, jostling with bodies, an ant hill of beings all locked in with each other, staff and inmates alike, shut away from a world which didn't want to know, unaware of this mass of misery. Yet, here was a quietness, if only for a moment. A balm for the spirit. 'A peace which passed understanding.'

The chips were down, in such a place. There could be no pretence. A man had ended up in prison because of his wrongdoing. Found guilty by a jury of his fellow men and women. Sentenced by a judge. Why was I here too? I had failed as well. Not in a law-breaking sense although that could have come about easily enough. "A fellow sickness makes one wondrous kind", as someone had written.

It was too pompous, too inappropriate, too smug, to think in terms of a confessional, a mercy-seat, an altar in this barren, brick desert spot, yet it was a place of truth where Scripture came strangely alive. People could not wear masks with each other in here. They did, of course, of a kind. Everyone had to put on a 'front'. The unworried, casual, 'no problems air'. The staff for the men and the men for the staff. Yet, everyone recognised the signs. Everyone knew that the others had 'sussed them out' too. There was no real deception. The moments of truth came in these personal talks if only time could be found.

The textbook concept of 'the unhurried initial interview' (when a man first came to prison) was a concept seldom possible to realise in the never-ending pressures of the army of men who confronted one daily. I had once asked my friend, the Roman Catholic Chaplain, how he managed. He had smiled wryly, "I hear confessions on the landings". Like standing on the platform of a busy railway station with other men clattering by every few seconds on the narrow slate-paved passageway outside the cells. "Come now, let us reason together," saith the Lord (Job 15:3). "Though your sins be as scarlet, they shall be as white as snow". Was there ever such a place for a man to bare his soul? Yet they did. And in a few words.

"Surely this is the gateway to heaven and I knew it not". (Gen. 28:17). That is what Jacob, another man on the run had thought.

Yet how to bring this about? I thought of Gladys Aylward 'The Small Woman' with a price on her head, being expelled with other missionaries from China, and going to the prisons of Formosa. "What good can you do in this ocean of misery?" she had been asked. "Take out my bucketful" she had replied. I was not a missionary, nor a chaplain, just a raw new Christian of some kind.

We were all on the run from something in here. Only God, - a Higher Power as Alcoholics Anonymous knew it, could provide a way out. Or perhaps in simple and secular terms for anyone who found difficulty with spiritual concepts, a total honesty of life and purpose. An acceptance that we were in the end, ourselves responsible for our lives and situations.

I thought of the leader of an A.A. meeting which I once attended, introducing himself as 'a sort of spiritual roughneck'. I had certainly identified with that. I was even on probation as a probation officer. It would now be 12 months before I was confirmed as such, if then. I was in some kind of no-man's land myself. No formal training, a back-door direct entrant from a shoestring-budget Prisoners' Aid Society. Into a conservative probation service which had reluctantly found a place for some of the ugly ducklings which Government expediency had thrust upon them.

I thought of the words of Jesus about being scorned and rejected, of having nowhere to call home. The Prison Service mainly looked askance at the 'do-gooders' who had been pushed in among them. For a great many years, the Chaplain alone had heroically somehow managed the welfare needs of the inmates. Now the ordered and familiar regime following Government reports was being upset. We had keys to come and go and to enter the cells, but no authority. The newest and lowest grade of prison officer could upset any interview plans at whim.

Yet with prisons beginning to become dangerously overfull and more and more ordinary human rights being sought for prisoners, the system had to change, somehow. And so I began to walk the tightrope of gaining the confidence of the prison staff, the same identification with those who were deprived of their liberty and above all, in simple welfare terms, to hopefully bring about what A.A. called 'a spiritual awakening'.

Wormwood Scrubs was on tenterhooks and I did not make a good start with authority. The spy Blake had just escaped to Russia. Security was aghast and smarting under the critical publicity which brought Lord Mountbatten to establish an enquiry. I had hardly set foot in the prison before a complaint was made that my plain blue van had been found parked suspiciously by the wall. I had not known of any regulations in this respect. The prison minefield again.

Then in my lunch hour I set off to walk around the inside perimeter of the prison as I usually had done, for exercise, during the previous eight years of my service in Wandsworth. I suddenly became aware of a body of prison officers rushing towards me. Then the Chief Officer, who was in front called

The China, which was displayed in part at Llwyn-yr-Eos Farm (Nightingale Bush), St Fagan's, 2 Sept 2000
for the Salvation Army 'Great Experience.'
Photography by The St Fagan's Folk Museum

out, "It's all right, it's our Mr. Preece". He had just been transferred himself from Wandsworth and knew me. Then to me, "You don't walk about in here, you know. The closed circuit cameras picked you up. We couldn't see from your back who it was". "It seems a different prison," I said. "It's a different service", he replied grimly.

Against the tension of the Scrubs, came the memory of the mountain-top, now nearly ten years before. Then I looked back to the warmth of Wayfarers. It is ideas which shape the world. If the vision was to be grasped, places like the Scrubs and all the other prisons could be half-emptied within a decade, instead of being best-part choked with people who were mentally ill and certainly no danger to society. We had been 25 years ahead of our time. Even in the Scrubs however came a great opportunity to work with the wives of inmates who wanted to see me, together with their husbands. It was all new and valuable experience for me too. A liberal policy of allowing these open welfare visits by an Assistant Governor played a crucial part in resolving marital problems. A coloured inmate serving a 5-year sentence for a sexual offence had his term reduced at least, to 3 years, on appeal, as a result of his wife's vital information. The man himself was almost incomprehensible and hardly able to defend himself. In the 'Scrubs' was where I should be, just then, I felt. But I had to complete my apprenticeship in the probation service too.

One day, after I had been through the prison and court system, I would go back to Aberdare and discover more of the woman whose influence from the other side of the grave had directed my steps.

The Author

Chapter 3

AGAINST THE CLOCK

"WE MUST GO before they are all dead," said Alice one morning at the breakfast table. We were reading our mail. There were several letters from unknown elderly ladies, in response to a request in 'The War Cry' asking for information from anyone who had known Grandma Shepherd. I agreed. My annual leave was coming up. It was high time to go to South Wales.

When Grandma Shepherd had gone from London by train to Aberdare with her four daughters, Kate, Pamela, Polly and Sally, a hundred years earlier, everything the five of them possessed went into a sack, we had read, "to save money". The steerage emigrants to the New World could hardly have travelled more lightly.

"Suppose we take the tent and the camping trailer," I said - that will be as basic as we can. We'll get some of the feeling of starting from scratch too, as they did. Another thing. Let's call on Fred in Oxford, on the way to Wales." It had been Fred, after all, who had encouraged me to write the book, who had pointed the way. He had been the first homeless alcoholic to recover when I had tried to put into practice Grandma Shepherd's concern for prisoners and those with drink problems in particular. Fred had fought his way from the bombsites of South London to waiting on the Dons at top table at an Oxford College. Now he even had his own council bachelor flat on the outskirts of the City.

It was a good time to call on Fred. A daughter had come all the way from Canada to meet her long-lost father. His son had come to find him at the hostel where he had become the assistant warden before his college job as a maintenance and general member of staff. His search for his children had finally been achieved with his settled way of life.

Fred was a quietly happy man but he was now seriously ill. He liked the idea of me trying to find out something of the woman who had inspired my work in the prisons and had brought us to know each other. Now he gave heart to me. Fred had put on cassette how he felt about it all and a particularly vivid account of his spiritual experience. We took photographs of Fred and his newly-discovered family.

My mind went back to the Salvation Army mercy seat at Wood Green Corps. We had knelt together, just to ask God's blessing on Fred's new drink-free life. "Isn't it hot here!" exclaimed Fred, and I thought of those two men on the road to Emmaus who had walked with the unrecognised, risen Jesus as he had unfolded the Scriptures to them. They had experienced that same, strange warmth within themselves. "Did not our hearts burn within us?" they had said afterwards, when describing their encounter to the other disciples left in Jerusalem.

We left Fred, the changed man whom we were not to see alive again. Cancer claimed him not long afterwards. We had seen Fred just in time. His daughter gave me a kiss when we parted after the funeral. I had not seen her before or since. It was reward enough.

That day, however, we had needed shortly afterwards to continue the journey on our own pilgrimage, our own search into the unknown. Merthyr was our first intended camp and we drove into it on a grey overcast evening, six hours later. We approached the town, strange to us, through the bleak, industrial wasteland of Dowlais, still looking like the landscape of the moon after the ravages of the Industrial Revolution. I thought of Alexander Cordell's vivid historical descriptions and his book 'The Rape of the Fair Country'. It did not seem to have changed over all the years.

In the rain, we had to find a farm on the outskirts, which had a campsite. We did not know a soul in Merthyr or the Rhondda Valley. I had grown up on the coastal fringe of South Wales. I felt a stranger here. It wasn't exactly camping country either. When we arrived at the farm, we were tired and somehow low in spirits. We found the proper ground flooded by the heavy rain of the previous days. A group of tents were jammed together miserably in a small, makeshift, rough and stony field. It seemed so desolate and unpromising a start for our long-anticipated quest.

The metal tent pegs bent as we tried to hammer them into the thin soil. We felt that it was not going to be easy after all and struggled to move the heavy camping trailer on the sloping, uneven ground. There was a heaviness on our minds as we felt that we didn't know what we were really trying to do or where to begin. Just a handful of little letters from people of whom we had never heard. We had to find them too in the small valley townships, villages really, where one street ran into another and one hardly knew where one was most of the time. And a faded snapshot of a grave. It seemed more than looking for a needle in a haystack.

Then, from the farmhouse, out of the gathering gloom came the sound of a little girl practising on an electric keyboard and we remembered that after all, we were in the land of song and our mood lifted.

The next morning, we crossed over the mountain to the cemetery in Aberdare. When we asked a caretaker for the whereabouts of Mother

Shepherd's grave, he told us that the manager was not in his office and suggested a far part of the extensive grounds. We wandered out into the endless expanse of graves, our little photograph in hand. There was a hedge and a pole in the background, so with this as our only clue, we set off along the edge of the cemetery, by the road.

Two hours later we were dazed with looking and sat down wearily in the heat of the midday sun. The overwhelming sense of frustration, of an oppressive mental wall of some kind, came down over us again. It was as if there was an impenetrable curtain between the past and us. A dark forbidding barrier which seemed determined to keep the secrets behind it. We were almost ready to give up the whole thing. It was all so nebulous, this historical trail. What were we looking for anyway, apart from a grave? We didn't know ourselves.

Then a man's figure appeared, walking towards where we sat dejectedly. It was the manager. "I'm sorry I wasn't here when you arrived," he said. "Come and I'll show you the grave." At the foot of a tall tree, not far from where we had first come in, near the gate, hidden in a hollow, with a hedge and a lighting pole behind it, we found her. It seemed like that. Not just a grave but a presence. It wasn't only a white headstone and surround. It was Grandma Shepherd and Auntie Polly. We had found them resting together and it was beautiful. Now we saw for the first time, the wording:

THE SALVATION ARMY
REMEMBERS WITH GRATITUDE
Mother Shepherd's
SELF-DENYING SERVICE IN THE EARLY DAYS
OF THE MOVEMENT WHEN SHE WON
THOUSANDS OF SOULS TO CHRIST
IN THE WELSH VALLEYS.

It was inscribed on the form of an open marble book, the Salvation Army's own memorial. With much imagination carved into the headstone were the Welsh daffodil and the English rose, standing for the half of her lifetime spent outside Wales. Much more than a grave, it all seemed like a shrine. Now, out of the mists of time, we had somewhere to begin. We had claimed a place in the very soil of the Valleys. Grandma Shepherd in that moment became real and, somehow, alive.

Chapter 4

THE LIGHT FROM THE RHONDDA

N OW BEGAN THE task of finding the folk who had written to say that they had known Mother Shepherd. All complete strangers to us. The small houses were strung in terraces along the sides of the mountains. Our first call was to Pentre, which had only been a name on a map of South Wales to us. The little place was part of the string of tiny townships, which ran, one into another, the length of the Upper Rhondda Valley. Its next-door neighbour however was Treorchy, made famous the world over by its Male Voice Choir. We were due to meet the Edmunds family.

Alf Edmunds' grandfather was one of the four men salvationists who had gone to prison with Louisa Lock for kneeling to pray in the town's Bridgend Square. Alf had sent me George Scott Railton's '125 Years Salvation Army', the earliest account of the Army's history which he had written as William Booth's first Commissioner. It was with fascination that I read the account of Mother Shepherd. Now another human link with all those events of 100 years ago was to be forged.

But before we reached Pentre, we had an unusual experience. There were no listed camping sites in the Rhondda Valley and we asked the Forestry Commission to help, which they did willingly when they knew of our historical mission. They found us a place on what seemed to be the former slagheap of the old pit in Blaen-y-Cwm (Before the Valley). The 'tip' had been landscaped and grassed over but as we tried to hammer the tent pegs into the hard surface, we discovered what it was and thought, 'A strange place to camp'. Never before had we been in such a situation. It was a curious site altogether.

A few hundred yards away was the sealed-off entrance to the mile-long railway tunnel under the mountain which had connected the Rhondda with the Avon Valley and the coal exporting port of Swansea, so vital to its trade in the latter part of the last century. Then coal had been king. During the War, Alice and I had travelled through the pitch-black tunnel in the train with my parents when we had all visited my Uncle Charlie (former Captain Charles Coole), great-aunt Kate Shepherd's widower. Now, forty years later, we were back on the very spot. We had no idea that we were going to end up there when we started out on our quest. It seemed uncanny somehow.

For some reason, Alice and I felt apprehensive and vulnerable, in this isolated spot, part way up the mountain, although the old mining village lay down in the valley bottom, only about half-a-mile away. "I'm going to sleep in my clothes tonight," said Alice. The long night passed uneasily for us both until the light of morning filtered into the tent. Then we heard a dog barking outside. I got out of my sleeping bag and unzipped the door. Two men, each with a dog were coming towards us. 'Good Morning' I called out. They returned the greeting good-naturedly. "We saw your tent," one said. "We usually bring our dogs up here for a walk first thing in the morning." "Pleased to see you " I replied. "We feel rather peculiar, stuck up here on the mountainside." "We've been keeping an eye on you, don't worry!" they said. Then they told us their story.

Both had been miners in the valley before the pits had closed. One had been badly smashed in an accident and he walked with a limp. "This place used to be a pit" they told us. My mind wandered. So many men killed or maimed in the daily battle underground. No wonder we had felt so strange. It was as though the very ground cried out with the agony of the past. We had camped over a graveyard.

This was our introduction to the Rhondda. A sense of some solid wall, of discouragement, of it all being such hard going, of not knowing which way to go, which way to turn. It was hot as the sun rose and we felt tired up there on the high land. Were we mad trying to do our research this way? Just camping in the Rhondda on these bare slopes was hard enough, but here we were trying to find out things as well. Yet in a strange way we were experiencing something else too, an element we had wanted to know. How had Pamela Shepherd felt, coming down to the Rhondda all those years ago? Here we were, with a car, a camping trailer full of equipment, clothes, money enough. All they had went into a sack and they even had to borrow a saucepan to make the tea, at first, in their bare rented cottage. They had slept on the floor and used orange boxes for furniture. What faith they must have had! How tough they must have been leaving the security and comparative comfort of the Christian Mission in London for this bleak, intimidating country. It would have been ravaged, treeless and torn in the desperate digging for coal. At least it was green now, not black and grey.

Yet, Aberdare had been the printing and literary centre of South Wales. Its handsome chapels provided the pulpits for some of the most brilliant preachers of the day. Even as Paul had ventured into the erudite Athens of his times and stood in the shadow of the mighty Acropolis to proclaim what had seemed a ludicrous account of a Jewish carpenter who had risen from the dead, so must the 'Hallelujah Washerwoman' have also appeared a 'vain babbler'. Like the man born blind, she had been made to see in a spiritual sense and her life had been changed beyond any learned argument.

But where were we going to find our facts, our story of what had actually happened? In Pentre Library, a bemused lady assistant heard our story that something dramatic had happened a hundred years before on her very doorstep but she did not seem to know anything. We had run into a stony corner, another dead end. Alice and I looked at each other. We did not feel like another strange night over the entombed pit. Where to go though? I said to Alice, 'We'll give ourselves a break and go up to the reservoirs of Tal-y-Bont, where I believe it is pretty and stay at the very first Bed-and-Breakfast we see'.

So, we headed for the outskirts of Merthyr, on the road to Ponsticillt and Brecon. It was a narrow, twisting, climbing road which claimed all my driving attention, so much so that after a while Alice said, "We've just passed a B and B sign." I stopped. I didn't really know where we were going. "We did say the first one, didn't we?"

It was not too easy to turn back to where a rough farm track led some distance up to a house. We drove slowly up the stony track until we reached the mountain farm. No one answered our knock on the door. Only a few chickens stopped to peer curiously at us. The place seemed deserted. I saw an

Hollesley Bay. Alice and the camping trailer which carried all our gear in our journeys in the Welsh valleys.

open barn door and peered inside. In the heat of the day, sweating and hot, a man was struggling to shear a sheep. He stopped as we looked in. He said briefly, "My wife will be back in a minute. She sees to the bed-and-breakfasts." Then he took a drink of cider and went back to the sheep lying motionless on the ground.

We had arrived at Pen-Gelli-Fach (Top of the Little Grove) and the base from which we now launched our endeavours. Like Grandma Shepherd and the girls, we now had a real roof over our heads. We too had been 'taken in' off the inhospitable mountainsides and stony places. We had found an oasis and felt that somehow, we now 'belonged' to the Rhondda and had come back to claim our heritage and to take possession of the land. It was to become another 'Shangri-La' for us.

At the back of the little sheep farm was the grove from which the place took its name. From that high point the glorious Brecon Beacons stretched away to Pen-y-Fan, 30 miles away in the distance, not a building in sight. An overpowering silence calmed the emotions with its peace and tranquility. It was like a glimpse into the Promised Land.

Some curious circles of stone heaps, we were told later had been studied with great interest by archaeological experts from Cardiff University who had considered them to be 5000 years old. What a perspective for our own fieldwork! A hundred years suddenly seemed nothing, like yesterday. The track of the old Roman road to Brecon could be seen. We had discovered our own way ahead in an amazing way too.

We found good friends as well and a family who warmed to our endeavours. The sheep-shearer was really a Bargoed schoolteacher and former RAF officer and navigator, Ken Thomas who worked his parents' farm in his spare time. Dinah Thomas, his wife, loved horses and was starting a little riding school. Her father had been a Squadron Leader on Blenheims in Malta when our crew had been there in 1942. We had done reconnaissance in our Beaufort for the Blenheims, attacking Rommell's convoys. It was a remarkable coincidence, if we could call it that. So, we found, in a way, an island fortress again for our trips into the Valleys.

We had written to Cardiff where we had been told that there was a good reference library and this was our next objective. There we were to make our great initial discovery. Came the morning when we waited while the archive copies of the 'Western Mail' and 'South Wales News' for February and March 1879 were brought to us and we eagerly turned the large pages.

There it was! A succession of articles, headed by 'Morien', the literary name of Owen Morgan who had been the author of the History of Pontypridd and the Rhondda Valleys. We could hardly contain ourselves. It was all there in professional form and detail. The Revival, which had swept the upper part of the Rhondda Valley, had begun when Auntie Kate had first preached on 8th February 1879 in the vestry of Shiloh Chapel where the Police Court was held on Mondays. Her very words had been faithfully recorded. Kate had spoken of herself as 'the daughter of a King'. A journalist from a London daily paper had been later sent to interview her, somewhat to his bewilderment at her spiritual replies to his questions.

We made our way back from The Hayes Library in Cardiff to our retreat in Pen Gelli Fach stunned by our discovery. We felt a sense of having a new mandate, a new authority. This wonderful piece of history, which had even found its way into the economic section of a schoolmaster's textbook, had been lost to the country in these faded archives. The Rhondda Revival had been one of those factors which had led to the later 1904 Revival which had spread around the world. The fog and darkness had been swept away.

The story was coming alive in our hands with a new relevance for today, a burning message to be communicated again. Not just an interesting series of facts but something urgent and powerful with a meaning for our times. If we had been guided so far in our blind quest we could trust now with renewed confidence to what we believed was our leading in God's purposes and we set out daily to clothe history with the personal experiences of those witnesses who remained alive.

THE HIDDEN ONES

The letter had come out of the blue. "There is mist over the mountain of Twmbarlwm. It is 6.30 a.m. and all is quiet as I write to you. The last time I saw you was as a baby in your mother's arms ... Jack Hynam."

Who was Jack Hynam? The years had passed, and now we found ourselves on the doorstep of a trim little council house on the mountainside overlooking the new town of Cwmbran, in Gwent, South Wales. We rang the bell. The door opened and a distinguished-looking man of about 75 stood there and said "Croeso!" (Welcome). It was third-cousin Jack. Behind him stood a neat little woman, his wife Bess. Inside was a refined old lady, Bess's widowed mother, Mrs. Davies. They were delighted to see us.

Jack spoke warmly of cousin Sally, my grandmother, fearlessly driving a horse and trap, overturning and carrying on unabashed. The past came alive as he spoke, as it had never done before. Here was an independent witness, a former R.A.F. officer who had known all my family when they had been in their prime and himself a boy soldier in the first World War.

Coming home on leave one day and visiting Mother Shepherd at the

'Nook', he had brought out a packet of cigarettes. "You don't want those Jack, good boy, do you?" his Aunt had gently asked and taking them from him, had dropped them on the blazing fire. "I haven't smoked since then. I was her favourite nephew", smiled Jack. "I could never stay at the 'Nook' though," said Jack wryly. "It was always full of girls, you see, whom she had taken in from the streets until they could be found somewhere to live. We always took a basket of food with us when I went with my mother. They always needed food there."

He lapsed into silence. "After I was wounded and gassed, the Army brought me to Penrhiewtyn Hospital. Aunt Pamela, Cousin Pam and Polly came to visit me. I was pretty broken and they didn't think that I'd live. I remember them all kneeling around my bed in the ward... You have some wonderful forebears, Charlie. You should be proud of them. I was named after Benjamin Morgan you know."

"Now you must have tea from the Swansea China", and Bess carefully placed the beautiful pieces on the embroidered tablecloth. It was more precious to them than any gold or silver service could have been. We were almost afraid to eat and drink from it. Not one of its 40 pieces ever broken. Over 170 years old, it had travelled from Wales to London, then back again, and yet once again to London and return, and many places in the Valleys. Bess could remember 14 different homes of their own, alone, which it had graced apart from all its travelling before Caredig, Jack's mother, Mother Shepherd's youngest sister, born in London, gave it to her as a wedding present. This was the third time that it had been such, passed lovingly from woman to woman.

What a miracle it was that it had survived. Delicate and fragile, a silken gossamer thread which had bound together generations of Morgan womenfolk in their family saga of struggle. What a story it could tell, a book in itself. One fell silent before such an heirloom. The living, almost human link which went back to Waterloo.

This was the first of many visits which we made to Bess and Jack over the years. Jack took us to the remains of the old British Ironworks in Abersychan, the spot where Benjamin Morgan's blacksmith shop had stood, the row where remained the houses he had built, to Talywain where Grandma Shepherd had been born in the house on the mountainside, to family graves, Noddfa Chapel where his mother Caredig was buried. Time fell away as we stood in these places. It might have been yesterday, so vividly did Jack recall them. His own story is told in 'Woman of the Valleys'. In their lovely little home, we prayed and sang while Bess played the piano. There was always the sense of great heritage there. It was certainly a gateway to Heaven and one to the past.

"Thank you for coming into our lives, Charlie," said Jack towards the end of his days. One of the nicest things that was ever said to me and humbling moreover. "It was Grandma Shepherd who brought me" was all I could say.

"If you only had a smattering of Welsh, Charlie, it would help you" said Jack. We were singing some of the old Welsh hymns with Bess, around the piano. These had been Grandma Shepherd's lifeblood and I felt that I was missing something because I did not know what they meant. As a boy in the County School, Port-Talbot, our morning assemblies had alternate English and Welsh hymns so I had learnt, parrot fashion, to sing in Welsh and no one had ever thought of translating them for those mostly English pupils who did not know their meaning. The melodies had strangely appealed to me, however, and now there was an even more powerful reason for understanding something more of Grandma Shepherd. I considered myself Welsh by upbringing, with both parents born in Wales although their families had come from Devon and Warwickshire in the days when the coal boom was at its height and Wales had been the Klondyke for the black gold which provided power for the world.

Jack produced a Welsh textbook and someone else some records, and Alice and I returned to London with a new resolve. My nearest evening class was in Westminster and as I registered to learn Welsh, I had a tremendous feeling of a new dimension coming into my life. My mind went back 50 years to being a boy in school and having to choose between taking Welsh and French. "Welsh...?" we had asserted with all the know-it-all of teenage youth. "A dying language". Now, I was seeking that which I felt I had lost along the way, my Welsh birthright.

Thus began another journey. At the end of that first Welsh lesson, in a plain-as-could-be-classroom, Eleanor Evans, our teacher from North Wales had said "We will ask Mair to sing something for us before we go." Mair, an advanced pupil from another class had come in and sang "Oes Gafr Eto", (Is There Yet a Goat?), the beloved folk song about the milking of goats wandering on the mountainside. Then we all joined in the chorus which all of us with anything to do with Wales knew at least in part from our schooldays.

Not far from Parliament and Big Ben, in the very heart of London, there came alive for us that night a corner of Wales, the country we had left, most of us to find work after the land had been pillaged and impoverised for its mineral wealth. It had been said that during the 1930s Wales had been denuded of its youth. Girls had come to London to go into domestic service, boys had worked in hotels, the miners had sung in the streets. For two years I had eked out an existence on a tiny Government grant. Now, I felt, we were recapturing some of what had been lost in those hard days.

The rich treasury of Welsh thought locked up in those hymns was thrilling to come to understand. A language 5000 years old, something like Hebrew, with a life and vitality which gave depths of meaning. Spiritual diamonds from the mines of the great ones of the past. Jack had been right. I felt a fresh rush of blood relationship with Grandma Shepherd, proud of her Celtic heritage and natural authority on her native heath, yet, with that love for the rose of England too, which had combined the two streams of her whole being in a flood of caring for the two nations. It was a tremendous combination. It was England which had provided me with work and a living, which I could never afford to forget. Welsh people, after all, had been coming to England for 500 years, since the times of Henry VII. It was a bond which went back a long way. A traditional home for refugees too. Alice's Huguenot forebears had been first made welcome by Queen Elizabeth I, the Tudor sovereign we shared in common.

The song finished in the classroom. "You must all come to the Cymanfa Ganu (Singing Festival) next month in Westminster Chapel," said Eleanor, adding with a smile, "You'll be speaking Welsh by Christmas".

So began a new quest, this time in London, with new friends, a new family, the London Welsh. Came the time when I linked up with Capel Holloway, a Welsh Presbyterian Chapel built a hundred years before when North London began to expand. To step from the cosmopolitan streets near the Nags Head pub into the oasis of the traditional Welsh Chapel was a tonic, like leaping across time and distance to the Valleys themselves. I was finding, recapturing something of the Wales I had left behind as a sixteen-year-old boy but always, I reminded myself, in the England which had been to me, like so many others, my refuge in those hard days and the place where I had met my wife. It was a boon to have the blessing of both worlds.

What new dimensions were coming into my life because of Grandma Shepherd? They seemed never ending. The next happening was the first Summer School at St. Donat's Castle and the Atlantic College, at Llantwit Major, near Cardiff, in South Wales. The reconstructed medieval castle had been built on an authentic ancient site by Randolph Hearst, the American newspaper magnate. Local tradition averred that Caractercus, the captured British chieftain of Roman times, was restored on account of his noble bearing, to his native land. He had become a Christian in Rome and founded a community in Llantwit Major, just two miles away. Certainly, it became a spiritual centre of learning.

Now Bryan James, a Welsh school teacher with a great concern for his language, year after year organised a Cardiff University extra-mural course for men and women learning 'The language of Heaven' - 'Y Iaeth y Nefoedd'. There I was introduced to many student choruses, swinging, lilting, catchy and full of fun. One, "Milgi Milgi", I believed to be a marching gospel song, something like "Onward Christian Soldiers", a 'good-going' tune, it would be called. To my surprise, it was the jolly story of a hungry greyhound who just needed a good meal!

I learnt a merry side to Welsh in complete contrast to the sad-sounding chapel hymns. There was a riotous, devil-may-care, rollicking side to the Welsh character too. Life was meant to be a bit of a circus, a holiday, in between times and the two went together. "We did have fun in Aberdare!" my Grandma Pope used to say of her days in the coal-and-chapel town of her youth. This was the side of Grandma Shepherd which somehow had become lost to me, concerned as I was, with her deep spirituality. The Welsh could slip from singing hymns in church and chapel to 'The White Hart' in Llantwit Major, without any problem. It was all the same to them. A simple expression of spirituality seemed to be the warp and weft of life, not something separate. I came to be reminded of this in Israel where the Torah was never far away from every-day affairs.

There was a great warmth at glorious St. Donat's under its cloudless blue skies and crash of breakers on the rocky cliff shore. We found another new family, young and not so young. The country dancing in the oak-raftered hall, the carefree fiddlers, the 'turns' of the Nosen Lawen (evening impromptu concerts where everybody did something to entertain), the treasure hunts around the Castle, the singing to guitars, the barbecues, it was all another facet of this rich kaleidoscope of Welshness, of a fresh existence.

"I am come that they might have new life, and have it more abundantly". (John:10:10). It was true. There was a story Jack told me which I hesitate to relate and yet it had happened and was in its way, a gem of that common touch, that honest humour, the market-place language of those tumultuous days which stole people's hearts and made them feel that faith in God was not a starchy, dressed-up parade for the 'respectable' but an earthy, sometimes uproarious transaction where ordinary people could have a good laugh in a heart-warming way.

It seemed that one day in the Aberdare open-air meeting, which was a new thing and, indeed, something the like of which had never been seen before in the town's Victoria Square, a well-known,one-time local gambler and owner of illegal fighting cocks had been converted. According to the custom of the day, he had been asked to tell how his life had changed. Now William Booth had discovered in the slums of London's East End that people listened with far more attention to the sometimes racy 'testimonies' and colourful vernacular of new believers than even to his own dramatic orations and gripping Gospel messages. Anyway, to come to the point, the man told the eager crowd, hanging on his every word that since he had come to know the Lord, he didn't have a cock any more. He had given both of them to Miss Shepherd.

The crowd was beside itself. The roars of laughter have come down through all these years in the family lore as a kind of heirloom of spontaneous, deep-inside, witness of Jesus. It was said 'the common people heard him gladly'. (Mark;12:37). Auntie Kate's blushes brought many nearer the Kingdom that night in the 'ring'.

Kate Shepherd was a character too, in spite of her saintliness. She had not been likened by the Press of her day to Joan of Arc for nothing. According to Jack again, Grandma Shepherd and Kate were walking down the street in Pontypool one day. They had been shopping and Auntie Kate was swinging their Sunday dinner by its legs, a dead fowl, ready for plucking. They were accosted by a man who proceeded to berate Mother Shepherd until Kate bluntly warned him to stop insulting her mother and when he persisted, promptly hit him on the head with her departed feathered fistful.

Souls were won in those days in all sorts of ways. He was probably at her next meeting to see what kind of Amazon the Shepherd girl-preacher was, what kind of young woman it could be who had transformed the Upper Rhondda.

GRANNIE PAXFORD OF ABERAMAN

It all started with the words "I am writing in answer to your letter published in 'The War Cry' of 20th May 1978. I feel sure that I could be of assistance to you in your search for information on Mother Shepherd. Although I am now in my 83rd year, I have clear memories of Mother Shepherd and the happy times I spent at her Mission in Johns Street, Trecynon, near Aberdare. Before she opened the Mission in Johns Street, she held services in a small cellar. My mother cleaned this cellar for her and many times, I helped her to scrub the floors. I have been a Salvationist all my life and still attend regularly, being the Home League Secretary for over 40 years but now retired. I have a picture of Mother Shepherd, published in a local book, in Welsh costume, which I would be happy to send to you, providing you will return it to me.

Mother Shepherd played a big part in my early life and there are many tales and stories that I could relate to you. I would not know where to stop writing about her..."

So it was that in July 1978, my wife and I came to knock at the door of a neat, tiny terraced house in the village of Cwmaman near Aberdare. A little old lady appeared on the threshold. I held out her letter and said, "You wrote to me... I am Charles Preece, the great-grandson of Mother Shepherd." Her face lit up. There was such a warmth in her smile. I felt as though she was putting her arms around me. "Come in!" She called out, "She is my mother too!"

We spent hours, after that, drinking tea in the kitchen with 'Grannie Paxford' as everyone knew her - but her Christian name was Phoebe and this is how Mother Shepherd would have called her. We were entranced with the stories of the spell which Mother Shepherd had woven around her, as a young girl. We took a recording of some of what she had to tell and as I listen to her voice now, more than twenty years later, those bubbling, joyful magical moments come alive with their enthusiasm. This beautiful, unassuming little lady became a living link with that legendary figure, my 'Hallelujah Washerwoman' great-grandmother.

Grannie Phoebe Paxford in her uniform, January 1980.

57

"She prayed for the devil to be taken out of you once", my own mother had told me. How Grannie Paxford had roared when my wife Alice had added "He was miserable, you see!" "She would, she would!" chortled Grannie Paxford "That's just how she was!"

Grannie Paxford continues, "There were hundreds of children in her Sunday Schools - she would be in every door fetching them out - we all had to go, even in our clogs and 'naily boots', but no child was long without shoes once Mother Shepherd came to know about it.

She had a wonderful way of winning. If only you met her once, you'd love her too. There never was a lady like Mother Shepherd. No never, she was marvellous, great, a spiritual woman. I just wanted to be like her, that was my ambition. If it weren't for her, I wouldn't have been the same person, I don't think. She taught me such a lot of things.

As long as I can go down to that hall (in nearby Aberaman) and see her photograph I am all right. I feel in tears when I talk about her. She was always so smart and tall. She was always joyful ... Every time I preach the gospel, I bring Mother Shepherd in. The thoughts of her are coming back so fresh to me now. I always feel her spirit when I go into that Army hall. I can't leave it out of my system."

So we reached back nearly a century and Grannie brought it all into the present of the little kitchen for us. Before she had been born, before she had come to know Mother Shepherd as a 16 year-old, she had heard the wonderful stories. 'They were throwing all the rubbish at her but she fought, how she fought until they all came to love her".

This practical little lady had buried a husband and two daughters herself and had known the hardship of bringing up a family in her mining village. She recalled those happy days when the Sunday Schools of Mother Shepherd's three missions went for their annual 'Treats' in their brakes (the open horse-drawn passenger vehicles of the day). "I was only a young girl then and my mother used to send me to the mission to keep me out of trouble."

There were saucy times when with her pals, she had stood up large at the back of the Mission Hall and sung out, noticeably aloud, to attract Mother Shepherd's attention so that she would remember seeing them before they ducked out of sight and disappeared for a walk. 'When Mam would ask Mother Shepherd later if she had seen us, then of course she had to say that she had. We could say that we had been there!" she smiled at the memory of the escapades of her girlhood.

Phoebe's own mother was a young widow at the time and thought the world of Mother Shepherd too, so Phoebe grew up feeling that she had two mothers. She told us that Mother Shepherd had a special concern for widows and used to make up parcels of food and clothing for the needy. Undoubtedly Pamela Shepherd's own harsh experiences in the slums and her 'Widow's Bonnet' had given her a special feeling for those many women, and their young children especially in the mining valleys with their heavy death toll of family men. The women were left in those days, to battle on alone. There was only the workhouse or the 'parish relief' to sustain them in their plight.

Of all the people we met, it was Phoebe who, at the very beginning, made a special contribution and was an inspiration to keep on with the research, because she was not directly related to the family. With her bright eyes, gleaming silver hair and robin-like round face, she had been a child and then in her teens, with Mother Shepherd in her late 70's, during those formative years which led to a lifetime of voluntary service in The Salvation Army.

Her undimmed recollection and regard was monumental. There was an unconscious note of awe in all she said which convinced us that we were not mistaken in feeling that the biography should be written. She was a living and independent witness and had little time for anyone 'official' understandingly - who had not heard of her spiritual 'mother'. Phoebe's life may well have been bounded by the Welsh Valleys but in them there was, in her view, no one to compare with Pamela Shepherd. She was indeed 'her girl'.

"There was a time, later on, when she embarrassed me so, though", went on Phoebe. Mother Shepherd had a stall in the market where she used to serve tea and cakes to raise funds for her missions. Phoebe had started courting and took her new young man along to the stall. He had not met Mother Shepherd before. She looked straight at him. "Her eyes seemed to go right through you sometimes." Phoebe said.

Mother Shepherd had seized upon the opportunity to take hold of the unsuspecting suitor's coat saying "Phoebe is my girl, you understand, and if anything happens to her, you will have me to reckon with!" Phoebe related how she had not known where to look and had wished that the ground would open up and swallow her. What the young man thought we do not know but he subsequently became her husband!

"There was a man once who would not give his wife her money for the housekeeping when he was paid on Friday nights. Anyway, the next pay day, Mother Shepherd was standing outside the colliery gates when all the men came out. She soon picked out her man and pointed her umbrella at him. 'You go straight home with your money now", she called out clearly "or you'll have me to deal with!' There's shamed he was! Before all his mates too. 'Mother Shepherd is going to sort you out, is she?' they would ask whenever they bumped into him at work. There was no more trouble."

Another story was of how one of her brothers - she was the only surviving member of her family was afraid of Mother Shepherd. "She had such winning ways but she could be a terror too. When she used to come visiting, he would run out of the back door and sit up on the mountain as soon as he heard her at the front door". When the visit was over, Phoebe used to go out to the back of the house to empty the teapot and that was when her brother used to know that the visitor had left and then he would come in.

"My daughters say to me sometimes 'You bring Mother Shepherd into everything'. They get tired of me always talking about her, you see", she said with an impish smile. This little woman was so clear, so captivated by her memories, so gripped by the wonder of the woman who had transformed her life. "My own mother was lovely", she said. "but Mother Shepherd was like my mother too. We both loved her. We were very close."

How I came to love this Grandma of mine. Here, nearly 70 years after Mother Shepherd had 'gone to Glory', her name still brought a strange light into people's eyes. "I keep asking these new Salvation Army people 'Have you heard of Mother Shepherd' and when they say they haven't, I tell them they don't know what they are missing". Granny shook her head in unbelief.

In her little home, we were indeed blessed. We remember her 'Promise Box'. A slip of rolled paper would be selected at random from the box offered by her to all her visitors before they left. The little roll contained a verse of Scripture which contained a promise which was then read out. It was a lovely benediction. Above all, Grannie Paxford provided those vivid pictures of bygone days and encouraged us to go on seeking out the countless pieces of the jig-saw of Mother Shepherd's life which had been strewn all over the valleys and beyond. Her life had been scattered liberally, like corn and had taken root and survived for 70 years and more. It was as though only yesterday that her fearless, winning ways had won the heart of a little girl for her Lord.

"All the 50 years, I have tried to do what she taught me", Grannie said. I felt somehow that she was near to meeting her spiritual mother again. There was that faraway look about her. Indeed, we were not to see her alive, again. "My days will soon be over", she had said quietly and so did the day come in late August of 1980 when a phone call from Wales told us that Grannie had been 'called Home'. Quietly and peacefully, she had folded up the garment of her life and put it aside, just after her corps officer had left her bedside.

When we journeyed down from London on August 29th, there was a great sadness in her daughter's house, among her sorrowing family. Welsh-cakes and coffee were waiting for the travellers as a reminder of the ever-free hospitality of her home. What a tribute was reflected from the community for whom she had so long cared. A great mountain of flowers which seemed to reach from floor to ceiling in the front room where the little figure rested, cradled in the blossoms.

Through Victoria Square, Aberdare, where the 'ring,' (the open-air meeting) like its own 'thin red line' had stood firm, went the cortege, then up Gadlys Hill, along the very same route of that other funeral procession of over 60 years before, to Aberdare Cemetery, past Trecynon where Grannie had helped scrub the floor of a cellar "not much bigger than this room" she had told us, in her little kitchen.

The rain lashed down without respite as though Hell itself was bent on withholding sunshine from the small woman. The cemetery was dripping with the chill of the torrent of the slate-grey deluge and then, as we struggled along the muddy path, the sound of brass instruments fought its own way through the downpour and I was amazed to see a group of bandsmen from Merthyr Corps, playing in more rain than I had thought possible.

At the head of the grave stood a bandswoman colour-sergeant, holding the Salvation Army flag. I knew she was Muriel, a policewoman by profession and I felt the link was very fitting. The rain streamed off her bonnet and down her uniform as she stood there, upright. I thought of the six stalwart police officers who had carried Mother Shepherd to her last resting place in that same cemetery, perhaps only a few hundreds of yards away.

At the graveside, bare-headed and undaunted by the teeming rain, the Divisional Commander, Major Lawrie Jardine, calmly conducted the service, a plastic sheet over his Bible. I was proud of the Army that day. We were wet enough. They must all have been soaked.

My last sight of the coffin as we filed past reminded me that there was another duty to be done. There was a story to write about Mother Shepherd's little girl. Over sixty years before, a triumphant note had been sounded in Aberdare by the stirring strains of the marching band, in spite of the drawn blinds, the stilled and hushed streets. Now it was Grannie Paxford, in the teeth of the rainstorm, going Home to the music of the band, to be with her own mother, her mother-in-God and, above all, to be safe in the arms of Jesus who had loved and won them all.

GWLADYS LEWIS.

"Charles, I've found someone who says she's your cousin - her name's Gwladys Lewis", said David, my probation officer friend from Aberdare. "She lives in Twynyrodyn (The Hill of the Lime Kiln). We looked blank. "I'll take you there," he said, seeing our lost look. Before going down to Aberdare on our first visit I had written to the probation officer to ask if he knew of any elderly folk who might have known Grandma Shepherd. This was the first result.

"Well, I never knew that I had a cousin by that name", I replied. "I'll take you and Alice to her this afternoon" said David. 'It's over in Merthyr."

So, a little later in the day we found ourselves knocking on the door of a little terraced house in Bryn Street, its name meant, "Hill Street", which clung steeply to a slope overlooking the town.

The door of No. 10 opened. A small woman stood there. "Here's your cousin, Gwladys", said David. We had never seen the dear lady before. "Charlie!" she exclaimed. "You were a baby in your mother's arms when I last saw you". She flung her arms around me and over 50 years vanished. "Come in", she said and led the way into her home. Another member of Grandma Shepherd's extended family had claimed us. David smiled and went back to his office.

"Mother Shepherd often stayed with us when my mother was alive, " said Gwladys. "She used to sleep with me". We sat down to tea. The photographs came out and our new cousin unfolded another hidden corner of the past for which we had come to look. We never did quite work out our relationship with Gwladys but I'm sure she was right. We didn't somehow have time in the enormous task of trying to capture all that Gwladys had to say. We were third cousins or something like that but it didn't really matter - Grandma Shepherd was our common link.

Little by little we learnt Gwladys's story. With an over-the-hills look in her eyes, she recaptured the South Wales of 60 years before, when she had been a young woman. She must have been a tremendous figure in her high days, well-known in the Valleys as an elocutionist. A chirpy little woman, a kind of Gracie Fields character whose feet went deeply into her native soil. Gwladys had been active in concerts for good causes, including raising funds for the starving families of miners on strike. The men had come home from the first World War, from the agony of the trenches' mud and horror, to the slump of the mining industry in the South Wales Valleys.

The secretary of the Gwent Relief Committee had been her one-time sweetheart, Jack Hynam of whom I have already written. They had not married due to his severe wounds. The young ex-soldier, still suffering from the poison gas of the trenches and a shattered ankle, had later been victimised by the employers and told after the miners had been driven back to work, by hunger, that there would be no work for him in the Valleys. Jack had gone to London and worked as a dishwasher in London hotels. While working in the kitchens, Jack had married Bess. All the time he had studied law until he obtained a commission in the R.A.F. This was the stuff of the people of the valleys.

Gwladys herself must have risked displeasing her own establishment with her radical help to Jack Hynam in the relief committee work. She had been bold enough to become a school attendance officer in a male-dominated preserve. One of her duties was to escort delinquent boys on railway journeys. She prevented runaway escapes by the simple expedient of removing their braces!

The barren, wind-swept, scarred hills were something of a no-man's-land themselves. The Valleys were lined with the huge heaps of slag and waste from the deep pits and seemed to have erupted from them like countless volcanoes. The soil was only deep enough for tussocky grass on which the mountain sheep plaintively struggled themselves to find something to eat. Coal was no longer King and the overseas markets had stopped clambering for the dynamic Welsh coal. They had found their own, more easily-worked seams and the British Navy had changed over to burning cheap oil for their fuel.

The wharves and piers of the one-time, busiest port in the world, Cardiff had sunk into moss-and-seaweed-clad wooden ruins and a cold paralysis had gripped the Valleys with a death-like iron hold.

Trapped between the mountains, in the economic blizzard of the 20s and 30s, with the desperate miners' strikes against the lowering of wages and relentless slide into destitution, Gwladys organised concerts, sang, recited, laughed and joked her way around the pits and the miners' halls trying to raise spirits and funds at the same time.

In the valley roads, the jazz bands marched and counter-marched with their 'gazookers', resonant simple wind instruments, grown-up, trumpet-like improvements to the primitive comb-and-paper children's toys. Trained to a high standard by former Army sergeants, their drill and drumming would have been a credit to the Brigades of Guards and with their big bass drums borne on imitation leopard skins and gleaming white tassels, dangling and swinging from their side drums they stormed through the townships in defiance of all that the world was throwing against them. It was so brave.

Their steady marching confronted the enemy of despair and depression. Drumsticks flashing through the air in a riot of movement, it was heart-warming and had stirred my blood as a small boy, only partially understanding what it was all about. They didn't have the chapel banners of the Chartists and the revival hymns of 25 years before but the spirit of care was the same. Somehow, the Gospel hadn't reached them in the same way and the Red Flag of Labour had been hoisted instead.

William Booth had said that you couldn't preach to people whose feet were cold, from concrete floors. So he had more expensive wooden boards in his halls. Perhaps the feet of people who were frozen from the chill of grinding poverty could not take in the Gospel either   so they expressed themselves in the flaming colours, the vocal music, the stage uniforms of their marching bands. They defied the dole, the hated Means Test, living on 'sop' - bread soaked in weak tea with a bit of sugar if you were lucky. Their names and costumes were as colourful and gay as a stream of butterflies against the grey hills: the Masqueraders, Orientals, Grenadiers, Kentucky Minstrels, Nelson's Sailors, Red Indians, Gypsies, the names fade but not the memories.

The world of white-faced people which hid the hunger at home lifted their hearts for a while at the carnivals where men with nothing to do had manoeuvered for hour after hour creating precision movements which compared to the Trooping of the Colour. The colourful floats were a sight to behold, long before the days of the Notting Hill Carnival and the jolly swaying steel bands. Old lorries were turned Cinderella-like into marvels of imagination. There was no anger against the suffering of the times, only good humour and fun. Into these valleys, The Salvation Army had poured its resources of men, women and such money as it had. Perhaps the Gospel would take new root but the first thing was to succour a desperate people. They did not forget it either.

The chapels and churches too had organised relief committees and soup kitchens, singing festivals, marches, parades, Sunday School outings. A day at the seaside was the height of a child's holiday-making. The people refused to be beaten, proud in their poverty. They stuck it out until it was clear that the valleys were all doomed and then quietly, with dignity, the men packed their few belongings and made for London - or any place where, at least, they could earn enough to eat. Wales was denuded of its youth as the Valley populations were halved through migration to an England which largely did not seem to know what was happening in stricken South Wales.

Sitting in Gwladys's kitchen, we began to see something of our indomitable forbears. "Grandma Shepherd gave me her Salvation Army brooch - here it is." Gwladys brought out the stainless steel brooch in the form of a shield and I took a photograph. It was the earliest badge which had been worn, sometimes by men as well as women.

Then we turned to Welsh hymns and Gwladys translated some of the gems into English. I came across the curious fact that Gwladys and other Welsh-speaking people of substantial educational background had to stop and obviously think hard when I asked for the literal English meaning or answered with a wealth of expressions which meant that a simple translation was too 'thin' or not rich enough to convey all the depth of the original Welsh. This was one of the reasons why I felt that I would have to learn my ancestral tongue if I were to understand the richness of the language which had been on Mother Shepherd's lips. I realised early through talking to Gwladys that while a number of Welsh hymns had been literally and beautifully translated into English, many had words completely different from their original meaning.

I remember a jovial English-speaking farmer living near Brecon who had learnt to sing Calon Lan ('A Clean Heart') in Welsh, imperfectly but recognisably, who declared: 'It.does more for me in Welsh which I do not understand, than in English which I do!' Again, I was recapturing something which had been lost to me, my unknown roots, my sense that there was something coming alive in my life experience, an element that was vital, and inspiring. I had not left everything behind, after all, when in my own time, the search for work had taken me from Wales.

It was no reflection of my love for the English language as I had been born of sturdy English parents who themselves had their birth in Wales, but a dimension which had even preceded it 5000 years ago and which could enhance it. I suppose it was like Hebrew to Jewish people, their own ancient language with all that it meant to them spiritually.

So, through being a superb English elocutionist, into the depths of her spiritual spoken expression, she had a plus-factor which came through. When I wondered where she found her strength, it emerged through her translations of Calon Lan in particular. This gem which comes close to the Welsh National Anthem in its popularity, it was for me the Gospel in song, a prayer for those who did not think of praying but wanted to be the best that they could be. It was a clarion call for a pure heart, for integrity.

I would not wish to labour this point about Welsh. To me it is a kind of experience, common to us all, of a deep-seated hunger for something which we know-not-what but which is real enough. We feel that it is something to do with our spiritual life, with our inmost being, with our very soul. It was a pathway to another plane of life yet I would not dare to suggest that one has to learn Welsh to understand something of Heaven! It can come in so many other ways to a seeking spirit.

I could see something of our Mother Shepherd in Gwladys too. Her recklessness of spirit and action, a fire which shone all the more in adversity. She had lived alone for 30 years yet her family was the world around her. My own grandmother, Sarah Ann ('Sally') had fearlessly driven horse-drawn traps over the rough mountain roads and ridden horses bare-back to the miners' meetings on the hills, like her grandfather Benjamin Morgan.

When my grandfather, Aaron Pope a Devon man who had learnt to speak and preach in Welsh was injured in a colliery and was denied any compensation, my mother had dug the mountainside garden to raise vegetables and Grandma Sally had carried sacks of sand which she brought from the Aberavon beaches, into houses to earn a few pence, in those years of depression. Sand was used in the stone-flagged floors of the cottages to absorb the mud and wet from the 'naily' boots of the miners, too tired for the business of washing, often, until they had eaten. Then they would bathe as best they could, in tin baths and tubs before the roaring fire.

As a young woman, my mother had been the church organist at the time and Grandma had said that there were some things she should not do, as such, and carrying sand on her back was one of them. This was the stuff of the women of Harlech who, when a French fleet was preparing to invade and the men were defending elsewhere, marched around the ramparts of the castle in their tall hats and red flannel skirts, creating a stage-army illusion of masses of soldiers. Then, they chased with pitchforks the few who did venture to land in Pembrokeshire. Again, I was looking into another world of thought and culture. Gwladys made it real.

The little old lady, now frail and often trembling with a nervous condition, seemed to gather new strength herself. She recalled the days when as a home-spun poetess, her monologues had held spellbound, audiences who had hung on her every word. She was a visionary and a mystic too. She spoke of Aunty Polly in her last days. "I was very close to Polly" she related. (Polly was the last daughter to live at 'The Nook' in Aberdare.) There was a mountain between Merthyr and Aberdare but transference of thought between them went on before any telephones or radar.

"There was a day when her face was before me wherever I went in the house - I just had to go and see her. In the end, I put on my hat and caught the bus over to Aberdare. When I got to 'The Nook', Polly lay, all alone, in bed, at her last. I took her hand. 'Thank God you've come, Gwladys, she whispered. 'I've been calling for you. I didn't want to die alone. 'Then she quietly turned her face to the wall and was gone. She died beautifully did Polly", said Gwladys. Her favourite hymn was 'O Love that will not let me go ... The tune was 'St. Margaret.'

My mind went back to Auntie Polly, converted in the iron town of Middlesbrough which she mentioned frequently. She was herself an early-day Salvation Army officer and Grandma Shepherd's redoubtable Lieutenant. My mind went back for a moment to my brother Raymond's wedding where Aunty Polly had been one of the guests. After the wedding breakfast, we had gathered in the house and had inevitably started singing the old hymns. Aunty Polly, sitting in a corner must have been 80 but had started to sing 'What a friend we have in Jesus'. Her fresh voice was that of a young girl. I was spellbound. I had never heard her sing before and I never did again.

Her life had been tragic too. 'Uncle Fred' her husband was always said to have been a nice man who drank. There was a great quiet sadness about her, like an invisible cloak. Her gaze always seemed to be far away. Poor Aunty Polly. She had adopted a little girl Cissie, who had got up to tricks with my own mother, putting the clocks back an hour when they were supposed to be in early. Teenagers have always been the same.

I wished that we had been with Gwladys when her own time came. For the whole of 1981 we were working in London, preparing for the Concert, and only went down to Wales, once that year, to meet the choirs at Port-Talbot. It was at Paddington Station, that London gateway to South Wales for so many exiles, that we found ourselves in conversation with a couple from Aberdare, also sitting on a seat, waiting for the train to arrive. Gwladys's name was mentioned. 'I believe she died a little while ago', said the man.

We were stunned. When we contacted friends in Merthyr, the news was confirmed. Gwladys had died in hospital following a fall when she had broken her hip. She seemed to have lost the will to live. Like Polly, she was very tired of life and must have known that it was her time to go to her eternal rest. She was now with all the other saints. Her songs and poems remain. Like Granny Phoebe, she had passed on her message to us.

Brave Gwladys. At 21 she had to have a colostomy and for the next 60 years she had sung and recited her happy way, like a little Pagliacci, so that everyone had known of her. Of what calibre some of these women were made. Over the years Gwladys sent us a number of recitations which she had given at her concerts, simple, direct and sincere, which spoke to the hearts of people. "Nothing fancy", as they would have said, but which made appealing sense to her hearers.

PROVIDENCE
by Gwladys Lewis.

Have you ever been broke, just broke to the wide?
With just what you stand up in, and nothing beside.
Living on scraps for best part of a week
When you can get'em and know where to seek.
I've been like that on a cold winter's night,
When the streets were deserted, with nothing in sight
But a slow-moving Bobby, whose job is to see

That the public's protected from fellows like me,
Who get put inside to answer the court
Why they're wandering round, with no means of support.
It always strikes me as a queer sort of joke
To pick on a man just because he is broke.
Do they think he enjoys wandering round in the rain?
Soaked through to the skin, with a dull aching pain
Thro' his stomach forgetting its last decent meal,
Just praying for the time when it's too numb to feel?
Life isn't worth much when you get to that state
Of just waiting to die with nowhere to wait.

I remember the time, it's a long while ago,
When I stood on a bridge, with the river below.
The last food I'd had was two days before
And I never expected I'd need any more.
That night was the worst that ever I've known,
With a dirty wet fog that chilled to the bone.
I set my teeth hard and I set down my heel
On the rail that my hands were too perished to feel.
When a snivelling pup came out of the fog
And whimpered at me - just a scrap of a dog,
Bedraggled and dirty like me, just a wreck
With a sad little face on his poor scraggy neck.
A few seconds more and I would have died
But he just licked my hand and I sat down and cried.
And I covered the poor little chap with my coat

And I carried him off, with a lump in my throat.
I took him along to the one place I know,
Where they'd give him a bed and a biscuit or two.
They didn't feel keen on taking him in,
But the sergeant in charge gave a bit of a grin
When I told him the dog could do with a meal.
He said "I'll fix him up but how do you feel?"
It may be perhaps that the sergeant had seen
The state I was in, I wasn't too clean.
The hunger and cold that I'd suffered all day
Exhausted my limits - I just fainted away.
Well, they fed me and slept me and gave me two bob

And the following day, they found me a job.
I've worked ever since and put a bit by,
I'm comfortable now and I don't want to die.
I've a nice little house, in a quiet little street
With a decent sized garden that's always kept neat.
I've worked there a lot when I've had time to spare
And I'm so proud of one little corner that's oe'r there,
With the pick of the flowers round a little old stone
That stands in a corner, all on its own.
It bears an inscription - not very grand,
The letters are crooked, but you'll understand
That I wasn't too steady, I couldn't quite see
At the time that I carved it - quite recently.
Here are the words that I carved on the stone:
'Here lies my friend - when I was alone,
Hopeless and friendless, just lost in a fog,
God saved my life, with the help of a dog.'

My mind went back to Grandma Shepherd poised on the edge of the canal lock and eternity in the Limehouse Cut with Kate and Pamela over a hundred years before, desperate beyond all endurance. Then my thoughts went to Billy Graham in the Kelvin Hall telling the story of a man who had been converted by the wag of a dog's tail. The man had simply called the dog to give it something to eat, and the gratitude the dog had shown, just for a meal, had made the man to think of all for which he had cause to be grateful in life. His whole outlook had changed. No sermon. No church or chapel. No scripture. No great flash of light. No huge experience. Just the wag of a dog's tail. When I didn't know or understand the half of the Gospel, I was convinced too.

"Convinced" - I reflected that this was the word used in the early days of the Rhondda Revival to describe the spiritual awakening which people experienced.

Among Gwladys's unforgettable literary endeavours were the English translations of 'Calon Lan' (A Clean Heart). I believe that she had given her mind to these when the late Lady Barnet had been the guest of honour at a local chapel function and a translation had been needed. Gwladys was proud that Lady Barnet had told her that she had never known anything so beautiful. This greatly loved of Welsh songs, ranks with Cwm Rhondda in its esteem among Welsh people.

CALON LAN

I ask not for worldly pleasures,
Gold and pearls I do not seek;
Seek I as my chiefest treasure
A clean heart, sincere and meek.

Chorus:
A clean heart, a heart of goodness,
Lovelier than the lily bright,
A clean heart dares sing with
    gladness,
Sing the day and sing the night.

Chorus:
Why should I desire great riches?
They have wings and fly away.
A clean heart of virtue reaches
Fortunes that can ne'er decay

Chorus:
On the wings of praises ever
Pleads my prayer, 0 God impart,
For the sake of my Redeemer,
Now to me a holy heart.

Though I seek not plenteous living,
Nor of gilded wealth a part,
I will ever be a suppliant
For a clean and honest heart.

Chorus:
Fairer than the sweetest lily,
In her gleaming bridal white,
Is the heart attuned by virtue

Into song, come day, come night.

Chorus:
If I cherish early treasure,
Time will prove my purpose vain;
But a heart with virtue stored
Finds a true eternal gain.

Chorus:
Songs that soar like winged wishes,
From my soul, are but a plea,
0 Redeemer in Thy mercy,
Let my heart from guile be free.

I learnt to sing this very much beloved Welsh song, by rote, as a boy in school. I wonder how many others there were like me, brought up in an English speaking part of Wales who did not come to know the meaning of the wonderful words.

Chapter 5

"INTERCEPTING INCIPIENT ALCOHOLISM"

An article by Charles Preece published in the *Journal of The Medical Council on Alcoholism.*

I WAS PUZZLED when in 1967, as a newly-installed Prison Welfare Officer at H.M. Prison, Brixton, I found that at the most, 6 - 8 men (4 - 5%) from the short term convicted section of about 140 men were being referred to the visiting Alcoholics Anonymous member for his weekly meeting. I knew that two years earlier, Martin Silberman, P.S.W. of the Institute for the Study and Treatment of Delinquency had established in the course of a survey of such men that there was an incidence of 27 % heavy drinking acknowledged by those inmates. (Royal London Prisoners' Aid Society Reports, 1963 and 1965.) Allowing for a number of men who might have been willing to attend the A.A. group being required for other duties at the time or on other educational classes, it seemed that either inmates were reluctant to admit to heavy drinking or that somehow, they were not being reached, probably a combination of both.

With colleagues in the Welfare Department, we modified the Alcoholics Anonymous U.S.A.-type questionnaire, in colloquial terms and endeavoured to put this to men on reception. It was also interesting that when a man was simply asked if he had taken a drink around the time of the offence, the answer was usually "Yes-but I was not drunk". It was later found helpful indeed when interviewing, to start by appearing to assume, in a matter-of-fact way, that the offence had some contributory element of alcohol, by remarking casually, "I expect you'd had a drink" or something similar. The man was then given the opportunity to deny this, if it did not apply but seldom was this the case. It was obvious however that there was great reluctance to accept the label of "alcoholic" and invariably resistance arose, almost by reflex action when an inmate felt that it was being applied and further discussion was likely to be blocked. Care had to be taken, therefore, at this delicate point.

I was greatly helped at this stage through reading "Alcoholism and Family Casework" published by the Community Council of Greater New York, covering an entirely new field in the training of family caseworkers.

The main achievement of the courses was seen to lay in attitude change. It was the faculty's stress on direct confrontation which appeared to be the dynamic which brought resistances into the open and the alcoholic to be seen as an appropriate recipient of normal professional services, rather than a "different" client for whom some other resource needed always to be sought.

In the simplest terms, I wondered whether, when so many colleagues used alcohol themselves, they found it difficult and uncomfortable to question others, apart from real frustration due to immense inadequacies of resources - hostels with waiting lists and difficult acceptance requirements, hospitals which refused to admit alcoholics, general temporary accommodation difficulties and apparently unmotivated clients. Social workers are said to share delinquent feelings with those they seek to help but there is a wide gap between the reasonable social use of alcohol and that kind of drinking whichleads to conflict with the law. A sort of "dangerous corner" does exist, however, where questions can boomerang too close for personal comfort.

In an endeavour to bridge the gap, World Health Organisation filmstrips in colour were obtained from Sweden and black-and-white educational ones from Finland which were used with small groups of men who had indicated some alcohol involvement. A certain persuasion was exercised here. It was said fairly that they would be given some information on drinking problems but the term "alcoholic", was, if possible, not used at all, at this stage and the description "problem drinking" employed instead. If a man appeared antagonistic in any way, he was not included. This did not happen very often and over two years of approximately 200 men, only 6 said that they were not interested. The initiative was taken by the welfare officers and without their quiet pressure encouraging attendance, at least on one occasion, the project would have stopped there.

Reluctance to talk strangely disappeared in subsequent group situations, held in a cell, with colourful curtains, freedom to smoke, half-light for projection purposes and a general relaxed atmosphere, distinct from the more inhibiting initial interview situation. When once the bubble of denial was burst, men were too ready to speak to someone whom they felt was understanding and who did not adopt a moralistic attitude. Men were, given Alcoholics Anonymous literature at this point if they wished and names were invited of those who were interested in going to the A.A. group proper. The work was seen at this juncture as being "pre-A.A.". It was remarkable in view of the earlier hedging, that only about 25% of these men subsequently declined to continue. Studies are currently indicating between 40-80%(1) (2) of prison inmates having some kind of alcohol difficulties. Although as these studies relate to two particular prisons, and not to the prison population as a whole, it is difficult to arrive at a possible overall percentage. Estimates made in 1967 for the Report of the Working Party on Habitual Drunken Offenders (1971) by medical officers of representative establishments suggested that in a total prison population which stood at 35,000 at the time (1967) there were about 5,000 men and women who had "serious drinking problems" of whom rather more than 1,000 were, when out in the community, "habitual drunken offenders" (neither term was defined for this purpose). The Prison Department suggested(3) that the total number of habitual drunken offenders was probably no more than about 2,000 of whom fewer than 100 were women. It was also suggested that about two fifths of all habitual drunken offenders in prison service establishments came from the metropolitan area of London.

This may well be. My work in Brixton, was however, with mainly younger men who had not come to the notice, to my knowledge at least, of the medical officers and my personal opinion was, that the official estimates for even "serious drinking problems" were conservative and not so likely to include considerations of "incipient" alcoholism before the more obvious "serious drinking stage" had been reached.

Apart from this, many have gambling problems, sometimes separately and sometimes combined but both capable of being dealt with in a modified A.A-type programme (Gamblers Anonymous) - the two have a great deal in common. Both find a meeting ground in feelings of aggression, anxiety, extreme tension, low self-esteem, depression, guilt, sheer social isolation, loneliness, inadequacy, low tolerance to frustration, inability to accept criticism and tendencies to act impulsively, to name but a few. It came as a surprise to men to learn that there were about 70 different A.A. meetings all over London during the week and all day on Sunday; apart from being widespread over the country as a whole.

The filmstrips were used, as much as a vehicle for accelerating group dynamics as for educational purposes and proved a definite catalyst in facilitating blunt speaking between the men. There were moments of supreme reality. A plainness was used which I would not have risked myself. A great sense of relief was evident in this free and frank confrontation with their fellows. I found that the most effective means of bringing a person to see and own up to his own difficulties was in this admission of a real problem, through honest discussion, with all pretence left at the door. There was an element of urgency in the exchange, as I pointed out that in the ordinary way, this was a once-only opportunity which was being extended. It was surprising how quickly the barriers of reserve were broken down in this kind of atmosphere, and stimulating to believe that motivation to at least discuss problems, could be evoked so readily.

In fact, the "real-life" situations led me to feel that if visual aids could be developed more closely related to the prison field, it would allow even greater identification. A commercial firm became interested, in the production of a set of British-type filmstrips and eventually a set of 7 were evolved, with scripts and tapes. Several of these dealt with the local rehabilitation projects including the D.H.S.S. Reception Centre with its Resettlement Section. St. Luke's and London House Hostels for alcoholics and a number of live stories of the residents themselves. A special contribution was made by journalist and playwright Archie Hill, with graphic stories of his own recovery in a moving description of family aspects of alcoholism.

These had an added impact on inmates and were also used for training purposes with volunteers and at public lectures. For early appraisal purposes, the material was shown informally to delegates at the Third International Conference on Alcoholism and Addictions, Cardiff, 1970.

Later, the Prison Administration gave permission for single-occasion daytime classes within working hours, subject to availability of inmates, under the heading of "Community Help" - something of a euphemism which was felt reasonable however as practical neighbourhood measures were indeed being portrayed. An interesting fact emerged by accident on several instances, when inmates could not be released from the prison duties at the last moment and obliging staff brought in men from the exercise yard, quite at random.

Even under these circumstances, some 50% of the men, after seeing the audio-visual aid programme, were willing to attend A.A. for further information. This indicated that if necessary, elaborate screening procedures and prior "orientation and indoctrination classes" as devised in American institutions could be dispensed with in the interests of time and labour saving on the part of busy prison workers. Referrals were accepted from all levels of staff, as a result of observation and common sense, without any previous special interest or training. The Prison Psychology Department became a valuable point of reference and in special cases, guidance was obtained from the appropriate medical staff.

In these days, when the value of prison is being held in question, it is interesting to record the expression of one man who said that he was glad to have been committed to prison because he hoped that there, some help would be forthcoming for what he knew was his drink problem.

Where criticism might be fair, is that often, full advantage cannot be taken of institutional custody - "the iron cure" - on grounds of over-riding security considerations and lack of educational facilities, which are understandable but nevertheless, frustrating.

The fact that in terms of the Habitual Drunken Offenders Report(4) overcrowded local prisons where most of them serve their short sentences do not have much time in which to deal with alcohol problems is not to be denied, nor the excellent attention which is given often to the allied physical ills. My point is rather that this careful medical consideration could well be extended to endeavour educationally to inspire motivation to seek treatment on release. Again, it is my personal view only but I believe that even single audio-visual aid talks significantly affected the attitudes of men thus counselled, especially where they were, again, younger men and had never had this experience previously.

The liberal circulation of A.A. literature through the generosity of a private sponsor was most helpful and this most valuable means of plain English dissemination of knowledge has since been officially increased.

Most of the men who came to these groups were married or were separated from their wives, on admitted drink problems and thus the matrimonial aspect of the work became very clear. Several wives, were, with the agreement of their husbands, interviewed following their normal visits, literature was provided, after sometimes, lengthy discussions and the wives were linked to the Al-anon family groups of A.A. Where wives were estranged from their husbands, they were sent special literature at the men's request, with the suggestion that they studied this material which might help them to understand matters better. Two wives actually stopped divorce proceedings which they, had instituted. One actually completed a questionnaire on alcoholic indications, as she believed her husband ought to have replied!

The work with wives is of special importance in view of the fact that some 50% of prisoners' wives have been found to be under 30 or suffering from some physical or mental illness. ("Prisoners and Their Families" - Pauline Morris, 1967.)

Endeavours were made to link wives with the Al-Anon family groups of A.A. as they were much in need of support on their own account and also seemed to be in a most important role insomuch that they could influence their husbands uniquely out of their own better understanding.

I felt that a new tool and some new principles had emerged for the detection and easier treatment of alcohol problems which could be used by any member of staff, needing only the filmstrip or slide projector with which most prisons are already equipped and a tape recorder or cassette replay unit. No specialised knowledge was required as the programme was independent and complete in itself. Simply enabling discussion to be developed by inmates themselves could lead up to the more personal, testimony-type Alcoholics Anonymous approach.

Our prisons present such an opportunity for dealing with, what, after all, is a problem accounting for at least, in some part, the committal of many of our inmates.

The views expressed are, of course, my own and are not necessarily those of the Home Office.

References:

(1) Dr. Griffith Edwards article *"New Society"* September 1971, stated that 40 % of men in a London prison had been found to have sustained damaging effects from alcohol although the homeless habitual type of alcoholic had not been included.

(2) *"The Fact Finder"* Bulletin of the Temperance Council of the Christian Churches (Educational) Ltd. October 1971. "In one British prison in 80% of the cases admitted, alcohol has been a contributory cause of the crime".

(3) Also refer to the *Report of the Working Party on Habitual Drunken Offenders (1971).* H.M.S.O. Para 4.25. Page 28.

(4) *Ibid.* 7.13. Page 56.

To my dismay, I had unintentionally upset the prison administration. It was a great pity. I had always enjoyed a good relationship with the Prison Service staff for over three years. Now I had written what was considered a 'begging letter' to outside bodies signing myself 'Prison Welfare Officer.' The letter asked for funds to be sent, not to myself but to the Church of England Board for Social Responsibility, to enable Archie Hill to develop his educational filmstrips for use with the alcohol education groups in the prison. Home Office approval had been given for scripts which I would prepare.

Only a handful of letters had been sent out to a few selected trusts, one of whom later responded favourably. If I had left out the word 'prison', it was said, it would have been a different matter. Trying to obtain outside assistance for clients, such as jobs etc, was part of my work. I myself had brought my endeavour to notice when I need not have done. As it was, I had upset protocol again.

Some time before, one of the visitors I had brought to speak to the A.A. group had served a sentence in Brixton at one time. I had not known that there was a rule against this. The man was eligible to be admitted to any other prison. With regard to my letter, I am sure that in holding me to question I was meant no harm and it had been said indeed at the time, that there would not be any repercussions. Mention had been made however to my superiors, I learnt later, of taking me off the work with alcoholics. I remember feeling quite tired and strained at the time. Without any problems I had done three and a half years of prison work. Two years was generally regarded as the normal tour of duty.

Prison was like a minefield. One never knew exactly where to step. Every officer had his own territory and like a robin, woe betide anyone who stepped on it, even unwittingly. There were no rules, no maps, because in many ways there were no fixed plans either. Each prison went its own way. No one seemed to have gone this particular way before.

I had always done my best to confer, to seek approval for any new developments. In this instance, I had not done so, mistakenly as it worked out. My only interest was the development of the work. Also, I was expecting to shortly leave the prison for my long-awaited probation course.

The prison saw its priority as security, quite rightly but this was also an inhibition against any kind of new development. Quiet containment was the order of the day. It was not unkind. The grim humour of prison alone made it bearable. You had to find something funny about most things to make them endurable, to survive.

I never had any rows with anyone. It was simply a monumental kind of apathy which gripped everything which was in any way different from the endless routine, the prescribed ways of undertaking the massive detail of prison life. To break new ground in any direction seemed a major upheaval. It was far easier just to take things as they were, to settle for the quiet life, to "just do one's bird" as the inmates put it.

In all conscience, with some two thousand men a year passing through one's hands, there seemed little time to do anything but the bare essentials. I had a young woman assigned to me as a trainee typist but there seemed little time to dictate letters. Most of the men wanted phone calls made to their families over urgent situations arising out of their initial receptions. It seemed that my best response was to try to maintain their communication, to prevent links, already fragile from being broken, to support wives who in turn could the better look after their husbands' affairs. So, my caring typist spent most of her time making the string of phone calls which accrued from each day's interviews with the never ceasing flood of new inmates.

I thought that she was doing a commendable job and we seemed to be helping a good number of men. One fine day, however, my trainee had to take a test and it seemed that her shorthand/typing skills through lack of practice had suffered beneath the pressures of communication work, although the matter was never raised with me. She was told that she would have to go. There was nothing I could do, it seemed, in the face of rules and regulations for typists. I stopped everything however out of respect for all that she had done, to immediately line up a job with a former colleague now in the local social services.

There was a price to pay for stepping out of line, even in a detail such as this. I used to think grimly at times, that we were like sparrows on the prison walls. We could come and go but we didn't really belong except on some kind of sufferance. When it came to hard-line decisions such as this, we had no say whatsoever, even how we used our own office workers and resources. Our own headquarters had assigned us to the prison and there we were left, for better or for worse. Only the good staff relationships which we forged stood us in any stead. Again, it at least gave us some feeling for the other inmates who had little rights either.

At this time we were aware of unrest among the men and I sought to calm some of this in a small way, with requests for family visits which I could supervise. This permission was often grudgingly given, if not denied altogether and eventually, after my time in Brixton, there was indeed, the trouble which we had feared, with sit-down strikes by the inmates.

I once heard a discipline officer say "I don't have any trouble with any of them. I just say 'No' to everything." It was a fact that the most junior prison officer to be recruited, could effectually make difficult my carefully designed welfare plans. Yet this very awkwardness, one day, led me to one of the most significant findings in my attempt to discover what proportion of the men had alcohol problems.

The governor had helpfully given permission for the convening or 'calling-up' of men for a single-occasion daytime class under the heading of 'Community Help'. These were younger men who had given an indication of having been drinking at the time of their offence. The procedure was to chalk up their names on a board on their cell-block as being required to attend, subject to the all-embracing discipline veto of 'being required for work'.

On this occasion, not a soul appeared when I arrived in the block to set up the projector and screen in one of the cells for the group discussion. Sensing some awkwardness, I asked the duty Principal Officer whom I had previously found to be very understanding, where all my men were. It did not seem reasonable that the whole ten were required for 'work', all at the same time. It had never happened before.

The officer looked at me quietly. "I'll get you a group," he said. He knew what was going on. Many of the discipline officers were excellent men. I saw one once, a former RAF officer with the ribbon of the Distinguished Flying Cross. I was sorry that I never had the chance to speak to him.

Another discipline officer was quoting Shakespeare to me with great ease, one day. A jocular man. He reminded me of a favourite uncle. This particular man was observing that another of his friendly colleagues had just left the prison service. "They should never have let him go" he commented. "Years ago, someone would have been down from Head Office to find out what was wrong. It's not like that now."

I knew what he meant. It was a very stressful job if one wanted to do any more than just the basic locking and unlocking, the 'slopping-out' every morning and that was bad enough. The hours were often long duties of shift work and living in quarters on top of the job. A lot of these men had domestic problems. An officer's wife had come into the welfare office one day and asked to see someone. I had to say that I would help if I could but that our duties were to see to the inmates.

The young woman was angry. "It's all for the prisoners" she said, and not for the staff." While she sat down, I phoned the Prison Service Head Office and asked if they had a welfare officer who could see the young woman. My opposite number made an appointment to come down to Brixton and see her. He went on to tell me that there was only a handful of such welfare officers for the whole country. "The staff are rife with problems," he added. "That's prison," I thought sadly. "A mass of concentrated misery with nowhere near enough staff to cope with it. All packed in, out of the country's sight and out of mind."

My senior had suggested putting up a notice saying that we were available to prisoners' wives for consultation, and vital as I knew this need to be, it seemed altogether unrealistic. We were in the prison most of the time interviewing and simply could not cope with any more work until we had more staff. One's mind was reeling by the end of the day at the best.

About this time our popular R.C. priest came out of the gate one night and drove his car straight through the red traffic lights at the end of the side road by the prison wall and was promptly booked by a policeman who chanced to be passing. Fortunately, there was no other traffic whatsoever on the road at the time. I knew just how full his mind must have been. I sometimes felt that I was sleepwalking myself, going home, down the little road.

The prison officers thought it was a huge joke and asked him how long he thought that be would get, as he was pleading guilty of course. There was further advice that he should ask at court if he could serve his time at Brixton when they would see that he was all right! The magistrates were sympathetic I am sure but the poor Father had to be fined and, as the unrelenting discipline staff pointed out, he now had a criminal record.

Underneath all the banter, I think that something unsaid emerged out of the traffic offence. It showed everyone the weight of the trouble the caring chaplain was trying to carry. He was a most composed man in the usual way. It was worth a court appearance, perhaps, to show the strain of being a man of the cloth in prison.

But to return to my principal officer friend, he went out into the yard where the men were walking around aimlessly, it seemed, on exercise in their endless circles. One by one, he called to individuals to come inside, quite at random, and told them to line up for the class. Such was his authority. No one was asked if they wanted to come and what the group was about. It was something like men being called in off the street for an identity parade.

I looked at my press-ganged crew with some sympathy, having been hauled in, bewildered, from their welcome exercise in the fresh air. I explained gratefully that they would be helping me particularly by taking part in a discussion group. This I hoped would be of assistance to them on their release. They looked at me without enthusiasm. At the back of my mind was the thought that they were older men than was my wont and had I been doing the calling in or selection, I would have left half of them out. These appeared plainly low I.Q. if not strange-looking. At a guess, I would have put many of them down as mentally disturbed.

Anyway, we settled down to the programme of showing Archie Hill's graphic story of his recovery from alcoholism. "A real tear jerker", said one man afterwards. Half of my hopeless lot said that they were willing to attend A.A. for further information and took some literature to read in the meantime. They would be braving possible scorn from fellow inmates and the deliberate taunting of some officers who would, I knew, be calling out "A.A. class for the alkies" when the time came to attend the evening classes and they walked along the landings, calling out the names.

A random sample of 50% with freely admitted alcohol problems. What a field of work, I reflected. It was an amazing finding. Half of the men in the prison were probably ready to respond to a positive programme. I had never dared to call up such a group myself. And all because of a disagreeable officer going against even the Governor's wishes.

Over 25 years later, as I re-read the article 'Intercepting Incipient

Alcoholism' which I wrote, I do not feel that I would want to alter a single word. A staff of 10 at Brixton is now twice the size it was then. There were odd times when I was the only welfare officer in the prison. Before us all, of course, there was only the Chaplain!

There was a lovely relationship with the Chaplains of all denominations. The resident ones were the Church of England chaplain and the R.C. priest. I remember a favourite joke with the Father was his own written work on his flock compared to the substantial records which we were supposed to keep. He had no typist at all and carried a large, diary-type journal with "one-line-entries" as he called them, describing the whole of his dealings with his men. The rest were all carried in his head. A former soldier and teacher, it was a tonic to talk to him.

In the face of the seemingly universal unbelief, all the chaplains presented a united front which was perhaps unique. There was simply no time, nor place for denominational differences in the face of intense spiritual darkness. Yet, individually and in the open sharing of groups, there was a readiness to talk about the deepest of feelings. In a sense, 'the chips were down' in prison. There was no room for pretence. There was no disguising the fact that prison was full of failures and as staff, to communicate, to empathise properly, I felt I had to keep in mind my own failures in life too. There could be no pedestal.

'Cons' (convicted men) are artists at recognising 'con men' among their fellows. It comes of long association where masks of all kinds are clearly perceived. Yet the tragedy is that prison lore requires that one's own mask is worn too. The 'front' must be kept up at all times. Any hint of softness is abhorrent. Men have to be known as 'hard'. I tried to follow the Governor's thought of all his basic officers (those in charge of a 'landing' of 40 or so cells) being the start of my 'welfare' duties. While there were always notable exceptions, many basic grade officers were afraid of being known by their colleagues as 'Welfare Screws'. It is only in the solitude of a man's 'Peter' (cell), if is he is fortunate to have one to himself, that the heartbreak can be unfolded. The fear of being different strikes deep.

Sometimes, as I walked out of the prison gate, I looked at my friends the sparrows on the wall and felt better. I was in the prison but not of it. With little official foothold compared to the uniformed staff and the establishment, as the birds. Detached from one's anchorage outside. Under the discipline of the prison as much as the inmates, yet with no charter of rights. I did carry a set of keys however. I could go anywhere in the prison, I reflected. This was authority of some kind. If the price was to be like the sparrows, to bridge the walls, the gap between the world outside and this sad place inside, it was worth it.

One beautiful place in the prison was the Chapel, tastefully draped and with a peace beyond description. I would go and sit there for a few quiet minutes, at some time in the day and marvel at the skill with which it had been made a sanctuary, all the more because it was in the middle of all the tragedy of broken lives.

Once a week, I attended communion there. There was just a handful of inmates, the Church Army Captain and Chaplain conducting the service.
One man was left until last, I remember when the wine was offered, as he had a real taste for it and did not leave it to the Chaplain to drain the residue in the chalice.

Kneeling with the cons, I used to think of something the Duke of Wellington had said when at the communion rail in a little country church. The 'Iron Duke' was intending to take the sacraments on his own, but an unwitting communicant had come and knelt beside him. Someone came to usher away the second supplicant but the Duke had restrained his neighbour saying, "Stay, we are all equal here".

The time came when Brixton made a maximum security section surrounded by a yard and a high steel mesh fence, inside the prison walls, adjoining the chapel. A small number of high-risk men were contained there, completely cut off from the rest of the prison. Their living conditions were perhaps better than the other inmates but otherwise they were like animals in a large cage. To compensate for the restrictions, I suppose, they were allowed to have a football and they kicked this relentlessly, monotonously, like a drum against the steel fence. They probably didn't even know there was a service going on. Inside the Chapel, we could hear the dull 'thud, thud, thud', of the ball outside. It seemed to epitomise the futility of their existence. The emptiness. The deadness. The gulf between the freedom which we knew, in spirit as well as body, and their bleak hell on earth. To see their wives come through the little gate in the fence, after visiting their men, with desolation showing unrealised in their faces, was devastating. Why did it have to be? Why did men prefer darkness to light? What monstrous powers of darkness existed in our midst?

The time came to leave Brixton. I had been asking for a course to enable me to work as a probation officer in the courts. A number of men and women of the highest calibre academically and of practical experience, had been recruited as direct entrants for the prison welfare posts in the National Association of Discharged Prisoners' Aid Societies which staffed the prisons. This organisation preceded the later Government approach, determined by financial policies, which had led to the existing Probation Service being given the additional responsibility, at the time, of prison welfare and after-care work which was not popular with probation officers who saw much less freedom in their way of working. Prison work, too, was not held in great esteem by many. It was even publicly admitted at the time that this was a temporary expedient, possibly not permanent. In other words, it seemed cheaper, if it would work.

There was a considerable body of opinion which contended that the Probation Service was already overloaded and did not have the experience, gained over many years, which had been developed by the Prison Welfare Service and some of the subsidised Discharged Prisoners Aid Societies which had always worked on very limited means. Most of these had now already been incorporated into the National Association of Discharged Prisoners Aid Societies as the after-care situation had been seen to be desperately in need of Government funding and support. There were alternative and forcible suggestions that either the Prison Service itself took over the work of the Prison Welfare Officers or that a new prison and after-care service was established, independent of both the Probation and Prison Service.

In the event, most of the welfare officers in the prisons were offered situations with the Probation Service and in due course I received the offer of a post as a probation officer (subject to confirmation after a year). We were required though, to take a short course of induction training or similar which was entirely reasonable, and for many of my colleagues, all this amounted to were a few weeks at a University.

I found myself having to make a difficult choice. My whole work for several years had been in the field of homeless alcoholic offenders in particular, for the simple reason that very little was being done from both inside the prison situation and outside probation, who then had no experience of general after-care. I would have to leave this specialised work for probable work in the courts as a probation officer and while I wanted to have this experience too, the pressing need was for something to be done for the hundreds of men in the London area whom I had come to know and who were not being catered for in this particular way.

I decided - with the support of my employers, the Royal London Discharged Prisoners' Aid Society, to ask for a deferment of taking up post in court-centred work and this was granted without question. My colleagues generally followed this 'main'-stream' exodus, took their short induction courses and then went into the courts or returned to their prison posts as fully trained probation officers by reason of their often considerable experience.

While continuing in Wandsworth Prison (I was attached to this prison for eight years) with a room by courtesy, in the hospital, I studied in my own time for the London University Diploma in Sociology, which many of my prison colleagues had already obtained. Most of them, with this theoretical background and their practical experience were well qualified. Most existing probation officers had trained usually under a Home Office course of about six months, I believe, for work in the courts. I knew that I would eventually need some kind of court-induction training, however, and requested this at the end of two years deferment when I felt that I had carried the work with the homeless alcoholics over the critical stage of establishing Wayfarers and seeing a hostel for homeless alcoholics coming into place. Then I felt that it could be taken over by the Probation Service.

Eventually I came to realise that I had made a mistake in not joining the initial general transfer with my contemporaries but there was no positive advice to me at the time to do otherwise. Indeed, everyone seemed happy for me to stay where I was! There was always a price to pay for trying to do something new, however, and I was to find this out again. Here and now, though, I was told that I would be posted to the Borough office pending the course for which I had now been waiting for several years.

Chapter 6

Enjoying a mug of tea. Fred is the tallest of this group of discharged prisoners being met at the gate of Wandsworth Prison by Wayfarer volunteers.
From left: Elizabeth, Charles Preece and Alice in light coat.

Chapter 7

THE OUTCASTS OF THE BOROUGH

W HEN I ARRIVED at the Borough, and my first experience of a probation office, I had worked altogether 12 years in prison and after-care, eight years in Wandsworth, six months in Wormwood Scrubs and three-and-a-half years in Brixton. The irrepressible humour of prison had given me a parting gift. When I mentioned my 'record' to an inmate, shortly before leaving, he said, "Blimey, Guv, you've done 'life'!" A 'Life' sentence at that time, was 12 years. However, more of this later.

I was grateful for the support which the generally helpful Prison Governors had given me over the years, at Brixton. I don't think that they ever refused any reasonable request. I had learnt a lot. Prison is a maelstrom of conflict, Brixton in particular was a 'hothouse' of emotional trauma ready to explode at any time. It was not for nothing that men sometimes took their lives behind its walls and physical violence lurked around every corner both openly and unseen, involving both inmates and staff.

To see the prison officers come off duty was a revealing experience. The long lines of two hundred or so men left through the gates like youngsters being let out of school, animated to a degree, conversation flying and their relief apparent. I never came out of prison myself without that same enormous sense of thankfulness, of escape even. I knew how they felt.

Years later, I was to emerge from a deep coal pit, the Lady Windsor mine, at Ynysybwl in the Rhondda and stepping out of the cage which had brought me from 1500 feet below the surface, to breathe the fresh air of safety as though I had never known it before. You can see on television sometimes, the smiles and obvious pleasure of miners, in orange boiler suits, their faces black and helmeted, pouring out of the cage as if they could hardly wait to get away. Now I had left prison behind me and a new life was beginning. It was almost like when I finished my tour of 200 hours operational flying during the war.

So, I took up my new appointment in the historic Borough High Street, halfway between London Bridge and the new Elephant and Castle shopping centre. A few hundred yards away was a remaining wall of the old Marshalsea Prison for debtors known to Charles Dickens and the Church of St. George's, recorded for posterity in "Little Dorrit". An old galleried coaching inn was nearby and the start of the road to Canterbury for Chaucer's pilgrims. It was the beginning of another thrilling chapter for me too.

I had a nicely decorated office to myself on the 5th floor. Not a sparrow on the wall any more! At one time, before things improved, in Brixton, I had worked by the kitchen sink! There was a view of the dome of St. Paul's Cathedral, seemingly only a little way across the River Thames. Floodlit at night, it was a beautiful sight. What a change from the walls of Brixton. It seemed a different world. There was only one ominous note. I had never had an office before fitted with the button of an alarm bell underneath the desk.

Now it was another kind of Mecca. To the Borough came men who had been discharged from prisons all over the country and who were, as a result, homeless and rootless in London. Drawn irresistibly to the capital, they arrived on our doorstep literally with only the clothes in which they stood. If they came from London prisons, they were, in theory, looked after by probation offices from the courts in which they had been sentenced but in practice because they were NFA ('No Fixed Abode') they found their way to us. They were not the 'skidrow' type homeless alcoholics which I had been dealing with at Wandsworth but in their dereliction they had much in common.

I soon discovered a curious aspect of the Borough. It was as if the Probation Service had decided to put all its own 'characters' in one place. I was to find out that most of my colleagues seemed to have 'ended up in the Borough' as we put it. The Borough was never afraid to be unorthodox in its own developed experience and to dispense with all the rules if thought necessary. It was stimulating. A demanding place in which to work but with lovely people. There were about 20 officers.

It was a large office in an old, unprepossessing block which might well have been a one-time warehouse - I never got around to finding out, but that was how I thought of it. Here, the Probation Service was hammering out its own experience of after-care on the anvil of trying to meet the needs of the most difficult homeless men and women it had known.

There was one thing which I thought endeared us to a wondering authority and that was our ability to contain some 800 or more of those just discharged from custodial sentences. This was the normal complement of a prison such as Brixton, and with a mere handful of staff, possibly about 40 people including the admin. and clerical officers instead of ten times that amount of prison staff. Most of our callers would have been in prison again had they not had the Borough and its band to which to turn. These were not probationers who had never been in prison but more like recidivists except that most were harmless in violent or serious criminal terms.

And so we were left alone in our little island of non-conformity and, apart from odd visits of headquarters people, we went our own way. If even an alternative to incarceration was demonstrated and at a fraction of the cost, it was at the Borough. Even the cost of supporting financially those discharged on what was at the time considered a high rate, was incredibly less than what would have been the huge expenditure for imprisonment of the same number of people.

There were some redeeming features. On the top floor, the Women's Royal Voluntary Service volunteer ladies had established a clothing store where they struggled with the worst of the clothing deficiencies of our callers. On one occasion, at least, a devout lady who was also a trained nurse, on duty there, washed and dressed the blistered feet of one of our callers. That wouldn't have happened anywhere else in London's probation offices of which I could think. Around the corner was a cafe called "The Willow", which took the food vouchers which could be given to our applicants. Here all repaired, men and probation officers alike when the going was hard and found a common refectory.

The outstanding feature of the Borough, as I was to soon find, was its officers facing the daunting flood with few facilities, although even these were greatly more than the means of the Voluntary Society for which I had previously worked, a fact which I appreciated. Rumour had it that one imaginative P.O. had been found interviewing his client with both sitting on the floor underneath his desk. It was explained that only there did the mentally disturbed former prisoner feel 'safe' from those who, in his paranoia, he was convinced were 'after him.'

The same probation officer, a former lieutenant-colonel in the Royal Army Medical Corps, was medically qualified and had, incidentally, in his former office kept a 'skeleton' in the corner. What part this piece of a medical student's learning apparatus played was not quite clear but I am sure it was vital in some way to the casework process.

Our colleague, the skeleton's custodian, was a charismatic character whose methods were not to be copied. There were callers who demanded by first name to see him and no one else. He was loved and something of a legend. His results in coping with the most weird of characters who defied all known categories, spoke for themselves. There was one man who turned up each morning in some kind of bizarre fancy-dress. One day he was an Apache Indian, the next a sort of Red Devil.

There was a large waiting room where men were quite content to spend a good part of the day. It was warm if otherwise comfortless and they knew that at the end of it, they would at least have a voucher for something to eat. With their prison records they might well have been otherwise, getting into trouble out on the streets so it served an useful purpose too. Anyway, on this occasion, the 'Red Devil' came to the reception desk and announced that he had "cleared them all out as they were only a lot of scroungers". How he had achieved this Herculean feat which would have daunted most of us was not clear but the waiting room was strangely empty and our Red Devil could claim undivided attention for himself. Another constant visitor was a young girl who called not simply once a day, which in itself was more than any other office could manage, by way of a reporting requirement but twice or thrice whenever she felt that she needed the particular support of the place. A brief word with the receptionist usually did the trick. It was this young lady who eventually requested that she be placed on 'perpetual probation' and, to her immense pleasure, the office artist designed a small, roll-up parchment scroll which testified to this fact. She was assured of permanent support for the rest of her life and after that, I think, she went on her way rejoicing, not to be seen again.

Over all this, although not a Senior, our medical mentor reigned as elder statesman, confidant and guide to all new officers who soon got the feeling that the Borough was beyond them. One of them was myself. I used to arrive at the Borough station rather early sometimes and on one of these occasions, on the way to the office, I went in to St. George's. I know that on this occasion, I wondered what that particular day would bring and how I would cope with its unpredictability. The sun was streaming through the east window and the church was flooded with light as I had never seen it before. I could only sit in a pew, spellbound. An elderly man whom I had seen once or twice before, one of the congregation, who had once shown me 'Little Dorrit's' vestry, came up and just said quietly, "Isn't it beautiful?" Somehow, the Borough seemed to be a different place. I went, restored, into the office and to our rest room on the top floor. From four stories up, the same sun poured over the Dickensian rooftops of South London, into our place of work. I sipped a plastic cup of hot chocolate from the automatic machine and life seemed good.

Came Christmas time and the office party. I had been told that all the stops were pulled out at Christmas as if to deny the rough-and-ready reputation of the Borough. Gleaming silver candelabra on snowy tablecloths. Colleagues appeared in fancy dress. How it appeared and where it came from was a mystery but magic. One woman colleague was gorgeous as a '20's' flapper in rainbow hues. I called her a 'Bird of Paradise'. That's where she was not so long after. Our colourful colleague never let on that she had a deadly illness and no one referred to the open secret. The lovely woman and mother kept going to the end. Whenever our ambassador's duties took her to court on cases, she wore the most stunning hats. What personal qualities, dear lady. An inspiration to us all. Again, I saw the Borough in a new and beautiful light. Other dimensions of our common denominator emerged. I knew that we did not fit somehow into the conventional 'mould'. A few, such as myself, had not had the benefit of any formal social work training but had learnt, as had done, so many of our predecessors, 'on the job'. Others had some undeniable skills, amazing backgrounds of experience and some, other academic qualifications. Individually they stood out as different and not too favourably, in the newly emerging ethos of 'training' with its 'civil service' approach which did not encourage what had been termed 'rugged' characteristics. Great store was now being set on line management and so-called supervision and control by the hierarchy. Traditional individual initiative and indefinable but real 'personal qualities' were not apparently appreciated in this new regime of conformity.

I suppose on looking back that, our administration was trying to find its own way to adapt to a fast-growing, unknown and bewildering sphere of new responsibilities, far removed from the traditional even though successful court-orientated probation work of the past decades. It was a pity that if in the search for a general form of training and duty that specialisations and again, those 'personal qualities' which had always been a hallmark of the pioneers were not recognised.   The last bastion was the Borough.

I had been given the job of the NAPO (National Association of Probation Officers) office representative and remember how it fell to me to hand in to the Senior Judge at our Inner London Sessions, as it then was, a notice as to why we were protesting and holding our one-day strike. This was the first in the history of the Probation Service and was not so much a strike as a demonstration and Lobby of Parliament against a grading system which had been introduced by the Home Office.

Briefly, we were to be assessed and re-graded into two grades, A & B (The 'sheep and the goats') and paid lower rates accordingly. No probation officer appointed had ever been told that such an arbitrary assessment would be brought about or of any existing 'deficiences' in their work. All had been equal since the beginning, after a 12-month probationary period and subsequent confirmation in post.

Our inner sanctum was a few doors away, the cafe which took the food vouchers and there we resolved a good many vital issues. In fact, "The Willow" became our own HQ when we spearheaded the strike. We set up an office more or less on the pavement outside the door of the building so as to look after the clients, in order that they did not suffer.

Since then, nurses, teachers, firemen, the coal miners, have struck out of desperation in not having reasonable requirements met. I remember my father, ex-soldier and miner saying "Strikes never helped anybody" and also adding, "but I have seen men treated like dogs." Why couldn't compromise be found, I asked myself that day, when the Judge in his legal dress said that he understood why we were protesting but not the way in which we were going about it. I didn't understand it myself. Why had authority seen fit to adopt such insensitive, divisive measures? The family sense, the fraternal way in which we all worked, vanished overnight. If there ever was a Phyric victory, it was then. It was a shattering blow to my own pride in my work. There was an appeal procedure and that was the only hope. It was a great experience to meet with the MPs at the end of the day, in St. Stephen's Hall, in the Palace of Westminster, to voice our anger at the injustice of what was happening to us, to tell them that the traditional Probation Service was being destroyed, the goodwill of 70 years being lost. It cost us all a day's pay.

This is now of course history, with all the contenders long gone from the scene, but many still do not know the anguish and struggle of those days which eventually brought about some rationalisation and a fairer means of assessment should it be necessary in the future. Such a pity! I record this now, years after, without hard feelings because in the long run, our management seemed to learn some kind of lesson. I just hope that the same mistake will never be repeated. It should never have happened. In the latter years of my service, I felt compensated by generous sick-leave prior to my heart operation and afterwards the facilities of the office to write my book.

About this time, we were provided with some very helpful courses which did show me that there was a lot more to learn. One was a group experience course. In one of our sessions, a colleague related how he had taken a group of unruly probationers for a weekend on a Thames sailing barge. The trip had been a seeming disaster from start to finish and they had narrowly escaped being run down by a ship in the middle of the night through some kind of failure to show their navigation lights. The probation officer concerned was almost overwhelmed by a sense of failure and disappointment until letters began to arrive from parents expressing their appreciation of what had been done for their youngsters.

We took the story to be something of an analogy of the probation service. A slow-moving, ponderous vessel, clumsy and difficult to navigate, with a mixed bunch of a crew making well-nigh disastrous mistakes at times and bringing one near to heartbreak and then, somehow, good being brought out of all the awfulness. I have carried that concept ever since. That some

Higher Power was holding us together in spite of human error and fallibility and would have the last word.

The result of my subsequent appeal was that I would not be given the higher grading until I had completed the awaited probation induction training. If my judges had known that years before, had I taken the few weeks which was then the case I would not now be in this situation. It might have made a difference but I was now at a considerable disavantage. It was ironic that when I subsequently came to be up-graded, I was still in the middle of the course and had not even taken up duties as a court-based probation officer after all. Perhaps the establishment had relented and was being kind. The best advice I had from Headquarters was to forget being a Direct Entrant.

The pain of it all had been quite unnecessary. I had confided my inner hurt to the psychiatrist who had earlier opened the way in the Maudsley Hospital for my down-and-outs. He had observed that some weakness in my work might reasonably have been observed but that this should not trigger-off a whole sense of inadequacy. It was good comment. I resolved that court work might well be the area in which I could be held deficient and that I would go all out to remedy this when the chance came, as indeed it would. As it was, I seemed to have some wonderful support from colleagues.

While I was at the Borough, I was given the opportunity of taking part in a group led by a psychiatrist who held an appointment at Broadmoor Hospital and who conducted a weekly group, one could almost call it a clinic, at the famous London Hospital where Dr. Barnado had worked as a young doctor. I would have thought that Mother Shepherd could have met Dr. Barnado when he came to the "Penny Gaff", the infamous, low music hall in Limehouse which William Booth had secured and turned into a mission station. Dr. Barnado had confided in William Booth his concern for the homeless, destitute boys on the streets (see "Woman of the Valleys") and had actually commenced with some small houses in the vicinity. Mother Shepherd had worked there in the early days of her conversion. Here I was, in some strange way again following her pathway through life.

It was a very new experience to me. The Training or 'T' Group approach, as one of its methods, took a group of people, sat them down in a room with no special agenda and allowed people to freely express their own needs and feelings of the moment. The leader acted as a skilled observer rather than a participant, often to guide and interpret the discussion, as it might seem appropriate from time to time, to explain what was happening in the dynamics of the group, what was going on, what we were trying to say.

I recall that at one stage our own leader suggested that there was a good deal of unexpressed anger in my make-up and that, having turned this inward, I had become depressed or even ill; that others were feeling the same way and that I was 'mopping up' their feelings too, which made me worse. I remember a young male colleague once asking somewhat incredulously "are you saying that we are making him ill?" Later our consultant said that while he did not usually take a directive approach, he thought I should see my doctor who subsequently put me on a course of anti-depressants for a short while and I felt much better.

There was some reluctance on my part to take the tablets, feeling that I should not need such with my Christian experience and confided this to my friend the Roman Catholic Chaplain. His advice was, "Supposing it was St. Luke ('Our Beloved Physician') who had prescribed the medication - would you feel happier about following it then?" My own doctor had said to me, "If you have been dealing with people with corkscrew minds for a long time, it is understandable that you may have gone the same way without realising it."

A young woman colleague once told us that she had an arsonist on her case-load and felt that the man was likely to commit the same serious crime again and that she could not prevent him. The belief and feeling of failure was proving too much for her. It was pointed out that, to begin with, she had now shared her sense of being powerless with us all and did not have to carry the burden on her own. We would have felt the same way in her position. We could do nothing to change people if they did not wish to respond to our efforts to help. She need have no sense of failure. We were indeed giving her release from her self-doubting. It was not a matter of higher training or skill either. There was no more anyone could do with such a client.

I recalled telling the Medical Officer in Wandsworth on one occasion of my fear that a man with whom I was dealing would commit suicide. "Nothing will stop him if he is determined to do it", was the reply.

The support group was a great help. Looking back, I can see that my years of prison work had extracted some kind of toll. I knew that I needed a break. I was angry that it was slow in coming. That there seemed no end to the remorseless demands of the multitude of men demanding time and attention. An error of judgement at Brixton had been the eventual result. I had not learnt sufficiently of the need to share one's self-doubts at all times, thinking that I could go it on my own. The devil exacts a high price for pride and I had to pay mine.

I came to believe a great deal in the value of these group experiences. For non-Christian colleagues and those of other faiths, it was a wonderful meeting point. Our common spiritual being became something very valuable, precious even, and I was grateful to the Service for having provided this opportunity both with our doctor and in other residential settings at Wansfell

1. *Jack Hynam with World War 1 and 2 medals. Boy soldier 1914, R.A.F. Flt. Lieutenant, American Forces Liaison Officer.*

2. *The grave of Jack Hynam buried with Military Honours by Members of the R.A.F. Association Cwmbran.*

3. *Mother Shepherd in the Welsh National Costume in which she conducted meetings and led street marches in South Wales.*

4. *Jack and Bess Hynam with Alice in their Cwmbran garden at the start of the research.*

5. *Alice and Penny who always loved to play with her.*

6. *The Gate, H.M. Prison Wandsworth where for two years, I met discharged prisoners.*

7. *Two former miners and their dogs. Our Guardians during the night.*

8. *Alice camping, in our Dutch tent, with wild flowers collected from the White Cliffs of Dover.*

9.   Our grandsons have fun with the goats at *Pengelli Fach. For a number of years we spent our holidays 'on the trail' in the valleys and tried to combine our research with lighter moments. The Thomas family were a great support to us in those uncertain days. We had memorable evening meals when, after the farm work was done, we would discuss the day's discoveries.*

10.   *I could hear Big Ben throughout the day when at work in the Crown Court, Middlesex Guildhall.*

11.   *The Farmhouse, Pen Gelli Fach, Merthyr. Our valleys base.*

12.   *Entrance: Middlesex Guildhall, Westminster. The original Crown Court.*

13. *Lilian and Alice with the camping trailer behind the 'Fox'. In the background are the village Church and school where Alice's mother attended. Her name as a child was Edith Threadkell and she would have worn a white lace mob-cap as was the custom. Her writing was always beautiful. The tall Church tower acted as a landmark for the local fishermen and a beacon by night when the weather was bad.*

14. *Hughes Hall, Cambridge University where the Direct Entrants' Course was held. Pauline, our youngest daughter with her husband Stanley Lewis and Alice.*

15. *"Expecting Storms Miss?" enquired a wit on Windermere while sailing on the lake. It was a real fisherman's sou'wester too and protected Alice's ears. Subsequently the hat was lost on the voyage. What a pity. It was a beauty.*

16. *Winter Jasmine outside Kings College Chapel while we were waiting for Choral Evensong and the sound of the 5 p.m. bell.*

17. *Springtime along the 'Backs' with the beautiful border of crocuses and Kings College Chapel in the background.*

18. *On Alice's 1985 Huguenot Trail which marked the Centenary of the founding of the Huguenot Society, also the three hundredth anniversary of the Revocation of the Edict of Nantes which ended the toleration of Protestants in France and resulted in the flight of over 200,000 Huguenots.*

In the reign of Elizabeth 1, an earlier migration brought 40.000 refugees, an influx which was greatly to the enrichment of the nation.

19. *Alice on Horseguards Parade with a Salvation Army Flag which she later carried past Buckingham Palace with the Band.*

20. *Caerphilly Mountain Top, at Christmas time, overlooking Cardiff and the Monmouthshire Valleys. The glorious vista is marked by a verse of Scripture in Welsh, inscribed on a cairn. Our eldest daughter Margaret with our grandchildren, well wrapped-up in the snow.*

21. *Where the 1904 Welsh Revival began in Loughor, near Swansea. The young people concerned took the flame to Aberdare from where it rapidly spread throughout the Valleys, to London and even India. The monument commemorates this amazing Spirit-led happening.*

22. *'Granny' (Phoebe) the redoubtable lady who grew up as a teenager under the wing of Mother Shepherd and who followed in practice, her teaching for 50 years as a Local Officer. Her reminiscences were invaluable to the research.*

23. *Fred the College servant at home in his Oxford flat. The photographs of his long-lost family and grandchildren are behind him. He died shortly afterwards, a happy man and at last at peace after being reunited with his son and daughter whom he had not seen since they were children themselves.*

24. *Alice and her sister Lilian outside the 'Fox' Hollesley, Suffolk. Their Mother, Edith Bonsey had been brought up (but never allowed!) into the pub. Within a stone's throw were the village Church and the Anglican school both of which Edith had attended, before venturing to London as a cook in service. Both sides of our family have kept good old-fashioned country pubs at one time or another.*

25. *A Family camp in the garden.*

26. *Mother Shepherd and Auntie Polly rest at the foot of a tall tree, in a hollow in front of the gates in Aberdare Old Cemetery.*

27. *Boris and Gitte confer in the Clinic. Gitte, a Concert Pianist was a considerable administrator and had an extraordinary rapport with all the patients, taking over when Boris had completed the medical side of the practice. All this against serious heart trouble herself. Truly a committed couple. It was a wonderful experience working with them both.*

28. *Canada 1975. Alice is seen with Mrs. W. G. Raymond who with her husband opened their lovely home in Montreal during World War II to Servicemen in the area. A truly hospitable and warm-hearted gesture. Alice and I returned to stay with these wonderful people for a month after the War.*

29. *Alice putting flowers on the grave of our son Alan who only lived for 4 days but brought a great change into our lives. We "entertained an angel unawares."*

30. *Madingley American Cemetery, Cambridge. A piece of the highest ground in the locality, gifted by Britain to America. Thousands of American airmen are commemorated here. An army of Crosses and Stars of David face the tall flagstaff from which the Stars and Stripes flies proudly over its men who flew for the last time from East Anglian bases. A most moving place to honour the dead. Alice and my mother visit to pay our own homage.*

31. *Retirement: Wood Green Crown Court London. Alice receives a bouquet from Judge McMullan our Presiding Judge who had always been most supportive in the experimental work with alcohol-related offenders.*

32. *Winston Churchill Statue, Parliament Square, London. He had brought hope to the Desert Air Force in dark days when he stopped in his flight and inspected detachments from our Middle East Command including our own squadron (No. 39) at Ishmalia on his way to meet Stalin at Teheran. We felt that we knew him persoally as a result.*

Adult College, near Epping, led by colleagues who had learnt the skills of leadership of such groups.

Another profound thinker who had helped me, even years before was a Dr. Joseph Singer of Israel, a survivor of the Holocaust who at one time, in the early days of the new Government of the State of Israel, had been its economic adviser. "No time (in business) is ever wasted", Joseph had said once when I had complained of a fruitless day's journeying with him. He had proved right. His meaning was that we had been working purposefully, that day and some good would come of it eventually.

There came a day when I was dealing with a young ex-soldier who was homosexual and who had ended up in Broadmoor for a violent attack on a man who had goaded him in some way, beyond endurance. Something had snapped in his mind and the result had been years in the mental hospital for criminal offenders. I felt completely out of my depth with my client. I had made all kind of plans for his probation supervision but I decided to first consult a well-known psychiatrist. This good man had been in a concentration camp. After I had recounted the history of my client, the specialist said simply "Just leave him alone. Some people feel so battered that the mere blink of an eyelid will make them feel that they are being persecuted." Later the doctor prescribed a course of tablets of some kind and the client showed me a bottle containing quite a quantity of pills which he had been given. "If I take too many", he told me, "the doctor said that they would kill me". "But I am trusting you not to do that", the doctor had told him.

One day my client mentioned that, in Broadmoor, he had come to know our consultant. I looked at him. "This is amazing," I said. We have both been treated by the same psychiatrist!" We roared with laughter and did not look back on our relationship after that. I never had any problems with my client who completed his term of probation without fault.

The Cambridge course, when it arrived, shortly afterwards was one of the highs of my life and, I reflected, still provided by the Probation Service. Truly, I was to find, "All things work together for good, to those who love the Lord, who are called, according to His purpose."

Chapter 7

CAMBRIDGE UNIVERSITY

WITH THE CAMDEN Wheelers Club, I had cycled past the Colleges of Cambridge University in the years just before World War 2. I wondered what would have happened if I had stayed on at school instead of leaving at 16. I had failed to obtain the required credits to matriculate. Maths had been my weakness. I hadn't worked on algebra and geometry, as I should have done. I couldn't face another year while my friends went on to sixth form. My Headmaster had suggested Llandaff Ecclesiastical College and the Church in Wales. "You are good at English," he had said. "I thought you had to have a vocation for that, Sir", I had replied. "It can come", was the answer. It didn't seem enough for my young heart.

I had ended up an office boy and learner in a firm of building equipment merchants and a warehouseman in a Poplar riverside railway depot. Just to get a job in those tough depression years of the late 30's was something. There was only one job going as a clerk in the steelworks in the whole of Port-Talbot when I came to leave school.

We didn't think we were poor, we just didn't have any money for anything except to live. When holidays came it only meant time to roam the docks, swim and climb the mountain. We schoolboys travelled just as far as our feet would take us. If, in dreaming of the unknown future, King Alfred burnt the cakes, mine was a wet experience. It was on one of these walks along the quayside that, in an absent-minded moment, I looked one way and stepped the other to the next paving slab except that it wasn't there, only a gap in the edge of the dock where I had been walking, so in I went for a cold, soaking experience.

I could swim of course. In search of new deep-water experience, we sometimes swam in the docks but this time I was wearing my newly-purchased school suit. Sopping wet when I climbed out, someone loaned me a bike to ride home in my bedraggled condition. My mother was taken aback at my abject appearance. "I fell in the dock, Mam", was all I could say. I felt so stupid. My brown suit was not expensive to begin with and it never seemed the same again. The stuffing had been knocked out of it.

When I went back to school after the holidays, a well-turned out older boy looked at my battered outfit and quipped, "That's a 'Twill' suit!" " 'Twill'?" I innocently questioned. " 't will never be any good" he smirked and raised a general laugh. I should have thumped him on the spot but instead decided that I must leave school. If that wiseguy had only known it, I had a smart, good quality serge suit in the wardrobe at home but that was for Sundays only. It would never do to use it for school. That would have meant I didn't have a best suit any more and my parents, with three growing younger children, couldn't afford another one just then.

I went to the Labour Exchange and asked about jobs. It would mean leaving home, of course. There was no work in Port-Talbot. The Ministry of Labour official flipped through the list of jobs away in England. He read out various office jobs, bank clerks and the like. I had visions of smartly dressed colleagues but only one suit. The adviser mentioned something about a learner with an engineering firm but then skipped it as unsuitable and went on looking for white-collar work. "What was that?" I enquired on impulse, and he turned back the sheets. Goodness knows what caused me to interest myself in the peculiar-sounding learner's job. I was no engineer. My interviewer referred to his notes. The salary was only £1.00 a week which would all go on lodgings, to be found, but I would receive five shillings pocket money and a grant to cover my employment stamps and fares to work. It sounded fabulous. In no time, an interview in London with free travel had been arranged over the phone. I hardly thought twice about it all. I would have signed up for the French Foreign Legion, the way I felt.

The next day I was on the train for my interview. I carried a suitcase

The Backs and St John's College Tower, Cambridge

which was largely empty except for a change of clothing, just in case I had to stay, and my first razor. Wearing my smart serge suit my father gave me a £1.00 as I went out of the back gate, to take London by storm. It seemed a huge adventure. I was given the job on the spot and did not return home as my parents had expected me to do.

Little did I know it but my real-life education was only beginning. One day I was in a Welsh County School classroom, having turned down the prospects of Llandaff Ecclesiastical College, and a few days later, I was on the Thames waterfront in Poplar, still in my blue serge suit, trying to direct a reluctant gang of tough dockers in loading light railway equipment into wagons. It was a considerable mystery and I just hoped that I was sending the right goods to the correct places. My hard-up casual workers thought I was a well-paid office worker of some kind in my Sunday suit, if underneath a dingy boiler suit, and wanted tips for their full co-operation. I didn't even have tips for myself and my £1.00 had long run out. It suddenly hit me that I had made a monumental mistake but there was no return ticket to Wales on offer and my pride would not let me go back home, defeated, weird job or not.

When I ruefully mentioned to the sales manager that I didn't like travelling back on the tube with a dirty face, and there was no wash place, I was told in well-intentioned encouragement, "Where's there's dirt there's money" but this was to elude me for a long time. When I was not over-keen on another occasion the advice to me was, "Do not to despise the job but to make myself efficient at it". Strangely, I was to discover that my employer was a German Jew who had managed to leave Germany with some part of his substantial assets. Shipments of light railway material came from his former Frankfurt works on the Rhine, by barge to the Thames waterfront. That was why we were at Poplar. Martin Eichelgrun was to become a friend and a good business teacher. The staff were kind to me in those hard and puzzling days and even helped me to learn to type and edit a cycling club magazine. (This was how I came to meet Alice!)

The firm later seemed to become a refuge for Jews who escaped from the Nazis. One engineer in particular had something of a 'Sound of Music' story to tell. He and his family had fled across the mountains with just rucksacks on their backs, leaving everything they had in the world, behind. The night before, Otto had picked up the phone when it rang. An unknown voice had just said, "Leave Germany tonight" and clicked off.

It was all a strange world for a teenager. On the long journey to Poplar I helped my elderly engineer friend with his English and he cheerfully told me his stories. He was an expert at peeling an apple with the skin in one long piece. It gave me some insights into life that I might not have known from behind a bank counter. So much for the strange feeling that I had to go for the job.

For the next two years I subsisted on my Juvenile Transference Scheme grant which I obtained, like the dole, each Friday from Camden Town Labour Exchange. After 12 months, I had a five shillings rise from the firm but it didn't do me any good as the Ministry of Labour rewarded my industry by deducting that amount from my grant so I went along for the second year to collect 4/3 instead. I found that it cost three shillings and six pence a time, to have my shoes repaired, frequently, with the heavy work and suddenly my five shillings seemed to vaporize. Cycling to work unofficially with my bike from Wales saved my fare money and my life. I was never positively hungry but after a light breakfast, one good meal a day supplemented by broken biscuits was all I knew as a 16-year-old. I seldom had a Sunday dinner in my first year, but a handful of sandwiches.

Amazingly, I was working some of the time within a mile of where Grandma Shepherd had lived in Poplar and where my grandmother had been born. The penury of the East End was to be my experience too, 50 years before I would come to write her story. The hand of God was upon me in this incredible way because I had no idea of it at the time. That awful job in the murky November days by the freezing river nearly broke my heart. I was convinced more than ever that I had made a huge mistake in mindlessly going for this miserable, dirty work in a railway sidings warehouse. Now I see. How could I have subsequently been able to enter into the lives of my forebears, as I imagined it, to write about it, without having passed that way, even in a very small part, myself?

I learned to love the East End and its people before I left it, to go into the RAF in September 1939. I remember the day when the dockside labourers accepted me. They were pretty poor too and asked me again for tips one day. I told them that I had barely enough to live on myself. I told them that when dinnertime came I couldn't even afford to go into the working men's cafe where they had their meal. They had seen me eating my sandwiches in the cold out on the waterfront and now, for the first time, I told them why. They asked me to come into their little shed and gave me some peculiar brown-looking tea in a funny cup. At the time it seemed the kindest thing which had happened to me, down in the docks. My 'apprenticeship' was over and after that, the job seemed to come easier.

These memories flooded back into my mind from the days of cycling past those lovely colleges which my life had bypassed. Now, the pendulum had swung back to me and it was time to leave all my friends at the Borough when the Probation Service sent me to Cambridge on a direct-entrants course,

It consisted of two periods of a month each with six months and a weekend session in between. It was one of the last courses of its kind as generally direct-entrance into probation was being phased out in favour of fully-academic courses of study and now at the age of 52, I was fortunate to have this opportunity.

Cambridge was a dream come true. In my mind, if not on paper, it placed a stamp on my experience over the years. What I learned academically was refreshing and useful but apart from the Courts procedures, did not add greatly to what I already knew. It was the sense of historicity, of belonging, even in a fringe way, to a great place of learning that I found deeply satisfying. I felt that, somehow, I had caught up with myself after all. I was to meet again with a wonderful lot of stimulating new colleagues. There was Dick who played chess in between times. He was an ordained Anglican clergyman, after being a reporter and had been in Zululand. What he had thought was going to be missionary work hadn't turned out that way and he had come home.

It was tough going financially and Dick went off at weekends to do pulpit supply to help out. One Friday evening when he was due to set off, his car wouldn't start so I offered to give him a tow. My Beetle had a proper towing eye to which I attached the rope, then I asked Dick if he knew where to securely attach the other end to his car. Dick said he did and got down on his knees in the road and did what was necessary then got in the car and I took up the strain. There was a jerk and off I went. It was dark and the ring road was one long line of homegoing traffic with blinding headlights. I couldn't make out Dick behind me in the glare and so got out. At the end of the towrope was a large metal part which was unhappily trailing in the road, but of Dick and his car there was no sign.

I was in a cold sweat by now. Then I found him. He was calmly standing by his car, with a smiling face, graciously waving on the occupants of the cars who had to get by his immobilised vehicle. He might have been warmly shaking hands with his congregation at the church door after the service had ended. I had apparently pulled some vital part off his front axle. I towed him to a nearby garage where he had to leave the car. In the middle of it all, I was due to meet Alice off the London train at any moment. We picked her up at the station, bundled Dick into the Beetle and sent him off to his flock.

Another time, I had set up a projector in one of the bedrooms at Hughes Hall where we had our course, and was showing some of the people on the course, Archie Hill's slides which I had used in the Brixton alcohol education classes. Dick produced some slides of his own from South Africa. One showed him in the centre of a group of Zulu women and the first question from the audience was, "Which one was your wife?" Dick was happily married as it was, but worse was to come. The Zulu ladies in traditional dress wore some elaborate beads but not a lot more! When I went downstairs later to the dining room the word had gone around hilariously that "Dick and Charles were showing porn upstairs".

One of the married women on the course was a real Gracie Fields kind of girl, full of vigour, straight from the shoulder. Her pithy comment was quite fearless. She told me that before becoming a probation officer she had made surgical needles, especially for operations on the eyes of small children. She had an unmistakable northern accent and a direct manner which went with it. "Are YOU the probation officer?" a magistrate had asked her once, she told me. I had thought, "What a probation officer too." Her rapport with her female clients in particular was something I could never have attained, from stories she told me.

These were things I learnt at Cambridge which weren't on the syllabus. To kneel alongside my tutor in Kings College Chapel and be lost in the cadences of the choir in the fan-vaulted roof, to feel the pounding and throbbing of the great organ was something which I shall always treasure. My fellow students, a handful of whom were mature direct-entrants like myself, often sitting together, soon came to be known as 'Dad's Army'. It was reassuring and fun.

I was grateful that the Service had brought me here and the strain of the past years began to melt away in the atmosphere of the University city. In the middle of the course, I was even given my higher grading and also shortlisted for a Cropwood Fellowship and asked to attend the Institute of Criminology for interview. I remember walking through the Backs that morning with the yellow and purple crocuses along the paths and feeling that life was good. In the event, the Fellowship was not awarded but I received a very encouraging response and it was not altogether a disappointment. To have reached that far seemed satisfying.

I had wanted to follow up some of the families and the men with whom I had dealt in Brixton Prison on the alcoholic classes, to see whether the prison work had brought about any significant change but this was not seen as a feasible subject for a period of study at Cambridge and in retrospect, I suppose it wasn't. I should have offered to write up my prison experience with the alcoholics. I was too far ahead of the moment, wanting to press on. I was beginning to feel that it was in the day-to-day work of the courts that I wanted to immerse myself now, to try to find out what was possible before the prison stage was reached. I had felt that I had made a mistake when my contemporaries of five years before had been absorbed into the Probation

Service, in 1967, but now it seemed that it might not have been such a disaster apart from the financial loss.

This Cambridge course was more substantial than the induction courses of those early days and the time in the University atmosphere was longer. I had spent five years over my London University diploma and now this seemed to provide a fitting conclusion. Whether it all added up to a contemporary social work qualification didn't seem to matter any more. The work with the alcoholics too seemed to have been recognised. One of the tutors asked me to talk to his students in his rooms. Cambridge gave me a certain confidence. It was uplifting. Hitherto, I had been struggling against the constant feeling that time and effort with alcohol problems were at the least ill-placed if not positively not 'proper' work, like dealing with the homeless at the Borough. 'Politically' it never enjoyed any great credit and had earned me the reputation of being 'single-minded' and even 'embarrassing the service', (Wayfarer Project) in my endeavours These experiences were humiliating.

Somewhere along the line, I had read in a learned medical journal that if alcoholism were to be a notifiable disease, a state of emergency would have to be declared in the country overnight. I remember seeing a television documentary of how concentration camp inmates were made to feel people of no worth. Their every vestige of moral fibre destroyed by their captors. Now I knew what the Van den Hoven woman doctor had meant when she said that no one wanted to inflict prison on their people. Our lot was nothing in comparison but it did provide an inkling of what our clients felt like and that was a tremendous step towards feeling for and understanding them. No university could impart that kind of knowledge. It had to come from experiencing something akin to desolation.

I took to before-breakfast runs around Fenners cricket field, to swims in the nearby pool and jogging, around the Backs. I was determined to get everything I could out of Cambridge. Out at Madingley was the American Air Force Cemetery, a piece of the United States in England. The great wall inscribed with the thousands of names of the American airmen was a living reminder of what I had been spared, what I had survived. It was a humbling thought. There must be some purpose to my being here.

In the midst of all this, I needed to remember the 'personal qualities' of the pioneer probation officers. We were in danger of losing sight of the indefinable meaning of those terms. They were nothing to do with academic attainments, desirable as those might be. If to them could be added the registration of qualifications, well and good, but these were the foundation of what could only otherwise be head knowledge, with not always a heart to go with it. The hard part had been fighting unspoken prejudice or polite indifference.

I brought away something I couldn't describe from Cambridge. Punting along the Backs, 'Moon River' concerts in the Cornmarket, the crocuses and daffodils along the paths, the frosty, February moonlight nights when with Alice, my lovely little wife, we wandered into the soft glow of King's College Chapel where David Willcocks, as he was then, later, Sir David, in shirt sleeves was rehearsing the students' orchestra. There was a sense that Cambridge had conferred something on me that was not a degree, but an assurance, a confidence for the future. I had found some of my lost youth, as well, the years which the War had taken away. This is where I might have been had life been different. University is where I could have found myself instead of being in the RAF for five and a half years. Not that I regretted my service either. No, I was proud to have been aircrew. It was that now, I had caught up with myself. It was great.

The mathematicians of Kings College, I had read somewhere had broken the German ULTRA super-code which had shaped the outcome of the second World War. I hoped that I was taking away from the University something too that would be of value in the battle with the dark forces of the outside world. The War which was still going on.

Alice, in background, with a colleague, Joy, in the Finchley Fire Station watchroom, London, during the Blitz.

Alice served with the NATIONAL FIRE SERVICE on 24-hour Watch (Control) Room Duty during World War II and as a telephone operator, at a large North London Station. With two colleagues she was responsible for sounding the alarm bells which brought the firement sliding down the pole from their canteen three stories up. They would race for their appliances pulling on their jackets as they went. Calls would come in from the street fire alarms, the Police, Air Raid Protection Wardens and members of the public. The Ambulance service also had to be alerted. On her rest days she cycled to her home where she cared for her father. In between times Alice wrote almost daily to me. After the War, alice was awarded the Defence Medal.

Chapter 8

THE FIERY CAULDRONS – THE MAGISTRATES COURTS

L EAVING CAMBRIDGE AFTER the first month of the course, I was attached as a kind of mature student amid a number of younger colleagues to the Wandsworth office, not far from the prison where I had worked for over eight years. I now flung myself into a new scene, South Western Magistrates Court in Clapham which the office served. I was determined to go through the Probation Service's own domain and to let it be seen that prison and after-care was not the only area in which I could work. There was a certain mystique, which appeared to be claimed by probation, and I was going to penetrate this.

"You have to keep your wits about you in here", was said to me in a kindly way by another mature and experienced officer on the first occasion when I sat with her in Tower Bridge Magistrates Court during part of my training. I certainly felt bewildered by the speed and newness of this strange legal world.

Once more came the 'sparrow on the wall' feeling. The police, the solicitors, the court clerks, the gaolers, the magistrates all seemed to have their well-defined roles and knew exactly what they were doing, but where did we fit in? Much of it seemed to pass us by until a report was needed, some information of occasion or someone to be seen in the cells. I soon sensed that even my own experienced colleagues were happier in their offices seeing clients than in the hurly-burly of the courts every day and knew their way around, rather than by only coming into Court on a rota basis of perhaps once a week or less and consequently not being so much a continuing part of the scene.

I took as many Court duties as I could, determined to become as familiar and competent as I could be, to the point where it was suggested to me by my superior that I was doing more than I needed. I had laid the ghost however. Court commanded my great respect and interest but it did not have the same terror for me any more. Also, I did not see any looking askance on my prison experience, the after-care work, the roughneck containment of the Borough, the struggles with the drunks. It was all equally valid if different. The care of the magistrates was impressive. I remember a day when a

Stipendiary suspended his court briefly while he came out and phoned me at the office regarding a client of mine who had unexpectedly been brought in before him. It was a minor charge and the magistrate wanted my view. I found an excellent understanding with one of the older magistrates in particular. Looking back on many years of experience with the probation service, he once said to me, "I used to ask the probation officer to see a man for me and then just to tell me if he thought that he could do anything with him. If so, I would put him on probation. It was simple." I realised that while court work had moved on to report-writing and more formalised approaches, the principle and possibility of intervention still existed.

I decided to intervene too in the proceedings, as it seemed fit. Usually, one 'stood up' if there was any factual matter to be brought to the Court's notice. If I was indeed an officer of the court, I had better play a full part. It seemed to come instinctively too. I thought of Grandma Shepherd in Aberdare Police Court, as it was then, 70 years before. I could hardly imagine her as a shrinking violet but standing in the very dock itself when it was necessary, as a Prisoner's Friend.

On the eventual completion of my course and placement at South Western Magistrates Court, I was offered a post as a full officer and several pleasant months followed, except that I began to feel tired and fatigued with the long journey each day from North London, which I had done for over 12 years. Now that I was free to move wherever I liked, my 'training' over, and higher grading established, I decided to transfer to Middlesex Probation Service when an appointment was offered me in the Tottenham office just fifteen minutes drive from Southgate where we lived. A colleague said, "You'll work just as long, except that it will be nearer home. That, I found was indeed the case. I had been with the Inner London Probation Service for eight years now and it seemed quite different.

Tottenham Magistrates Court was very busy. There were no Stipendiary (full time, paid magistrates, usually former solicitors) at Tottenham and with a large number of non-professional magistrates, including one of my former volunteers (!), whom I now addressed as "Your Worship"! It was not so easy to achieve that personal relationship which had been the case at South Western. It was a very busy complex of courts serving an area with a large number of immigrants and I found the tempo and work load increasing in momentum across a wide range of involvement. However, I took on a large caseload and at one time had 70 people for whom I was responsible, about twice the normal. Then no one questioned my judgement in taking on so many, and trying to cope with whatever came my way seemed a fair-enough approach.

When it came to writing up records, I realised I was cutting it fine. I kept thinking of Father Tony in Brixton and his one-line entries and wondered how he would have fared in a regime which regarded case-notes as a sacred duty. Also trying to combine intense office pressure with making home-visits as well as court duties, report writing, prison and hostel visits to such a number of people proved impossible. I had the idea somehow, that clients were meant to report to me and not me to be chasing after them. When they did not do so after fair warning, I brought them back to court, quite properly, for breach of their probation orders in failing to report. This caused a few eyebrows to be raised especially when the police, on my evidence charged a probationer with assault on me, during a critical intervention. I realised that I was becoming an odd man out with my firm approach, doubtless influenced as much by my RAF experience as a warrant officer in charge of discipline on a small station at one time, as any casework theory.

However, the moment of reckoning came when the Home Office inspected our records and in some - not all - my 'one-line entries' came to light in all their horror. My observation as to the double caseload I had undertaken failed to impress and I was under fire. I decided to 'appeal to Caesar' and an Assistant Chief Probation Officer came down from Head Office to see me. He was sympathetic and helpful, observing that I should have worked more within the limits which was quite right and showed me again that I had much to learn. I couldn't blame the Home Office people either, just doing their job. They hadn't known Brixton and the avalanche of men every day. Ultimately twice the welfare staff came to be employed, which was a good thing.

In the unremitting grind of this large and very busy court, I was probably over-keen again. I still had to learn to switch from the prison methods of absolute brevity and emphasis on personal dealing. "How would the inspectors have fared in that situation?" I asked myself. What would our supervisors know of the R.C. Priest's dimension of 'confessions' on the landings? In human terms, more important anyway. It was a different world out here and most of my colleagues knew little of or wished to work in a prison. To have to conform to the regime of prison, with its host of regulations, themselves, did not come easily. Curiously too, it meant being severed from the probation service, in many ways. One came under the jurisdiction of the Governor, understandably, but also under the thumb, it seemed, of many others. It felt sometimes you forever had to play an unscripted part in all this or else one settled for a narrow role which had been delineated.

There was one occasion when I was on Court Duty, and decided to simply ask defendants informally, after they left Court, if they had been drinking at the time of the offence. Nothing more and they were free to answer one way or the other. It was a harmless enquiry well within my duties, outside the court room door. I should have cleared it with the Court Clerk first, however as one of the police was quick to point out.

The result was like being in Brixton all over again, when the men were called in from exercise. Out of ten people, men and women, eight said that they had been drinking. I left it at that. No one else had asked them. If they had, it would have taken time to explain about A.A. or some form of advice or treatment and there wasn't time or anyone to do it. Here was our army of offenders, I thought, riddled with a common characteristic. I thought again of the doctor who had said that if alcoholism were a notifiable disease, a state of emergency would have to be declared.

If one was not dealing positively with alcoholism as such, one was certainly confronted with an immense problem of some kind which was being disregarded on an equally monumental scale. Where drinking was some kind of widespread element in offending, it should not be so but here one was on dangerous ground in taking a stand, when drinking was so much part of social life, a subject on which so many were touchy beyond reason and made it seem improper even to enquire.

I remember, once, a woman Salvation Army officer telling of being asked why she did not drink. Her answer was simply that if others saw the amount of trouble caused by drink as she did, in the nature of her work, she did not think that they would want to drink either.

About this time, a more sinister spectre appeared on my horizon. I had been experiencing some chest pains from time to time and some of the dizziness I had found in Brixton, climbing up the four flights of steel stairs to the top landings. Now my G.P. Dr. George Macdonald had sent me to the local hospital for tests. After these had been carried out, I was handed my documents to take to the X-ray department for a further appointment. I took a quick look at the top sheet. The word 'ANGINA' jumped out at me. 'Heart disease' I thought and my heart sunk. The findings had to be reported.

My next visitor from Head Office was the Chief Probation Officer for Middlesex. "We would like you to go to Crown Court at the Guildhall, Westminster. You won't have to go travelling so much and there won't be the same pressures of court work. We select our officers very carefully for this kind of post." The Chief put it very kindly. Near Tottenham Court in the old Bruce Grove Castle was the regimental museum of the Middlesex Regiment. I used to wander in there during my lunch breaks. They had fought in the Zulu Wars when my Aunt Kate had been leading the Rhondda Revival. What caught my attention however was their nickname "The Diehards". During the Peninsular Wars under Wellington, one of their Companies had been surrounded. They faced hopeless odds but refused to surrender. "Die hard, my men!" their Colonel had told them. The name had stuck over all the years.

"If I have to go, I'll take a leaf from their book" I thought, in quite a matter-of-fact way. It didn't bother me. There was no need for heroics. I was a survivor already from my aircrew days. I had lived on borrowed time long enough already. It just meant that I would have to pull out all the stops if my days were numbered. There was now a certain urgency and perhaps no time to pull any punches.

Assembling on Horse Guards Parade. Alice with the Salvation Army contingent, about to march past Buckingham Palace with her own flag.

Chapter 9

PARLIAMENT SQUARE and WESTMINSTER CROWN COURT

T HE FLOODLIGHTS HIT me like coming out on a brilliantly-lit stage, the first time that I emerged from the Guildhall at night. Beside the oak, castle-like doors, Abraham Lincoln's statue surveyed the flag-bedecked Parliament Square. In front, Winston Churchill's monument stood like a bulldog in the heart of our empire. Big Ben towered as a sentinel with its lantern alight, showing that the House was sitting. It seemed a long way from the clattering iron staircases of the prisons, the bleak mornings at the prison gates, the bacon sandwiches in the Blackfriars Cafe, the steaming mugs of tea in the freezing mornings by the murky river. I wondered what Benjamin Morgan would have thought as he rode his horse to Parliament to give evidence, if he could have thought that 130 years later his great-great-grandson would be there too, inspired by his life. "The oldest Crown Court of the Land", as one judge used to say, was awe-inspiring.

If magistrates court had been such a contrast to prison, this was like Heaven itself. Certainly, the main courts had angels carved into the massive, cathedral-like roof-beams. I felt overwhelmed by it all, with colourful robed judges and barristers in wigs and gowns. Again, it was another world. I had more of the 'sparrow-on-the-wall' feeling in the face of this massive panoply of the legal system, its etiquette and formality as never experienced before.

Strangely, as a young man, I had been a juror in the very court in which I was now sitting as the probation officer. It seemed incredible. The oak panelled elegance of the historic building; the magnificent curving staircase carried its own sense of being a cathedral of the law. I felt that I had arrived at somewhere very special.

Middlesex Guildhall has a fascinating history. The present building, formally opened on 19th December 1913 by Prince Arthur of Connaught, stands on the site of three previous Guildhalls, the first in 1762, then 1808 and the third in 1893. It cost over £111,000. The site is one of the finest in London and wonderfully situated for the State ceremonies which take place at Westminster Abbey, just across the road. At the coronations in 1937 and in

1953, the building was used as a relaying centre for broadcasts to the whole world.

I found it thought-provoking that the site was that of the old Sanctuary building which had been constructed by the benevolence of Edward the Confessor. The interior of the original building had been a chapel in which the fugitive had to confess the reason for his seeking sanctuary before he was allowed safe shelter. Of astonishing strength, the vaults of the original Sanctuary had survived until finally demolished when the present building was erected. The cells for prisoners being tried would be on this very spot.

Just across Parliament Square outside were Big Ben and the Palace of Westminster. All day long could be heard the famous chimes and I would think of the ditty which went with them

"All through the day
Be though my guide,
That through thy power
No foot may slide."

It seemed strange that within a few hundred yards of the House of Lords and St Stephen's Tower were these cells where men and women were held in custody while their cases were being heard in the august, carved courts above. The tourists milling by in the heart of the Empire little knew of the shattered lives hidden beneath the pavement.

One evening it was part of my job to see a man face-to-face who had just been sentenced to seven years imprisonment by a judge upstairs. "I'm surprised to see anyone," said the newly convicted prisoner dryly. "Usually I just get carted off right away to the nick." "The probation department tries to see everyone before they go", I said quietly. "To see whether there are any immediate problems", I added. He smiled wryly. "I don't suppose you can sort out the legal system for me. I feel just now as though it isn't much good." He complained. "I could have done better myself". He added bitterly.

"What do you mean?" "Well I pleaded 'Guilty', didn't I, as my counsel advised me. So what happened? I saw him for a quarter of an hour before I went into the dock. How could he properly represent me on the strength of that? If I had stuck in a 'Not Guilty' plea, I would have had a proper defence speech, been in the witness box myself, telling my story. No, that Judge didn't even hear the sound of my voice."

"Often a judge will ask the defendant if he has anything to say before he is sentenced". "It didn't happen to me did it?" said the man. "No probation report asked for - just bang - seven years of my life taken from me." (This procedure has now thankfully been changed.) "A counsel may have studied his brief for a long time, unbeknown to you" I offered. "They can be very quick in talking to you. There is a lot of pressure on time. Seconds count." It did not convince even me. "There's parole to be considered, after a couple of years. It's not so hopeless as it seems now." He nodded. "Maybe. That's a gamble though. Not so many get parole and nobody says why." He drew heavily on a cigarette. "I might as well make the most of my fags while I've got them."

Then the lights went out. It was a power cut. We had had several. In the pitch darkness I could just see where he was by the glow of his cigarette. "It's as well I'm doing this cell interview", I thought "and not one of the women. It could have been awkward. Anyway, I expect the prison officers will come in a minute to see what's happening." But no one came. I didn't know why. Normally there would have been all sorts of flap, the prison staff rushing around. Perhaps they thought it was a joke. One saw the beginnings of prison life down here, the unpleasant side. The officers played little tricks like keeping you waiting for ages outside the locked door leading to the cells while sometimes they played cards in their mess room. Or they locked you in with a prisoner and then did not appear to hear when you called out for an officer to come and unlock the cell door at the end of the interview. Probation officers and even defence counsel were not always popular. This is what seemed to be happening now.

The aggrieved   and unhappy man could have attacked me in his frustration and anger. After all, I was part of the system. Who would know what had happened? We were both buried deep in the black darkness. It was like a tomb. The huge bulk of the Guild Hall above, pressing down overhead.

"I'm glad he's got that cigarette", I thought. "I can see where he is, at least." There was a deep silence. We were reading each other's thoughts. My voice when it came, trying to sound calm, seemed like a disembodied spirit. He couldn't even see me. "These power cuts don't usually last long. There is some emergency lighting as well." "Don't you smoke?" he asked, lighting up another cigarette from the glowing end. "No" I answered. "Not now. I used to. I was a heavy smoker. I remember what it feels like to be gasping for a fag" "How did you come to give it up?" He asked. "It would save me a lot of trouble if I didn't." "It's a bit of a story." I replied. "I reckon we've got some time before these screws come tearing in. It's my immediate problem, I reckon. All the others can wait until seven years time." I thought hard. I might find myself in deep water here. I was supposed to be interviewing him not giving my life story. Some of these cons. had a way of twisting well-intentioned related personal anecdotes. One had to be careful. Yet, he had asked me a direct question. Anything less than the simple truth would not be a proper answer. "Well, you've heard of Billy Graham haven't you?" I started hesitantly. "I have. The American hot gospeller - who hasn't?" "That's what I thought. Even that he had a nerve coming over here to tell us how to live. My wife wanted me to go to bear him at Haringay when he first came over but I didn't want to know. I was doing all right in business and I didn't like some of the characters I heard going around singing his songs."

I fell silent as it all came back to me. "But something happened to make you change your mind?" "Yes. A year later I was in Glasgow when he came to the Kelvin Hall on his Scottish Crusade. A lot had happened. My little business empire had come unstuck. I was a near bankrupt. I didn't feel so clever after all. What had this man to say, I wondered? He must be quite a salesman too. Half of Glasgow seemed to be flocking to the Kelvin Hall. There were huge queues every night. Well, I went. 'This chap means what he is saying,' I thought. 'This is no con.'

When the end of the meeting came, he asked those who wanted to know more to come out and stand in the front as enquirers. It seemed to make sense to look into this religious stuff. It didn't seem religious somehow, either, the way he put it. I was aware of a great burning sensation within me. My old heart seemed to be going like a sledgehammer. I had never experienced a sensation like it. I just got up and walked out. In fact, there was no one else there and someone pointed out an empty room where I went and sat down until hundreds of other people started pouring in. A young man came and sat down beside me, asked me if there was anything I wanted God to forgive for in my life. I said there was. He told me to tell God about it and to pray. I dimly remembered something from my boyhood in church about 'the peace which passeth understanding' and asked for this. It all seemed natural enough. Then I dried up. I couldn't understand anything else. Then an elderly man came to us, sitting in our little island in the midst of the buzzing multitude. I did not know it at the time, but my new young friend had put up his hand indicating that he needed help in his counselling. 'What's the problem?' He asked in a warm way. The young man in his smart Bible College blazer murmured that I did not seem to understand some of his expressions. I felt pretty thick somehow. My head was beginning to reel with all this.

The old man looked at me thoughtfully. 'Do you feel that something has happened to you tonight?' 'Oh yes,' I replied, 'but I don't understand these religious terms at all - they even seem to get up my nose.' He nodded. 'Just hang on to what you do understand' he said. 'Never mind about all that you don't. It will come clearer later on.' Then I seemed to find myself on the pavement outside the Kelvin Hall. It was all over.

All I had to do was to get a tram back to the hotel. I felt strangely calm. I realised that for hours I had not had a cigarette and reached in my pocket for my cigarette case and lighter. In the ordinary way my hands would have been shaking for so long without a smoke. I would have been tense and trembling. As I opened the silver case, my wife had bought me for Christmas I realised that I had no desire to smoke. For twenty years I had been smoking. I couldn't live without it. I stared at the cigarettes in my case. They meant nothing to me. I snapped the case shut.

"Something had indeed happened. This was no figment of my imagination. This was no heated emotional reaction. I felt as cool as a cucumber. I had to recognise that the ingrained, addictive habit of twenty years' standing had somehow vanished. I might never have smoked in my life for all the interest I had in it. A long story" I ended lamely. "But that's just what happened."

His cigarette glowed fiercely. "I need a bit of a miracle, too". "If you want it to, I think it can happen to you too. I was on the floor myself. My world had fallen in on me. I couldn't see a way out. The Bible says, 'There is lifting up'. Why not have a chat with the Chaplain when you get to the Nick?"

Then the lights came on. There was a fumbling of keys at the door. "Finished?" asked the officer.

And now I began to see another aspect of the legal system. Once more came the query; was I meant to be an efficient provider of formal information, the link between the outside probation officers and the court or something more, bringing to the court what I had learnt in so many other situations? Was I to be an active participant as the system allowed or something more, an intervenor, an intercessor even, of occasion? There were no rules here for a probation officer. A good relationship with the judge was vital. He was in complete charge.

The balance between intervention and improper contribution was finely balanced. As in prison, so much depended upon human relationships, more so than on rules, especially ones which hadn't even been formulated. As a client said once, of a probation officer in court, "I could see the way you looked at the magistrate and I could see the way he looked at you." There was regrettably, I thought, not always as much out-of-court contact between the magistrates and the probation officers; understandably in a busy court with a large number of magistrates on the Bench.

Often, in Crown Court too, I used to think of the Judge "If you only knew as much about the defendant as I do, I think that it would make a difference." Unfortunately, it is only in the evidence that is presented in court that a judge can be expected to form an opinion. Sometimes, there would be an opportunity for me to see a man while the Jury was out, or the case adjourned, to ask him if there was anything which he would like to add to what he had already told his counsel or the probation service. Of occasion, there was an opportunity to indicate to the clerk that I would like to be called to give additional information which I had gleaned, neither for the prosecution or the defence, but as an officer of the court. The matter of trying to inform the Judge of as much as possible, in a neutral position, seemed vital.

My mind used to go back to my Rugby playing days where, within the rules, anything was possible on the field of play. You made your own game until someone stopped you. The barristers played their hand, confident in their legal status, the well established rules. It was difficult to see the man or woman in the dock being increasingly disadvantaged by a defence counsel who had only seen him very briefly before coming into court and who plainly did not have all the facts, who may have only received his brief the night before. "What could one do? I asked myself against such an entrenched legal system.

I knew that many of the barristers were excellent at grasping their instructions in a very short space of time but there was so much more to it than that. I recall hearing a barrister tell his instructing solicitor "You can't let me know too much". What if a solicitor didn't have too much time either or worse still, if a client didn't go to see his solicitor through some mental quirk or other so that everything had to be put together like an ill-prepared conjuring trick, at the courtroom door. The stakes were often high and the grim gates of prison the price to pay for a badly-prepared case.

I used to feel that once a case started, it was like being caught up in the rapids leading to a dangerous waterfall. There was no stopping. It was too late to do anything very much. The time had gone. There was no time to talk to anybody any more. The opportunity had been lost. Lives were going to be broken and smashed when they might have been saved. I wondered whether anything could be done when I retired, to go into this grey area of non-communication.

I remember once, in Crown Court, a man had pleaded guilty at the last moment, on his counsel's advice, so that no social enquiry report had been prepared. There was no request for an adjournment for this to be done, so all depended upon the counsel's grasp of the case. I knew that he had only seen the defendant for perhaps fifteen minutes before going into court. (This length of time, incidentally, as I had discovered in Brixton, was often all a prison doctor had in which to prepare the medical report for which, with a long line of others, the man had gone through all the procedure of remand). There was an element of 'rough justice' present all too often, in the harsh reality of court, despite all the impressive ritual.

It soon emerged during the counsel's evidence in mitigation that he plainly did not have all the facts, which was hardly surprising. I wondered whether the judge would ask the defendant if he had anything to say before being sentenced but it did not seem that this was going to be so. I could not catch the judge's eye - not always easy - much like an MP trying to 'catch the Speaker's eye' in Parliament. With my heart pounding, I half rose in my sat. The Judge then noticed me and murmured that he "thought the probation officer wanted to say something." "With respect to learned counsel ..." I then offered the fact which I believed had not been brought to his notice. This intervention was a touch-and-go situation, in Crown Court, more so than in Magistrates' Court where the same degree of protocol did not prevail. On one occasion, a barrister took me aside and told me I was not following court practice. His legal arrogance was a pity. I was only trying to help his client. "So long as the judge did not criticize me, I was all right" I thought but it was that minefield again. I was going to be the one who would face the defendant in the cells if he went to prison. It was me who would be scorned if he knew that I had information which could have been brought to the Court's attention and had not been made known by his counsel. The possibility might be that an alcohol problem had just come to light. The moment of truth for a man often came suddenly. The judge might consider an adjournment for a full medical and social enquiry report. All hinged on a few minutes beneath the angels in the roof.

Even when I failed to persuade the Court of the need, as happened, I had the feeling when I later saw a man in the cells that I had communicated with him anyway at a deep level through my efforts and that, when the time came, he would be more likely to listen to my suggestion of treatment. It was worth it after all. The stakes were high though. There was one Judge who referred to me openly as a 'do-gooder'. Even the barristers were shocked and after court told me not to take it personally. I had submitted that he asked the man in the dock a question directly before sentencing - not an unknown thing to happen. "I am not going to ask HIM" retorted the Judge with a withering look at me and the unworthy epithet, ill found in a Q.C. The same judge had once sent a court usher to fetch an overcoat from his home during the lunch recess, for a man in the dock who said that he didn't have one and was being released on bail.

It was down in the cells that I saw a side of the law, which I will always remember. A woman alcoholic had been sentenced to prison. She had been found guilty but the reason for her offending was clear to her barrister. Now, the woman had sunk in an hysterical heap, on the concrete floor and refused to get up. Her counsel, still wigged and be-robed from court had come down quickly from upstairs. While we all stood around the disconsolate woman, the young man got down on his knees on the floor, gowned as well, trying to persuade her not to be so upset. It was defence counsel at its best and not to be found, I suspect in any of the law books. I saluted the law that day. It could be so human after all.

It was the 'adversary' system which I felt was at fault. The prosecution sought a conviction, however fairly, the defence, an acquittal. The truth as I saw it, impartially concerned, was often midway. A man might well be guilty but his sentence called for some understanding of his need, especially if it was a matter of alcohol dependency. It all depended on the evidence before the court and that was often not complete.

The probation service had a unique opportunity, having heard both sides, often for the first time, to suggest to the judge that alternatives to imprisonment were available. Frequently this was in the light of what had only just emerged in court and outside of prepared 'scripts' to the extent of almost being 'new evidence,' if one had been able to follow the whole of the case through being in court as the duty probation officer. This was simply not possible in long trials, particularly with a number of other courts to be looked after.

Sentencing could not be dragged on indefinitely ("At the end of the day, when you have all done, I HAVE to decide ... " had declared a judge once, at a conference). The legal system would grind to a halt if every case had to be adjourned yet there was a case for a final attempt to sentence fairly if prison was seen as the last resort.

If a man pleaded guilty, rather than contest a case because he had little hope otherwise of not going to prison, I felt he should be asked as a matter of practice whether he had anything to say for himself, not withstanding whatever may have been said on his behalf.

"Ask for an opportunity to speak for yourself," I would suggest to a man waiting for sentence. "Let the Judge hear your own voice. Write down what you want to say, if needs be and if you are afraid of being tongue-tied". Otherwise, it was all left to his counsel for better or worse. A man could be sent down without uttering a word on his own account because he had honestly pleaded guilty and thereby saved the court a great deal of time and expense. Some counsel, of course, did a brilliant job in speaking in mitigation but there were sad instances where men faced with long prison sentences had complained to me afterwards, in the cells, that their story had not been properly told to the court by an illprepared defence counsel.

Having decided, with the support of my senior and colleagues, on an experimental programme of intervention in the cases of offenders coming to court, pleading guilty of admitted alcohol-related offences and asking for help with their addiction, a positive strategy had to be adopted. The number of cases would have to be limited to six, a very small number but it was felt that this would be the maximum with which I could cope in addition to my general duties as a liaison probation officer. There was no special provision for time to deal with this experimental work and, indeed, we were not expected to have a caseload as the administration work was enough in itself. I have never had to do so much writing by hand, for the typists, and colleages outside in my life.

I have to refer now to the basis for the intervention policy, the principles and practical work of the clinic known as the Conservation of Manpower Unit.

The Conservation of Manpower Unit, a stone's throw from The Mansion House was both highly professional and amazingly friendly and welcoming.

Here, Gitte Serebro the Administrator, Boris Serebro her husband and Medical Director are seen with one of their nursing staff and a patient. This man was in charge of a 100-ton crane.

Chapter 10

REGIME OF HOPE

THE CONSERVATION OF MANPOWER UNIT

THE MIDDLESEX PROBATION Service in 1978 had formed an Addictions Committee on which I became a member. One day, we were told that we were to be addressed by a Dr. Boris Serebro, medical director of a clinic known as the Conservation of Manpower Unit. We met on the due date in the conference room of our training headquarters at Hendon.

A genial man in his sixties stood up to talk to us. He had a relaxed and easy manner, looked directly at you and immediately seemed to establish rapport. He was more like a friendly uncle than a medical director.

"Now I want you to hold out your hands, palms upwards", he told us next. Wondering what was coming, we did so and out of a small bottle he dropped a few spots of a blue liquid into our hands. A stain appeared on the skin and spread into a spot, the size of a 10p coin.

"Now please close your hands tightly", he instructed us. "I will tell you when to open them." about five minutes later, he stopped giving us an account of the clinic to say, "Now open your hands". To our surprise, the stains had disappeared.

"It's quite simple" he smiled. "The dye I put on your palms has dissolved in the sweat your anxiety generated. What degree of anxiety, however, are you experiencing? Wondering what all this is about? What notes you should take? Possibly about some of your alcoholic clients and what you can do about it? Not so much to worry about really, yet you are all anxious people.

"Suppose however that you didn't know from where your next meal was coming. Where you were going to sleep tonight. Where you could get some money on which to live. If, all the   time you had a monumental sense of foreboding. Of impending disaster. A nameless fear of the unknown day ahead of you. Every minute your nerves stretched as taut as violin strings. What degree of anxiety would you feel then?

"Imagine that you had found a swift and certain cure for all this malaise, readily to hand and socially acceptable. The oldest and most efficient tranquilliser known to mankind ... you would take it without hesitating. That drug and I say again, drug, is of course, alcohol, in its myriad flavours and forms but with the same effect on the nervous system.

"Rum was the naval 'sawbones' anaesthetic of Nelson's day and to a lesser extent, it is used today to 'amputate' shattered nerves from a suffering mind and body. An elixir of relief and forgetfulness. The certain release into the half-world of sedated problems which for a brief while would go away. As the gin dens of Whitechapel advertised it:

> "Drunk for a ha'penny,
> Dead drunk for a penny,
> Straw for nothing",

"In our stressed world, it is not the down-and-outs (only 10% of our alcohol-dependent people) that the Conservation of Manpower clinic deals with but with professional people. Doctors like myself, dentists, magistrates, judges, ships' captains, engineers, radio and television executives, journalists, teachers, lecturers, clergymen - the whole gamut of intelligent, trained, educated men and women whom you would think would know better than to so carelessly expose themselves to such risk of addiction.

"The cumulative effect of literally thousands of drinks, doses of this drug alcohol, that is, just one or two a day, is close on a thousand for a year and for a period of 5-10-20 years produces a dependency which is irreversible without medical help.

This is why the daily intake of alcohol has to be replaced with another drug which can allay those feelings of anxiety but as a carefully monitored, closely supervised daily programme such as the clinic provides. Alcoholics define alcoholism as 'a physical allergy coupled to a mental obsession".

I went back to the office with my mind in a turmoil. I had never known the problem to be so described. This clinic was literally an open door, only 15 minutes from Westminster Crown Court where I was working at the time. The doctor claimed that if he could treat offenders on a daily basis for only 20 minutes at a time, they would not want, or be able to drink that day. No complicated referrals or case-histories were required. It did not seem possible after my 10 years of struggle with what William Booth, a hundred years before had said, was like a disease. How could it be tested out in practice however? If it was true, there was new hope for the 70-80% of men and women in our prisons with some kind of alcohol problem. The opportunity soon came.

Just as God has been put back into the state philosophy of the Soviet Union, I wondered if the religious belief which I had come to know myself could be properly brought somehow into my work, into the now largely secular probation service. In the meantime, I had to find out more about this clinic and one day shortly afterwards, found me munching an egg sandwich with Boris Serebro on the other side of his desk, within a stone's throw of the

Serebro, Boris

2 Devonshire Place, London, W1N 1PA, BA, MB, BCh BAO Dub. 1939, AFOM 1979, Vis. Med.Off. Pound Lodge Reception Centre, DHSS, Med. Director Conservation of Manpower Unit, Lond, Assoc. Fac. Occupat. Med. Late Scientif. Adviser Trade Union Council. S. Africa, Med. Admin. Workm. Rehabil Centre, Johannesburg, Mem. Miners' Pneumoconiosis Certification Comm. S. Africa. Author:' Recruitment of Alcohol Dependent Working People into the Productivity Drive' Jl. Alcoholism 1974; 'Compliance in Treat. of Alcohol-Dependent Individuals (Alcoholics), Jl. International Medical Research 'Behaviour Analysis of Factors Leading to Alcohol-dependence & Excessive Drinking' Jl. RSH 1981 &c.

Mansion House.

To sit in Boris's consulting room when a patient entered, was a new experience for me. I was invariably introduced as a probation officer specially interested in alcohol problems. I immediately became aware of a tremendous rapport between Boris and the men and women who came in. "Let Charles see how you take the gas" he said, early in my visits, to a stocky man who was in overalls and seemed to be a mechanic. The man grinned and hoisted himself on to Boris' examination couch. Something like an oxygen mask was held casually near his nose and gas from a small cylinder was inhaled for a few minutes.

The man seemed a little flushed when he climbed down but I thought he looked much the same. Cheerfully, he chatted to Boris for a few minutes, took some medicine next door from one of the nurses, then with a wave he was off to work with his 200-ton lifting capacity crane.

"Would you like to try it Charles?" asked Boris - come on - I'll give you a whiff." The sensation was a little like what I remembered, when as a boy, a gassy lemonade had 'gone up my nose' in a tingling sensation which made my eyes water. Nothing unpleasant, just unusual. In fact, it was carbon dioxide, the very same gas. "It relaxes the system", was Boris's simple explanation.

Boris was an amazing mixture. On the one hand treating me like a fellow physician one moment and then, the next, airily dismissing my questions with "You wouldn't understand Charlie", when I asked him for a simple description of his methods of treatment.

"I don't need to", I would retort. "I dare say that your laughing gas does some kind of medical trick but I think there's a certain amount of mumbo-jumbo about it all. What you say to your people seems to be the main medicine. You are a bit of a witch-doctor, I suspect!

His fund of stories, his grip on the realities and details of their lives was amazing. I could have sat all day listening to him and seeing the exchanges between him and his patients.

The next patient was a Merchant Navy Captain, a man of great experience and engaging personality. "I used to be addicted to alcohol", he beamed. "Now I'm addicted to him", pointing to Boris. It was true. There was something about Boris, a kind of magnetism. "We trust no one", he quipped - "where alcohol is concerned, anyway - otherwise, I'd trust them with my life".

Then I heard Gitte, Boris's wife, a charming woman, or a nurse taking over the patient, cheerfully with mortar and pestle making up the liquid Antabuse which had to be swallowed on the spot. They all seemed to think it a joke once inside the surgery. Out in the waiting room, there seemed to be a cloud of silent tension between those waiting to be seen. The reality of a huge problem hanging over them seemed very evident.

The time sped by when I was with Boris. Each patient was a fascinating study of a person trapped by a drug which had found their own Achilles heel, the chink in their own armour. "Without help" said Boris emphatically, "they are doomed."

"How am I to explain your method in non-medical terms to my colleagues who would like to know how you treat the patients?" I asked. "It takes time to train people" he said and proceeded to expound his theory of equations. "It's too technical", I commented after a while. "Make it simple".

I told Boris once that I felt very tense myself and he gave me some tablet or other to take before going to sleep. I seem to remember that it made me stagger when I got out of bed during the night and I felt that I had been given something very potent. "Knock-out drops", I thought.

I felt that Boris was not afraid to prescribe strong tranquilisers but strictly under daily supervision, with only a day's supply to take home until the following day. He told me the drugs he used were not addictive and could be 'unwound' in any habit-forming tendency. He was always stressing that his patient's nervous systems were 'shattered' and that without medication to relieve their anxiety, they could think of nothing else but alcohol as the only means they knew of coping with their monumental tension. He said he monitored the degree of anxiety, and adjusted the sedative effect accordingly, providing the minimum necessary to preserve their balance, neither sedating them so that they could not work or function and at the same time, taking the raw edge out of their depression.

He had a cartoon drawing on the wall showing a man's face reflecting emotions on a scale from being on top of the world to being in the depths of misery. "How do you feel today?" was his first question to a patient who would point to one of the various revealing faces without saying a word. Boris would nod, understandingly. "You won't need any medicine today", he would declare, "just the gas", if the patient seemed happy. A man or woman plainly under the weather, whose tension shouted out, would receive a sympathetic nod and "The nurse will fix you up with something to make you feel better. You'll feel different tomorrow." Then his time-sheet would be stamped.

Boris's idea of the time sheet was novel. The idea was that where a firm allowed a man to retain his job on condition of daily attendance, the Clinic would literally stamp a daily record sheet of his treatment so that he could provide proof to his firm that he had been to the clinic each and every day. The system worked well where the man worked within easy distance of the clinic and later, where my own clients were concerned, provided a conclusive piece of evidence of a massive amount of daily treatment and control which could be appreciated by judges and even the police who might challenge a client seen on their 'patch', as sometimes happened.

Behind Boris was Gitte. I used to think of her as another Golda Meyer. "Benign Compulsion" was a phrase she adeptly coined to describe the tenet by which the clinic lived. If there was a 'Rule' by which this little clinic community lived, it was the unshakeable belief that only daily treatment, backed by sanctions of some kind, could keep a person sober. The sanction could be that of a supportive spouse, an employer and, in my work, the alternative of imprisonment which the court held over a man's head, but only if he had originally asked for the court's help of his own accord and had agreed to conform to the clinic's programme after it had all been carefully explained to him in writing and in practical terms through an initial month's trial visits.

I used to think that Boris was unnecessarily rigid about this and thought that alternate days or weekly visits might suffice, but in time I came to see that in the case of so many, if not all, there was no other choice. Boris had a fund of stories of patients, often high-powered executives and professional people, who after a while 'thought that they were all right' or those in authority who thought the same and let up with the sanctions.

It was not simply the mechanistic application of anti-alcohol medicine or tranquilisers either but the warm human contact of Gitte and the nurses, the understanding attitudes. It was the way they cared. The way they had time to talk. The concern with social problems. It was the care for the whole person.

But it took time, if the patients wanted to talk after they had seen Boris. What seemed a very reasonable complaint on the part of patients was that their worktime was greatly invaded by the time taken to travel to and from the clinic. Boris' answer was blunt. Without daily treatment, they would have no job anyway. Half was better than none. While they were at work, they would at least be functioning properly. In my case of court referrals, if my clients were locked up in prison, there would be no financially gainful work of any kind behind bars as well as costing the state and taxpayers hundreds of pounds a week.

In this respect, I was to learn a terrible lesson which I was never to forget. I had a young man whom I will call John. Literally at the court room door, John admitted to an alcohol addiction and in the brief moments before he was due to be sentenced agreed to attend the clinic daily as an alternative to what he knew was going to be a prison sentence for the serious offence to which he was pleading guilty.

The judge gave John his chance, put him on probation to me and treatment began. After a month or so, his very appearance was transformed and while his nightly visits to his favourite pub continued, his drink was orange squash because the medication would not allow any intake of alcohol. He lived a good hour's journey from the clinic and, of course, there was the cost of fares. After several months and feeling so much better, the inevitable excuses for non-attendance began to appear, usually that his new job - he had been out of work - was making it difficult to travel the distance involved. When I phoned his parents from time to time as, unfortunately, he lived some distance from the office too, I was assured that he was not drinking.

Boris became alarmed and demanded that I brought John in myself. This was easier said than done with the pressure of my daily court work. I did, however, tell my probationer that this is what I would have to do if he did not attend, with breach of probation proceedings a certain prospect.

Then a medical certificate arrived, issued privately by his local doctor stating that he was suffering from some condition or other. Boris smelt a rat and I contacted the doctor concerned, advising him of the court requirement to attend for treatment and requesting caution in the granting of a medical certificate.

Next came a rather cynical call from the local police. Was the clinic aware they asked, that our former alcoholic patient was now on heroin? He had been arrested on some kind of charge, then released. When examined, however, his forearms had revealed the unmistakable signs of drug injection. I contacted his parents. They had no idea, they said. I collected him and took him to Boris.

The police had been quite right. John's appearance so shocked Boris that he took a photograph of him. Very soon afterwards the young man was taken to hospital with jaundice. Of what happened then, I could only obtain hearsay evidence but John had been visited by a 'friend' in hospital who was said to have there given him the heroin for which he craved but the overdose had not killed him until after he reached home.

At the funeral, I have never seen a mother so broken and disconsolate with grief. She leaned desperately against the crematorium wall, wracked with sobs. My own responsibility hung heavily on me although my part was not questioned. From that day onward, I knew that the work had literally life-and-death dimensions and I could think of it in no other way.

Boris and I held our own inquest. "But the programme has to come to an end sometime, on probation at least," I said "and what can take its place then, unless there is personal motivation?" "Hopefully it may come to them, in the light of their sobriety for a year or two, in normal life", Boris said carefully. He did not seem certain. "Nor could anyone", I thought. But it was a start. Prison did not offer even that.

The force of law now seemed to be the only hope. There was that part of me which agreed with my probation colleagues, in the belief that no one could be forced to comply against their will. I could see that Boris's uncompromising attitude was difficult to accept, even as I had experienced it. His remarks had been described as 'abrasive' and in the 'gloves off' conversations which we had, I told him this. His reply was dismissive. I could only observe that the criticisms levelled against the probation service could equally be made against his own and the legal professions who largely 'did not want to know either'. Even the Christian church cannot escape criticism although in what might well be the latter days of our world, it is striving for greater involvement with suffering humanity.

My Christian belief told me that without a positive change of heart, a 'coming to oneself' or a 'spiritual awakening', as Alcoholics Anonymous put it, there was nothing complete to be done. "Plenty of people need A.A. but they don't want it", was an expression I had heard; even simply an absolute honesty with oneself. An acceptance of one's own ultimate responsibility was a new beginning. Evangelical expression would quote Christ's own words to the learned Nicodemus "Unless a man is born again", Yet this approach would hardly make sense to people whose thinking was not on Christian lines. I remembered the words of my psychiatrist friend "If someone spoke to me in Christian terms, Charles, I would feel as you might if a Buddhist priest started talking to you about his faith." It was true.

"It wasn't the preaching that did it. It was the way they looked after me". Into my mind came words of Rebecca Jarrett, the reformed procuress at the time of the White Slave scandal in which The Salvation Army had played such a part with W.T. Stead of the Pall Mall Gazette. They had brought about an awakening of the conscience of the country to the horror of the ways in which our girls, usually doped with laudanam, were being smuggled abroad to the brothels and worse of the Orient. Our laws, alone in Europe did not recognise the widespread social evil and left our young women, or even children unprotected, to be snatched from England. The opposite to the incoming tide of today's refugees to our 'sceptred isle'.

Looking back on her conversion in her later saintly days, Rebecca had uttered these words. She had gone to prison, as had W.T. Stead, for their efforts to expose the evil that was happening. Bramwell Booth, son of The Salvation Army founder, had stood in the dock, at the Old Bailey, in his deafness, before being acquitted by a jury, recording their gratitude to all three for what they had so bravely done and at such risk to themselves. This incredible action won the heart of the nation. The whole amazing story has been told in "Maiden Tribute". A plaque on the Embankment, later placed there by his Fleet Street colleagues, pays tribute to Stead's memory.

Thus, I took heart from the plain caring of the clinic. Neither Gitte nor Boris, ever claimed to be practising Jewish people.

They were modern-day Good Samaritans. I seem to remember them once describing themselves as humanists. They encouraged any patient to follow whatever spiritual leanings they might have and certainly suggested A.A. with its non-sectarian approach. One A.A. Secretary was actually a patient of the clinic too, they told me. If there was any real change of heart on anyone's part, it ought to come about through their caring.

"Why do you drink?" my great grandmother had asked her own son-in-law, Polly's husband, a well-liked man known as Uncle Fred and an alcoholic, like herself, in those far-off days before medical science had come to the aid of people who were often mentally ill. Whether she was able to help the 'Uncle Fred' I had never known, I cannot say. Her question however was so simple and so profound and remains so for anyone who wonders whether they have a problem, whether the misuse of alcohol has in some way, even known only to themselves, damaged their lives.

There were no hostels in her day either. Little understanding; no doctors who understood all that is now known. She was cast back on the 'Great Physician' and she identified herself out of her own past misery with the suffering of those who trembled with anxiety before her. She did not flinch from exposing her own deep hurts in recognising and challenging theirs. They knew that they had a source of support and strength as never before. What heart-to-heart transactions took place in that little cottage we shall never know, but take place they did. This was no remote, professional discussion but one soul in agony for another, with present life itself as the issue at stake, and everlasting life the reward for believing.

Grandma Shepherd never managed to get her methods into print. Her close links with the community and families in her small town meant that she had a grip on every aspect of a man's life. Her door was ever open to any parent whose children were becoming wayward. Her very name was a power no child dared to defy. She was constantly to be seen around the streets of Aberdare, a visible presence of authority. She left no memoranda to guide others along the paths which she had pioneered. What she did leave were individuals whose lives had been changed. Thousands of them, her memorial tells us. Individual 'hand-picked' fruit rather than huge evangelistic rallies, although in time all rallies come down to the faithful individual dealing of counsellors with their enquirers.

Neither has Boris left us his secrets but a good many clues. Certainly enough with which to begin. Like another physician in America who was signally successful with alcoholic people but who could not be emulated after him.

The time had come again to move on, this time to a new Crown Court which was being opened in North London, in Wood Green near to my home. Westminster Crown Court was due to close when the Guildhall would be taken over for Parliament to have additional office accommodation. It would be the end of an era.

An article 'Regime Of Hope' was published in 'ALLIANCE NEWS', the magazine of the United Kingdom Alliance. The work with the group of alcohol-related offenders was summarised as follows:

1. Of the six men, not specially selected and taken simply as their cases came to court, virtually at random, three were working and doing well and had not re-offended over the two-year duration of their probation orders. Regrettably, I lost contact with them as a result of moving but the point had been made.

2. Certain principles had been demonstrated:

(a) I had enjoyed willing co-operation from the courts who are often nonplussed when dealing with alcohol-related offenders. The lack of readily-available facilities being a barrier to non-custodial measures.

(b) The men concerned had been gainfully employed, paying their taxes and fines and functioning profitably instead of being committed for a period of costly and sterile incarceration.

(c) The compliance with the regime of daily Monday to Friday treatment agreed to by the offender at the time of his court appearance as an alternative to an immediate prison sentence needed to be under-pinned by sanctions and the strictest of supervision.

(d) The ever-present acute tension experienced by alcoholics living in open community required medical support initially before any other approach could be safely considered, where the safety of the public must be the first consideration. This could only be ensured by the use of anti-alcohol medication which would not allow a man to use alcohol. The daily monitoring and treatment only took 10-30 minutes. The inconvenience and cost of travelling to the clinic would have to be accepted as a positive alternative to imprisonment. Possibly more local secure arrangements could be made over time once the treatment and support regime had been properly established. Initially, it had a specialist element, which had to be preserved.

(e) The programme's first essential was a thorough assessment by the clinic and report to the Court with preferably a period of a month's trial when the full extent of the programme could be experienced and accepted or not, by the offender before the long-term commitment as a condition of a probation order was established.

(f) A court having a mind to ultimately make a probation order could safeguard its concern even further by deferring sentence for six months, initially, making use of a bind-over in the meantime with a condition of daily clinic attendance. An alternative to a probation order could be the imposition of a suspended prison sentence, which could be activated by the commitment of a further offence, in addition to any new imposable sentence. Supervision could be on a voluntary basis if there were difficulties with supervision.

(g) If possible, the medical facilities should be adjacent to the Court and closely related, for maximum communication. There should also be a close understanding with local police regarding immediate arrest back-up in the event of breaches of daily reporting.

(b) There should be no discretion allowed to supervising probation officers in the event of non-compliance without the express authority of the court to vary the conditions of the order.

This was the experience which I was now to take to a new Crown Court. The stakes were high. The programme needed to be taken further and with larger numbers. Further refinements were needing to be made. Above all, a new medical resource had to be found, close to Wood Green Crown Court.

Chapter 11

WOOD GREEN CROWN COURT

THE RISE OF THE PHOENIX

IT WAS EXCITING to make a new beginning at Wood Green Crown
Court. Then the YMCA at Hornsey came to the rescue and provided Boris
with the use of their boardroom in which to interview offenders whom I
was able to refer from the court. Boris gamely managed to visit every morning
on his way to the West End Clinic and spent an hour there. I was generally
present myself before going on to court for my own duties. The arrangement
worked well although it was a struggle. In May 1985, temporary funds
enabled Boris to install a Registered Nurse for daily dispensation of the
medical treatment which he prescribed and the YMCA provided extended
accommodation.

During this time, the Hornsey Journal published an excellent article
which is now reproduced here with permission.

... AND SALVATION BEHIND A WHITE DOOR

Reprinted from the Hornsey Journal of Thursday February 2 1989

Every morning more than 70 alcoholics and drug addicts, most of them
young and unemployed, climb an outside staircase behind the Hornsey
YMCA in Tottenham Lane (in North London) and push open a plain, white
door. Behind it lies their chance of salvation.

For four and a half years Dr. Boris Serebro, an expert in the treatment
of alcoholics has been running a clinic. It is his proud boast that he has never
turned away a dependent and he has not hospitalised a single patient, the
terminally ill apart.

The idea is simple: anyone will be treated but they must come every
day and take medication under the supervision of a nurse. Dr. Serebro is
Medical Director of the Conservation of Manpower Unit which also runs a
clinic in Devonshire Place off Harley Street. There he caters for executives
with a drink problem, trying to ensure they stay in a job. In Hornsey he is
trying to get his patients a job.

The clinic is housed by the YMCA which also runs a job club where the patients can learn practical skills and get help in the job search. Companionship is an important factor because many patients turn to alcohol or drugs out of boredom.

Without the support of the YMCA, the clinic could not exist. As it is, it's future is in doubt. Two charities are providing money for the next two years but this only covers the cost of employing one nurse. Dr. Serebro's treatment depends on daily attention and one nurse is not enough for 70 patients.

"If the scheme is going to be useful to the community, it has got to be put on a proper basis" said Louis Lewis, B.Sc. and J.P. the YMCA's director. "The worst thing you can do is to provide a service to people who really need it and then withdraw it."

Dr. Serebro wants more staff for the clinic so that its full potential can be realised. To give proper attention to patients he needs a doctor, four nurses, a therapist and a secretary.

"It would be a good investment by the state, much cheaper than hospital or prison". he said. It costs £1,200 a week to keep someone in hospital (1989 figures) and we see 70 men and women every week. That works out as a saving of almost £4.5 million a year. It would cost the NHS £80,000 a year to set up a unit such as ours and it simply does not have the resources, but we already have the facilities and can do it much more cheaply. (Hospitalisation as they might well require for only a week for this number of patients would cost £84,000 - Author's note).

Haringey Health Authority has refused to fund the clinic despite the report and has written to Louis Lewis earlier this month saying that they will already be spending £50,000 on their drug service and had no more. Mr. Lewis claims they have refused even to come to see the scheme.

The Haringey Community Health Council has said that Dr. Serebro was working outside the existing system. "The Health Authority already runs a drug service at Stuart Crescent Health Centre supervised by four doctors and we run a service for alcoholics."

"The health authority has very little money this year and had to close 200 beds. There is no money for an independent service."

The Health Authority may also be suspicious of Dr. Serebro's methods. In 1984, the British Medical Council attacked a similar antabuse medication treatment because the drug, used on alcoholics caused vomiting and nausea.

But some probation officers support this type of treatment and Wood Green Crown Court has studied it as part of a pilot scheme. Convicted criminals can submit to daily medication as an alternative to prison and then must take it every day as a condition of their probation.

Charles Preece, a probation officer for 25 years claims the scheme could halve the prison population in five years if applied nationally. At present about 40 per cent of prisoners are in jail for alcohol-related offences.

In 1981, Lord Avebury raised the matter in the House of Lords during the prison debate: "The Home Office should spend much more on prevention by encouraging, wherever possible, voluntary effort such as that of the Conservation of Manpower Unit, which aims to treat and give support to alcoholics within the community."

Seven years later, his words remain unheeded with no sign of a national scheme. Is Dr. Serebro a prophet in the wilderness destined to be ignored? Or is he the peddler of an ineffectual, irrelevant treatment? His critics say that they have seen no figures that prove his worth: his supporters point to a long and distinguished track record. For the sake of the demoralised individuals who come to Dr. Serebro's clinics each morning let us hope they come to some agreement.

Author's Note

My comment on this article is that there may well be some kind of drug service in Haringey but it is not court-related and without the sanctions which only a court can impose, such as probation orders, it is unlikely that there would be compliance with a treatment programme. To what extent the existing facilities are dealing with convicted offenders would be illuminating. Many of the patients attending the YMCA clinic have freely admitted to criminal activities to finance their addictions. They have not yet however been caught. Their cost to the community might be staggering.

The use of Antabuse, at one time called "The Danish Wonder Drug" because previously there was no other drug to help alcoholics to maintain sobriety, has to the best of my lay knowledge only been criticised when not properly administered and without adequate supervision. One of the clinic's main reasons for requiring daily attendance is that the drug is only given in carefully monitored dosage in the controlled situation of the clinic itself. Adverse effects, such as vomiting and nausea, are only brought about through deliberate and wilful flaunting of the medical advice and counselling provided.

I have been advised medically that drinking on top of Antabuse treatment has been known to be fatal. I have never failed, even as a non-medically qualified probation officer, to warn would-be patients of this. Nevertheless, in 25 years of service even with irresponsible clients at times, I have never known any other than normal and uncomfortable reaction when alcohol has been taken. A small risk and price for the thousands of damaged lives with which I have had to deal. A poor excuse even for doctors who do not wish to have in their practice the time consuming attention and trouble an alcoholic patient can cause as one practitioner freely admitted to me when I sought help for a client through the normal NHS channels.

It should be remembered too that each patient at the clinic comes to treatment as a matter of choice and of his or her own free will and accord. There is no forced treatment. Even if convicted people decide to accept a stringent programme rather than go to prison - a poor option as it may seem at the time and as they would otherwise inevitably do - they do so, in best practice, after careful thought and a trial of the clinic's methods. There is ample opportunity at any time to withdraw from the treatment. It does however require a convicted person - often of a serious and danger-to-the-public crime to be returned to court to explain a change of mind from the time when they first stood in the dock and asked for help with their admitted addiction. Such people for both their own safety and certainly that of the public, need containing in the security of a prison and not freed in an unprotected community.

The life-and-death dimension of my work came to me anew. I had been asked by a judge to do a 'stand-down' report on a young woman who had pleaded guilty to an offence. These hurried reports were never considered satisfactory, as there was simply no time to obtain all the necessary background information. In this case, the young woman appeared honest enough in her request for help with a drug problem. At that time, I had no experience of drug programmes, certainly not locally or readily available. It was obvious that the court did not wish to impose a custodial sentence. The young lady was working as a nurse. A former nun, she was placed on probation with a condition of taking medical treatment. I had never had such a refined client. She seemed to wear her spirituality, her previous vocation, like an invisible habit. I felt at a loss as to how to deal with her. Delicate and smiling wistfully, I could see why the court did not wish to be harsh, if there was some other way.

While trying to arrange the treatment which often took time, I arranged for her to visit the chaplain of her faith whom I had come to know and greatly respect in one of the prisons where I had worked.

She kept the appointment, going some way to see the Father in his prison office. She phoned afterwards to tell me that she had been helped by the counselling of the priest. Her duties at a new hospital situation however were presenting her with some immediate difficulties in coming to keep her first office appointment with me and I agreed to wait for a fortnight before

On 7th February 1989, GENERAL EVA BURROWS, accepted the first bound copy of 'WOMAN OF THE VALLEYS'. Lt. Colonel David Guy, Literary Secretary at International Headquarters who has advised on the original manuscript introduced the author Charles Preece, a soldier at Wood Green Corps.

The book has been described as "A classic of Salvation Army History in South Wales". Nearly 1000 copies have been distributed in the first three months of publication to the many people, a large number outside of the Army, who have helped in the preparation of "this magnificent story". A second edition of the book is now being commanded by Divisional Commanders of the Salvation Army to their Officers, throughout Great Britain.

The frontispiece is a reproduction in colour of the artistic treasure 'Applications for Admission to a Casual Ward' by the Royal painter Sir Luke Fildes, R.A., by Courtesy of Royal Holloway and Bedford New College. This world-famous painting is very relevant to the story.

Its gripping human, down-to-earth Gospel message has proved inspiring to a great body of people. "It packs a punch" one reviewer declared. It was an indication of appreciation for the years of research which had led to the writing of the story of Captain Pamela (Mother) Shepherd, Charles' great-grandmother, a former helper in the home of Catherine and later Hall-keeper to William Booth, at his first Headquarters.

The General's gracious and encouraging gesture, culminating in a prayer for its success, will set the seal on the launch of the bold, large reprint.

The historical kaleidoscope joins the past to the present and points to the future. "Mother Shepherd is a Window on History"-deeply and revealingly personal-" It made me laugh and cry" wrote Rev. W. J. Griffiths who arranged with Crowned Bard Dafydd Owen for the first-time ever translation of the Welsh Literary gem, the poem on the 1904 Revival by Professor Sir T. H. Parry-Williams.

The writer hopes that this book, in its daffodil-yellow covers, will convey a yearning for a new era of spiritual development which will reflect something of the great days past which are recorded in the narrative. The personal encouragement of the present leader of The Salvation Army, General Eva Burrows is gratefully acknowledged.

seeing her again, as she had followed my instructions regarding the religious support which I felt she needed particularly.

It was the local coroner who was to see me, however and not the little nun. At her inquest, The verdict was a drug overdose when found dead at home, not so far from the office. There was no criticism of me. It was accepted that I had not been able to arrange immediate treatment of some kind. The counselling had not been enough.

Boris would shake his head. "Let me treat them on my medical programme Charles," he would say," and then you can obtain spiritual counselling - if you can find it - as much as you like."

There was also an incident where I had brought back to court for breach of probation a man with a long record of offences when drunk. He had been warned that failure to report to the clinic under the terms of the order to which he had agreed would result in this. At the courtroom door, his family told me that were he sent to prison, as could well be the outcome, he had said that he would 'top himself'. My reply was that if he did kill himself, his blood would be on their hands and not mine. My duty was to bring him back to the court, which he had chosen to defy. Their duty was to make sure that he attended the clinic, living with them, as he was. I told them that I could not be with him 24 hours a day. They were.

I remember the silence in the midst of the hubbub when this sunk in. I had never spoken so bluntly before. Then his son replied that if his father were to be given another chance, he personally would take him to the clinic again, to renew the regular attendance. He was as good as his word. With some minor 'skids' which the court treated sympathetically in view of the man's overall record of compliance and treatment, he went on to complete the order, at least. Whether there was any spiritual 'awakening', I would not like to say. If pressed, I would doubt it. Nevertheless, a pattern had been established, for all to see. A positive alternative to prison for a man who was never more than a petty offender, who was pleasant and likeable and showed a capacity to lead a much improved if not completely changed life. Whatever might have happened, if he had gone to prison, that better self which we saw in sobriety would have perished, I am sure.

These people were not the seven-day drunks of the prison-gate days, the ex-servicemen of much my own age. They had been magistrates' court cases mostly. The new delinquents had been sent on to Crown Court for sentencing and were often skilled in some way but manipulative and devious. They had often a good number of 'previous' (offences). Their crimes were of violence and serious property lawbreaking. Yet, their dependence on alcohol was no different from their humbler brothers in crime. Whisky and not surgical spirits had been their poison. They were 'high-risk' in many ways. I thought of the Dutch clinic and its recidivists. The public's protection must be my first duty too. Yet after that, prison was no real safeguard either. These individuals would be released again, some time, with their problems probably worse rather than better. "Desperate maladies need desperate remedies", had declared a judge once, when considering the Conservation programme.

Now and again, there were lighter moments. A Scandinavian seaman who had been in trouble came to see me once, voluntarily, asking for help with his alcohol problem. He told me that he had been a ship's engineer and was rather hard to understand in conversation. He was estranged from his wife and hoped that I could help to bring about some reconciliation. To this end, he gave me her telephone number. In the meantime, I suggested that he started on an Antabuse programme through his local GP whose name he volunteered. He had previously taken Antabuse, he said, but had not kept it up.

When I spoke to the doctor concerned of the daily need for medication under supervision, he responded readily to my suggestion that if he gave his patient the required prescription, we could ask the man to come into the office each morning, with his tablets and take them as directed, in our presence, so that we could confirm his treatment. Like a lamb, our client presented himself day after day from his place of abode, around the corner from the court. With an air of resigned fortitude he took a tablet from the chemist's bottle, smiled and left.

After a week or so, I telephoned the wife and told her how her husband was regularly taking his anti-alcohol medication again. Her reply was to say that she thought I would find that the anti alcohol medication was a well-known brand of yeast vitamin tablets which looked very similar and had been substituted in the bottle for what had been prescribed. When our prodigal next came to the office, he was asked if he had heard of this brand and he left abruptly, never to be seen again.

Quite another story had been that of a wife whom I had taken to court to speak for her husband who had been on the Wayfarer programme but had had a relapse. Arrested and kept in custody, he was now facing a prison sentence. She stood up in the magistrate's court when the moment to be heard, came. Shaking and almost speechless, she could only hold up in the air a large half-empty bottle of Antabuse tablets. "He's taken all these, in the last six months, your Honour, and I love him", she said and sat down. We were able to collect her husband from the cells and take him home, on probation. He never drank again.

Another client had been a head waiter but under the influence had badly assaulted a fellow employee. He did some frequent reporting to me, together with the medication. He developed a way of sitting over a cup of coffee at my desk, for an hour at a time however, until I sent him to the canteen for some refreshment after a brief word. I think he would have sat in my office all day, talking incessantly. He stayed out of trouble though and never seemed a violent man to me. Nervous, and excitable, I could imagine him becoming unbalanced under stress but he was no thug.

I have a vivid memory of a European whom I had to visit in a prison hospital, pleading guilty to murder. When I went to him, before I knew what was happening he was on his knees before me and kissing the ring on my hand.

"I never meant to kill her", he said. "I had only drunk two pints of beer". "I am not a priest", was all I could think of saying "just a man like you. There's no need to kneel. Just tell me what happened".

One of the nicest men we have ever had staying in the house was a man released on parole after a number of years' imprisonment for a capital charge. He had no recollection of his wife's death as he was drunk at the time but he did not deny that he was responsible.

With memories like these, alcohol abuse became the very devil. It was a barrister once, who said that he thought that there should be a new offence on the statute book. That of drinking when the individual concerned knew that doing so would lead to serious trouble of some kind. A willful flaunting of common sense. Not so much the offence itself when he was incapable of knowing what he was doing.

A sad case was that of a youthful cadet in one of the Services who was arrested for driving at 90 m.p.h. through red traffic lights. I had to prepare a report. I could only tell the judge that in the ordinary way the young man did not drink to excess. He cared for a disabled mother, carrying her up and down the stairs every day. The strain had got to him somehow and the drunken bout had been the result on this occasion. Clean cut and erect, he had told me his story. I felt I had to tell him that despite his good record, I had to look on him as a potential killer if I had to supervise him.

The judge, after hearing my report, said, "He might be an angel at home but I have to consider the safety of the public." He was quite right of course. I could only say that I had told the defendant the same and that he was prepared to accept the anti-alcohol medication for a long time if he could be shown some leniency. He was sentenced to Borstal training instead of a prison sentence. I hope he made it eventually.

With retirement came an immediate possibility which I had long awaited, that of contacting solicitors more thoroughly in advance of a case coming to court. Generally, there was not much co-operation between probation officers and solicitors. Probation officers usually took the view that solicitors made use of them to do the work which they were paid to do. Certainly, their clerks and representatives could hardly wait to get hold of the social enquiry reports on the morning of the cases coming to court. The probation story was that they then got their barristers to read out the reports as the basis of their defence. They seldom seemed to have much that was new to offer.

Their remuneration was infinitely more than what the probation officers received. On the other hand, an article I read once in a law journal was the rebuttal of this by solicitors who challenged salaried probation officers to run a law firm if they wished and to find out that it was not all they thought it was. Probably the truth lay somewhere in between, I thought and the only way was to try to find out. Into this arena I then, ventured, again with the 'sparrow-on-the-wall' feeling. Another 'no man's land' where, my appearance brought curious looks.

At Crown Court, I had tried the experiment of suggesting to solicitors that they simply tried to arrange for discussions with their clients to begin well in advance of their court appearances, certainly if there was any question of an alcohol problem. Through having access to the court records I was often able to observe from statements made by police, that there might well be some relationship with drink, as there had been evidence of this at the time of arrest.

The sooner this could be investigated, even in a simple way, the better to avoid the awful business of being called in at the very last moment by counsel advising their clients to plead guilty, and the pressure to provide the court with verbal reports on the spot and the absolute inability to do this properly. Courts were often naturally reluctant to adjourn cases for reports at this late stage and, more often than not, it was the defendant who suffered and often went to prison, when the clinic in my opinion offered a safe and realistic alternative. All this needed explaining and time was needed.

I began by visiting solicitors who were frequently practising at Crown Court, in the convenience of their own offices. I was taken aback by unabashed disclaimers of interest in legally-aided cases, on the grounds that they did not pay well in comparison to private practice and that there were long delays in obtaining payment, even then. I pointed out that some firms seemed to thrive on their legal-aid work.

My own view was that often their cases were not very well prepared. One solicitor went so far as to suggest that he was not going to obtain much business if his clients thought he was lining them up for alcohol treatment. Another mentioned the difficulty of getting clients to even come and see him until the very last moment. I offered to see them myself on behalf of the clinic.

The fact that I had to ask for the reasonable costs to the clinic, as a voluntary registered charity was looked at askance with comments that the court wouldn't pay. When I discussed this point with the Chief Clerk at Crown Court, I was assured that any reasonable application would be sympathetically considered. Certainly, in my experience, our judiciary was altogether helpful and quite prepared to order special reports where prison was the only other alternative. The procedure had to be properly outlined in court, of course. One judge described the approach as 'Novel' and so it was. A new approach to an old problem.

In a word, it all came to naught. I saw that the legal system was going wrong. That people were often going to prison to little real purpose when there were alternatives. It was costing our tax payers huge sums.

I loved the atmosphere of the courts. The last bastion of courtesy and good usage. Where our language reached its highest mark. Where the idea of law was so fine. Where the legal system had been honed to a fine point. Where our judiciary seemed so open to good argument. Where dignity and graceful manners were so much in contrast to the world outside. Something inside me wept to see the canker within.

My other approach was to the police. I thought of how Grandma Shepherd had been carried to her grave on their shoulders. Not many probation officers could claim that respect, I thought. I tried to establish good communication with them. At one time, we had been given a 'pep-talk' on co-operation by the local police coordinator, where men on parole, were concerned. Over the phone, I betook myself to New Scotland Yard to talk to this man, an inspector. It was not easy to tell him that when I had tried to put dialogue into practice at a local level as a result of his advice, I had been told that "they were real policemen". 'Not very good public relations' was all that he could say. It did not get me very far in trying to protect a patient of the clinic who was being 'leaned on' but it might have prevented something worse from happening. Since these happenings, some years ago, grave miscarriages of justice have been revealed. I have too much regard and too many friends in the Police to wish to denigrate their high values.

I simply wish that accountability should be expected of all in the legal structure of our society and where it is found lacking, there should be fearless action to cleanse our systems. I have to look again at my own field of work, the probation service.

Boris, at one time, asked me to define 'dependency' in its alcohol and drug senses. With the help of my Roget's Thesaurus, I came across words such as subjugation, conquest, loss of freedom, yoked, fettered, enslaved, forced labour, loss of freedom, captivity.

All of these terms evoked thoughts of the condition of the thousands of men and women, I had met with over the years, in 25 years of work in court and prison situations. It was no figment of the imagination, no 'going over the top' to see these elements in their lives. The myth of respecting a person's 'freedom of choice', in the face of this thralldom was an absurdity. They had no choice because they had already lost their freedom.

I could never ask a man or woman to live without alcohol where they had a self-confessed dependency, unless I was prepared to live that way myself. It is said that 90% of our society drink thus and it follows, that, while not all have a problem, too many must do, to be able to resolutely seek sobriety from their fellows. Boris himself drank on occasion but so rarely, I observed, as to make no difference. No one would say that he had a problem. As A.A. have put it, "Alcoholism comes in people and not in bottles." Sobriety of itself was not enough. For some, it was simply a step on the way to 'being the best that one could be' as the Scouts put it.

When I went out to try to talk to solicitors, I had to have some visiting cards printed. The title given me by Boris was Forensic Administration Officer. I looked it up to be sure as to what I was supposed to be. 'Forensic - pertaining to law courts' 'Medical Jurisprudence - medicine applied to the science and philosophy of law'. A tall order, I felt and I have shrunk back from attempting to write about such a profound matter. Yet my experience is valid and my own and if I stick to that, rightly or wrongly, time will tell if I am mistaken but speak I must. Boris and Gitte must not have died in vain. It wasn't my personal office or function, anyway.

The Forensic approach was the work itself. Boris's 'industrial' medicine now applied to the courts. As simple as that. There came into my mind the thought that if all the 5000 or so probation officers of the day took on just two cases each in the course of a year, that would account for 10,000 cases a year. With a prison population of around 50,000 at the time, if those men could be kept out of prison, as we knew could mostly be done, our prisons could be emptied in 5 years. There would always be the hard core, of course, those who would never want to change their life styles. Even William Booth had sadly concluded that a certain proportion of our criminals would have to be segregated from the rest of the community for the remainder of their lives. A harsh judgement from such a caring man, but he was a realist too.

But that proportion did not have to be inhumanly treated, simply separated, 'during the Queen's Pleasure' we already had the concept - and the numbers were comparatively small, nothing like the army at present incarcerated. These were modest figures. Just two per officer. If the number was doubled, the prisons could be well nigh half-emptied in a couple of years. Instead of millions of pounds going in new super-prisons, if the money was spent in community measures on hostels and clinics, and the prison staff with their experience switched to run them, there wouldn't be a prison population as such. It sounded too Utopian to be true but it hadn't even been tried yet. We at least had our Open Prisons, to prove that in good part, walls were not needed.

An OUT OF BOUNDS sign was sufficient where there had to be a demarcation line. I thought of a talk I had heard once from a doctor at the Van den Hoven Clinic in Amsterdam given at the Mary Ward Settlement in London. They had a policy of even allowing, dangerous criminals to be at liberty in the community during the day, returning each evening for treatment and residence.

There had been a kind of stunned silence for a moment when the speaker had concluded. Then someone had asked, "But how can you allow hardened criminals, rapists, dangerous, violent men to be loose in the community?" The doctor had paused for a moment. "During the war", she said "almost every Dutch family had someone in prison. We wouldn't wish anyone to be there, if there was some other way." "What could one say?" I asked myself. It was the attitude which mattered. The Dutch had thought of men and women in prison as part of their families. We knew there were great differences. I thought of Corrie ten Boom, in a concentration camp for helping the Jews. The patriots, the Resistance people, helping our shot-down airmen to escape the Gestapo .... what a small price in comparison we had to contemplate if we tried to follow their example.

"Go and write your book", Boris had said, at the last when the work with the courts, the solicitors, the barristers, the probation service, the police, had all failed and his fast approaching illness, his loneliness without Gitte, had worn down even his own resilient spirit. I hoped that it might bring about some warmer climate of opinion, some better understanding, some kind of epitaph, some greater hope for the future. Was the story of Grandma Shepherd going to help in some way? I felt that I wanted my colleagues in the Probation Service at least to know about her, to understand something of their origins. There was a spiritual basis still, as with A.A., but it had to be conveyed in language which today's generation would somehow understand. In the last resort, did it have to be in language? I thought of a saying attributed to St. Francis. "Preach the gospel at all times. Use words if you must."

My mind went back to the Wayfarer days. The Christian workers had been bothered because we didn't seem to be "saying a word for the Lord" very much. It had been Fred Aldred who had said once, "We know what you believe. You don't have to say anything." Now, I thought I understood what A.A. meant when they spoke about the groups who, without any kind of criticism, were the 'God-bothering' kind, where they began or ended with the Lord's prayer. That was simply their persuasion and why not. On the other hand was the kind where they weren't 'bothered' at all. There was a place for both. The same belief in a HIGHER POWER was shared and people found it or God where they would. Without this intervention, however, there seemed to be nothing to be done. It was all too hopeless. And yet there was 'HOPE FOR THE HOPELESS'. My mind went back to something I had written, 30 years before and this I have now included in my notes at the back of the book.

In the meantime, our spirits were to be lifted. In the midst of all the agonising was to come a breath of new life, a foretaste of something out of this world. It was the CONCERT.

Penny from Pentonville.

She was a real little lady. Her manners were impeccable and she loved to sit with us at the table.......She would sit at an upstairs window waiting for Alice to return from work. The children loved her. When we put her in a local cattery while we were on our camping holidays, Alice's sister would go and talk to her every day.

She was game to the last, until her health broke down and she was mercifully put to sleep. I held her while the Vet. gave her the injection. I kept thinking of the refrain "Going Home ... Going Home ..." It was like losing a child. She had been so much part of the family, our life together, our hard times.

When we returned from camping on the last occasion, she painfully and stiffly got down from her favourite garden seat in the sun, to plaintively greet us. It was time for her to go and I believe she knew it. She did not murmur once when I carried her to the surgery.

Chapter 12

THE CONCERT

LOOKING BACK AT the Concert, nine years afterwards awakens a new thrill. It had begun at the Royal Albert Hall at one of the wonderful 1,000 Voice Welsh Choir Concerts when I had first met Glyn Jones, Organising Secretary of the Welsh Association of Male Choirs at the time. It had been a brief moment when someone came to tell Bryn, whom I was seeing backstage that the Prince of Wales was on his way to the Royal Box and Bryn had to rush off to receive the Royal guest, but not before he had suggested, bringing up one of the better-known choirs to sing at one of the larger London halls with all the proceeds going to the CONSERVATION OF MANPOWER UNIT and the work with the alcohol dependants.

The idea was in both polarities. We were drawn to it irresistibly and repelled at the same time by the thought of our complete lack of experience. In early 1981, we visited Port-Talbot to discuss the matter further with Glyn. We decided eventually to do it by starting the work early in the year, over six months in advance, which should give us plenty of time. (We thought).

First, Alice drove Glyn and myself up the Afan Valley from Port Talbot and over the Bwlch (the high pass) which led over the top of the mountains, down into the Rhondda Valley to see the printers in Pentre to discuss having the tickets printed.

Somehow, I felt that the enterprise should begin where Auntie Kate had taken the Rhondda by spiritual storm in 1879. A good job was made of the printing, and the sight of the date and names of the choirs later gave me an enormous realisation that come what may, the die was cast and for better or worse, we were launched on something tremendous.

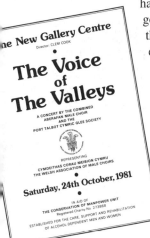

It was a shot in the arm spiritually, too. For three years we had thought of nothing but the research, the hunting for we knew-not-what. We seemed to be collecting hundreds of bits of jig-saw without having any idea of the finished picture. We never knew which were the red herrings of historical information and which were vital clues. All the months of preparing mailing lists and personal invitations both took our minds off the earlier grinding research and subjected us to new pressures.

We found there were clashes in dates, with other major events. There was the last-minute failure to obtain advertising space in one of the Salvation Army papers. Volunteers somehow failed to respond to the effort of selling tickets in advance although strangely, to our amazement, the money came in steadily from well-wishers, and we were able to meet our expenses as we went along.

When I was trying to involve the people of the clinic, the Medical Director of the Conservation of Manpower Unit said at one stage, "You can't rely on alcoholics for anything." The force of the advice came home to me in a marked way. In conversation, the clinic's patients were enthusiastic, interested and responsive but the intentions seemed to evaporate. The old Alcoholics Anonymous adage about will-power being soluble in alcohol became very clear, even although these men and women were not drinking. Their vital life strength seemed to have been sapped. They had become hollow shells, still fearful and unsure of themselves. Confidence was a thing of the past. They had sobriety now and the worst excesses of life were controlled by the daily medication, but otherwise, a vital spark seemed to be missing. Where they had formerly-acquired skills, happily these remained, which was a great gain but anything new seemed out of reach.

The Right Hon George Thomas, MP, Labour. The House of Commons Speaker. Later, Lord Tonypandy.

Speaker's House   Westminster   London   SW1A 0AA

I am delighted to learn of "The Voice of the Valleys" Concert in support of the Conservation of Manpower Unit, which is doing such splendid work in helping alcohol-dependent individuals to regain their freedom. This is a life-saving work which deserves support throughout the land.

I very gladly commend this cause for your sympathetic help.

George Thomas.

From the Voice of the Valleys Concert programme.

A good example of this was the recording of the Concert. With the music of previous Albert Hall recordings of the 1,000 voices in my mind, I had begun with a vision of having these cassettes made by a professional company but the cost of this emerged as quite beyond our resources apart from the uncertainty as to how many we could sell anyway. Then two of the patients revealed some experience of recording and one even arranged to borrow some of the required equipment except for microphones. These we were able to hire, and with the marvellous acoustics of the New Gallery Centre in Regent Street, a good recording was obtained. There were hair-raising technical problems which were overcome for us later by the Audio Department of the Seventh Day Adventist Church at Stanborough Park, Watford, and eventually hundreds of cassettes were produced and sold cheaply to the delight of many listeners.

What troubled us however as the months slipped by was that the tickets themselves were not being taken up. People sent in donations but did not want to commit themselves to attending. There was a terrible moment only a few weeks before the choirs were due to come when I felt that I had to phone South Wales and say that while financially we were meeting the costs, including their transport, I had doubts as to how many, perhaps only a few hundred were going to be in those 1,700 seats. The Choirs kept assuring me, "It will be all right on the night", and were game to travel to London despite my uncertainties. I resolved, if need be, to stand in Piccadilly Circus and give the unsold tickets away and even made up something like a sandwich board to use if the worst came to the worst.

There have seldom been times in my life when I have been so filled with misgiving and the sheer weight of heaviness of spirit when every decision, every step seemed dragged down with the ball-and-chain of dead inertia and doubt. George Thomas's commendation shone through the dark like a lighthouse although neither H.R.H. the Prince of Wales or he could attend. The contingency plan went into operation a few days before the Concert. Alice sat down and phoned every hospital nurses' home, handicapped club and Salvation Army social centre within easy travelling radius of Regent Street and offered free seats with or without tickets as time was running out. We delivered thousands of leaflets locally, door to door, even on the very morning of the concert. The final blow was the non-delivery of the vital 1000 concert brochures.

A phone call from the Rhondda the night before, said that they would be awaiting collection at Paddington Station. On phoning the parcels office, we were told that they were not open on Saturday mornings. I begged them to arrange for us to pick them up as hundreds of pounds of printing would be valueless otherwise and they said they would leave them out on the back of one of their vans. Alice and my son-in-law Michael were dispatched to pick them up, as I had to go to the New Gallery to erect the staging for the choirs. We could not obtain admittance to the building until a few hours before the doors were due to be opened and also a tea had to be arranged.

The choirs had asked for staging for their 100 men and no one seemed to know how to obtain this. In the end, I had been to a builder's scaffolding hire firm in Islington which had amazingly conjured up in their yard a collection of planks and stands which made up into an impressive if

'Applicants for Admission to a Casual Ward'

"The Picture of the Year". Exhibited at the Royal Academy in 1874 and at the International Exhibition, Paris in 1878. By Sir Luke Fildes, R.A. 1844-1927, later to be entrusted with royal portrait commissions of the Princess of Wales in 1893, Edward VII in 1902, Queen Alexandra in 1905, and George V in 1912.

A detailed account of this amazing picture is given in 'WOMAN OF THE VALLEYS' (Pages 57-60). We are indebted to Charles Dickens, social reformer as well as writer for his graphic pen-pictures of scenes similar to those in the story of Mother Shepherd. Luke Fildes added force with his vivid drawings. They were both seen independently in an almost incredible way to a comparable incident in the most moving part of the book, and at the very time (Winter of 1863). We are told that real-life individuals were used. It could almost have been Pamela Shepherd, Kate and baby Pam, "Down Whitechapel way", seen in their awful desolation. "Dumb, wet, silent horrors! Sphinxes set against that dead wall, and none likely to to be at the pains of solving them ... it is by virtue of that Act (The Homeless Poor Act) that the group before us will obtain food and shelter tonight ... they present themselves at a Police Station and ask for a ticket for admission to the casual ward of one of our great workhouses."

unorthodox piece of platform staging. All depended upon things going smoothly as it had to be carefully timed. There was no allowance for disasters. In the event, after a near fruitless search of the parcels area for an hour or more, the brochures were indeed found on the back of a lorry and arrived about 20 minutes before the concert began. There was a frantic effort to distribute them by Major Arthur Westwood who appeared like an angel from nowhere. They were nicely printed and it would have been a tragedy not to have had them. In the meantime, my volunteer alcoholic ushers failed to arrive and I can still see the two nurses from the clinic in their crisp white uniforms struggling with me to put up the dusty planking on the metal stands.

Then, like the United States Cavalry, the choirs arrived, full of fun and many strong hands providing the final arrangements for what turned out to be a striking, tiered position for all the men in their own smart blazers.

It was a fact indeed that the acoustics of the New Gallery with its high domed roof were remarkable. So much so that London's leading opera companies conducted their auditions there. Also, organists travelled from all over the country to play the famous Wurlitzer, only two of these famous 60-year old organs existing here at the time. Behind the scenes, I raced to change from my working clothes into a dinner jacket as I could hear the Wurlitzer starting up the programme. I managed to get up into the auditorium minutes before the choirs came on the platform.

Roger Chilcott turned around from the organ, looked at the people who seemed to be steadily coming in and gave me the 'Thumbs Up'. We had made it! Later, the hallkeeper estimated that the best part of a thousand people were there. I still don't know where they all came from.

The moment came when Huw Morgan, the conductor of the combined choirs, mounted the rostrum. Concealed beneath a brown ground sheet, part of our camping equipment, was our old wooden household step-ladder, quite safe but much improvised at the last moment. Only I knew what lay beneath the plastic covering as I showed Huw where to place his feet. Part of me flinched when I thought of all the Heath Robinson touches, which were present in this presentation. I felt weak at the knees.

Huw glanced down to Roger Chilcott at the Wurlitzer, nodded, and the strains of the National Anthem, sung in a soft, quiet key, filtered through the auditorium. Then came "God Bless the Prince of Wales", the Choirs' customary salutation, followed by the triumphant "Roman War Song". I must have leaned somewhere for support. It was immense. I was overwhelmed. The stress and strain of the last year fell away beneath the magic of the music these men had brought from the valleys.

When I introduced Anne Edwards, the internationally-known Welsh soprano who had donated her artistry to our cause that night. I could only say "There is HWYL here tonight, which means everything from just having fun and a good time, to the presence of 'Yr Ysbryd Glan, God's Holy Spirit'." It seemed like that. In the midst of the struggle, the dead hand of dark opposing forces, was this overpowering glory, this irresistible movement of strength and conquering purpose. The concert programme opened with the projected, wonderful picture of the Speaker, George Thomas and his message "I am delighted to learn of 'THE VOICE OF THE VALLEYS CONCERT' in support of the CONSERVATION OF MANPOWER UNIT which is doing such splendid work in helping alcohol-dependent individuals to regain their freedom. This is a life-saving work which deserves support throughout the land. I very gladly commend this cause for your sympathetic help."

I stood at the door as the audience eventually filed out. The number of friends and well-wishers we had, was a blessing in itself. A woman said to me simply, "Thank you for bringing us such a concert". I could only smile and say "Thank you for coming." Words had now failed me. The men from my home town of Port-Talbot, the men from the Afan Valley had come to our rescue. I just wanted to go home and think about the wonder of it all.

We covered all the expenses but in terms of fund-raising there were only a few hundreds of pounds as we had given away a great number of tickets. It was the encouragement of it all which mattered most. The sense that we had been in high places that night.

Gitte said afterwards. "No one has ever done anything like this for us before." None of us knew that it was to be their epitaph.

Chapter 12

BRUSH WITH DEATH –
The National Heart Hospital

"**Y**OU COULD DROP dead at any moment, Charles," said Doctor George Macdonald, our family practitioner. "Sounds drastic", I replied. "I haven't any great pains or anything. Just tightness of the chest - like when walking down here to the surgery this morning. Mrs. Macdonald met me in the park the other day and said that you wanted to talk to me." "Were you worried because you had to see me?" "No, I don't think so. It just came over me so that I had to stop." He nodded. "That's it, you need a proper check up." "The local hospital did that some time ago" I replied. He shook his head. "They haven't got the equipment. No, you must go to the National Heart Hospital. The sooner the better". I fell silent.

"Charles", said Doctor Mac. "I wanted you to come down because since I had my own operation I have been going over all my records, picking out those former patients whom I suspected had heart trouble as well. You were one. I've spoken to others too. I have felt that my own life had been restored so that I could help others better. Ask for a referral and lead an 80% existence while you are waiting. 20% of your day - 2-3 hours is not too much to give up. When you feel tired, when you are writing, for instance, don't even wait 'til you get to the end of the line - stop".

That had been six months ago. After extensive tests I had been told "You need this operation" by the surgeons of international repute. Here I was now, the night before my heart surgery. The book was still a lot of jumbled notes. I tried to leave some instructions as to how it could be assembled. I thought that my youngest daughter Pauline might manage it. Eight years work and still, I had not completed it. Where had the time gone? Some of it must have been wasted. Now the moment of truth had come. Tomorrow I might not be here. I wrote a short letter to Alice, in case I should not survive. I thanked her for all she had been to me and that I was sure that my death would not be the end of our love and being together. I felt at peace somehow.

As I was drowsily wheeled to the operating theatre, the following morning, I noticed from the big clock that it was 9 a.m. and then I was put to sleep. When I awoke, the ward clock said 11.30. "They have been quick, I thought" until I later came to know that I had been unconscious all day, over 14 hours. I could hear two voices speaking behind me. "He's still bleeding internally." "It's not unheard of." "I'm going off now. Will you take him back in and open him up if it continues? "How long shall we give it?" "30 minutes. Till 12 o'clock." I looked at the nurse who sat continuously at the foot of my bed, watching some instruments intently. I had an oxygen mask on, a tube in my throat, and various wires connected to me. I could not speak if I'd wanted to. I thought, "Lord, I don't want to go back in to the operating theatre. Something seems to be going wrong. I next came to at the sound of a doctor's voice again, speaking to the nurse. "How is the bleeding?" It's just stopped," she said and sounded surprised. "At twelve o'clock exactly" she added. "All right, we'll leave him then. See how it is in the morning."

A grey dawn crept over the West End rooftops. We were on the top floor of the hospital. Then it began to rain. I thought of the men painting the house at home - not that I could do much about it. The surgeon arrived and conferred with the nurse. "We'll move him now." The nurse seemed to demur. "He's not very well", she murmured. "He'll recover in the ward," said the doctor and I was trundled out of intensive care.

An early visitor was the young technician who happened to know me. He came and sat by my bedside, still in his operating theatre gown and wooden-soled shoes. He was responsible for organising the blood transfusions which had kept me going. Someone else's blood had helped to save my life. I would always feel a new sense of unity with my fellow beings, black or white, after this. I had other peoples' blood in my body. My young friend had something to say: "We were short of your kind of blood towards the end" he said, "but you made it". The story was not finished though.

It was some weeks later that I was talking to a little group of Christian nurses from Scotland, now living in London. One was Mary the daughter of the Manse in which I had stayed after the Kelvin Hall spiritual awakening. She had been a teenager then. Now a very competent sister tutor and in charge of a cancer ward. They had come home late to their flat, the very night of my operation which they knew had taken place. "Let's pray for Charles," said one. "It's almost 12 o'clock" observed one." But that is what they did.

Back in the ward, I noticed that the bed next to mine was empty. The night before, I had been chatting to the occupant, who was due for his own heart operation. "Where is the man who was there?" I asked the nurse who came to attend to me. There was a pause. "He didn't survive his operation", she said and went on with her work.

My thoughts inevitably turned to Grandma Shepherd, how her influence transfixed my life. Her concern for prisoners had led me into work with the alcoholics. This had brought me into association with Dr. Macdonald. His own experience of heart surgery when this was still a major operation had brought me to the point of highly-skilled treatments at the hands of surgeons of world-wide recognition. Finally, a group of Christian girls had prayed for a final healing, when, for all I knew, my life might still have hung in the balance.

"You are a miracle of medical science", declared Boris roundly when I told him the story. If God wanted it to be that way, I was content. I had been restored to life and that was what mattered. But like Doctor Mac, I must make something of my recovery, I thought. The book must be completed. After my convalescence, the Probation Service put me on relief duty at the Crown Court and, when I was not required, in the courts, told me to use the office facilities.

Not knowing how on earth my book was going to turn out, this was a noble gesture. If ever I had felt rejected in my special interest, this was a handsome regard and I hoped that I might produce something worthy of such trust and one which might help my colleagues.

I recognised the counselling skills, the training and academic understanding of human problems, the expertise of report writing, the practical knowledge of resources and the dedication of professionally minded men and women. I just yearned however for my colleagues to feel that, when all was said and done, the change of heart which they sought in those committed to them by the courts could only come about through the intervention of a Higher Power and that they too needed that grace in their own lives, as I had done, if they were to truly be able to befriend in the deepest sense of that word.

A rare archive snapshot of over 60 years ago showing Mother Shepherd sitting in the little front garden of her cottage, 'The Nook', 7 East Avenue, Gadlys, Aberdare. She was fond of this vantage point where she could be seen by passers-by. With her is her eldest daughter Kate, the 'Joan-of-Arc' of the Upper Rhondda Revival of 1878. This undoubtedly led to the National Revival of 1904 led by Evan Roberts which spread directly to the London Welsh Chapels in particular and even to India.

Chapter 14

THE RECORD COMES TO LIFE

W E WERE AT last in the Public Record Office at Kew. It was modern and impressive. There was a sophisticated computerised system for obtaining the particular volume which we required but help was available and then we sat back and waited.

Our earlier written enquiry had secured a reference number so we had a good start. (ZH.C1 /1376 85239 1842 Sessional Papers of the House of Commons: Reports from Committees Vol. IX) Then the thick 150 year-old volume was brought by a member of staff.

REPORT

The Select Committee Appointed To Inquire Into The Operation of the Law which prohibits the Payment of Wages in Goods, or otherwise than in the Current Coin of the Realm: and into the alleged Violations and Defects of the existing Enactments, and who were empowered to report the Minutes of the Evidence taken before them to The House; and to whom several Petitions were referred:-

Have, pursuant to the Order of The House, examined the matter to them referred, and have agreed to report the Minutes of Evidence taken before them to The House.

20 July 1842

It was going to take some time and we didn't know where to begin to look.

"Start at the beginning, Alice", I said. "Go through it page by page. Benjamin Morgan's name must be there somewhere".

Time was precious in this place. Not a moment to be lost. I decided to leave Alice to search and to go upstairs to study the prison records to try to find my great-grandfather William Shepherd. I didn't know which prison or the years, and not all the big, heavy registers were available. After a while I felt I was on the wrong track. It was all fascinating, these careful hand-written records of the past, but not what I was looking for. I thought that I would go back downstairs to see how Alice was faring. Her face was radiant. "I've found Benjamin Morgan. I was coming to look for you."

There it all was. Pages 93-96, 127, and 327/21. The complete verbatim account of Benjamin's evidence to the Select Committee.

Alice's find established in factual detail what had been barely referred to in the original War Cry account which had said that, as a child, Pamela Shepherd had remembered her father going to London to give evidence to Parliament. She had just been six and a half years old then.

Now, the shadowy, unknown character of my great-great-grandfather came to life through his replies to the searching questions of Sir John Guest, the Earl of Hillsborough, Mr. Villiers, Mr. Ferrant and Mr. Cobden.

With pride, I read how this proud man had said goodbye to his livelihood, his home in his Welsh Valleys, all he held dear in his native land by his uncompromising stand against those employers who had flouted the law of the land which had already outlawed the Truck System. They were defiantly continuing to rob their workers through their iniquitous Company Shops.

Grimly, Benjamin had weighed the cost of giving the evidence for those thousands who had sent him and had told the Committee so, before stepping down from the witness stand.

"There is one thing I wish to say: that I fear that, in consequence of my being examined, I shall be discharged when I get home, in consequence of my being here as evidence: I hope the Committee will consider that."

"What makes you think you shall be discharged?" "Because I am much against the system: but I am only one of 3,000 who have the same feeling against it."

How those words ring through the century and a half. They revealed the power of the coal and iron masters of those days who held a man, his wife and his children, their home and their future in their callous hands.

Benjamin may have escaped transportation three years before after the Newport Rising but now it was exile from Wales instead.

What emerges from Benjamin's evidence was his years of work as a blacksmith, his struggle to survive, walking the miles to his work in the remote Glenavon Colliery, only able to come home at weekends. The journey to Bridgend for an occasional sheep's head.

This was a voice from the heat and hell of the ironworks, the blast furnaces, the rivers of molten iron, sometimes exploding like a volcano in the crude processes of the day. Or the dark labyrinths under ground where women and children crawled like harnessed dogs dragging the tubs of coal in tiny tunnels.

A nation was struggling to find its soul in the shattering change from an agricultural people with its sheep and its cornfields to the industrial heart of the new world. Struggling to maintain its ancient standards in the face of the catastrophic birth of a strange new life. Abandoned in the bare, stony, stricken valleys, denuded of every tree, long-since burnt for fuel, the very grass poisoned by the fumes, they were slaves in all but having fetters of iron. Their chains were the bondage of the wretched Truck System.

We left the Record Office. We had found Benjamin. We carried home photocopies of Alice's discovery. It was a scoop. Probably the first time the story had come to life in all these years. It was a foundation upon which we could go forward. Like The War Cry articles. It was history and not hearsay. Our forebears were real people and now across time, they were speaking to us, in a new way.

The Parish Church of Saint John the Baptist, Aberdare. From a watercolour by Goronwy Owen. The church which Mother Shepherd would have known before 1852 when Saint Elvan's was founded.

Chapter 15

POSTSCRIPT

ACASE CONFERENCE had been asked for at the local hospital. The tests on Alice had been referred to the Mental Health Department by the other local General Hospital which had been checking her long-standing thyroid condition.

We sat outside for a moment before going inside to the reception desk. Alice looked up at the MENTAL HEALTH sign over the door. "How did I come to end up here?" she asked me, quietly. "It's simply that this is where memory problems are checked" was all I could offer. "It's nothing to do with questions of sanity. Remember the probation officers' group which I attended for over a year which was under the guidance of a consultant psychiatrist from Broadmoor. It was invaluable to us all". Inside, we were directed to the sensitively named "Memory Clinic".

Alice was asked to wait outside while the conference took place. I said that we were hoping for some feedback after several years of investigations and waiting, without information. My son-in-law was more direct "Has there been a diagnosis?" he asked.

"Dementia of the Alzheimer type we think." was the consultant's reply. "The condition is irreversible".

"What can be done?" I asked. "We have a day centre and a psychiatric community nurse could visit you monthly for support and advice. It was a bleak pronouncement. Alzheimers Disease.

"Can we start with the Day Centre?" I enquired. "Would, your wife be willing to go?" asked the consultant. "Could we ask her? We have always shared everything. We are not afraid of Alzheimers".

Alice was called in and I have never been more proud of her. She stood smiling before the eight or so nurses and health care professionals. Would she like to attend a day centre where it was hoped that her memory problems could be helped?

Without batting an eyelid, Alice affirmed that she would do anything she was advised. So it was arranged and we came away. I felt determined as never before to explore every avenue, from my own experience of alcoholism in particular also incurable, to fight what I knew vaguely was potentially a devastating condition out of love for the gallant woman who had been my loving wife and a devoted mother for nearly 60 years.

The story of what happened will be told in GOLDEN YEARS WITH ALICE, our next book.

THE TALE OF THE PRISONER'S WIFE

BEFORE I START my talk on the effects of a man's imprisonment on his wife and family, I must say a few words about Prisoners' Wives Service of which I was a member and voluntary visitor for 10 years from 1966-1977. The service for London only was started in 1963 by Lady Chancellor who, as a J.P., realised how little was being done for the families of the men who were going to prison.

The Probation Service was doing all it could but there were not enough officers to do all the home visiting necessary to help these families with their problems. So after training as an Associate of the Inner London Probation Service, at the final interview I was asked whether I would like to do Aftercare or work with the prisoners families and obviously, I chose the latter.

At times, I was looking after some 14 families who could call on me for help and advice at anytime, including evenings and weekends when all the official workers were unavailable. When I started, there were only about 25 visitors for the London area and so my area in North London included Stoke Newington, Hackney and Islington and when I also became an Associate of the Middlesex Probation Service, I had families in Enfield, Edmonton and Tottenham. The work involved getting a phone call from the office which at that time was in Bishop Creighton House in Fulham, requesting a visit to a wife and particulars were given of the husband's imprisonment, length of sentence, number of children, any other organisation involved and the source of the referral. These were made from the Prison Welfare Officer, the Chaplain, Probation Officer, Health Visitor or Social worker.

Sometimes, the prisoner himself made the request for a visitor to see his wife and there were self-referrals from the wife herself who had probably heard of the Service through a friend or relative or had seen the posters displayed at the prison or visiting Centres and some had been in contact with P.W.S. during a previous sentence. Almost half the referrals were for families of men held in the four London prisons with the remainder spread widely from Dartmoor and Durham to the I.O.W. Our task was to visit the wives in their homes, to find out their problems and to deal with them by giving help, and moral support. One great advantage we had was the fact that we wore no 'official hat' and so we were able to gain their trust and friendship. Sometimes when just to be there with a wife in an unembarrassed and accepting way, could be far more helpful than a multitude of well-meant advice.

After the visit, a full report form had to be filled in and sent back to the office, stating details of children and schools, health of wife and name of doctor, financial arrangements and other problems. If further procedures were necessary, our consultant probation officer would advise on these matters. I always tried to visit my wives once a week on a regular basis and encouraged them to phone if any kind of emergency arose. This was a lifeline for them which I felt was very important if some times inconvenient.

Imprisonment produces a double crisis for the family - demoralisation plus dismemberment. Many of the problems are similar to those encountered when a family member dies, but there is one important difference - the man is still very much alive and one day will probably return to the family. In addition, his absence from the family has usually been caused by acts which are socially unacceptable. Thus at the same time as a family are dealing with the shock of dismemberment, it must also deal with shame and with the creation of a new relationship with the family member who is living while dead!

To understand the dimensions of this crisis, we need to look at what may have happened to the wife prior to the husband's imprisonment. There will probably have been an extended period of time between the man's initial arrest and final sentencing. During this period, the wife has undergone a series of shocks: the initial arrest, often occurring in the home itself - if the man gets bail, he often loses his job, either because of the arrest or because of the time lost in having to make repeated court appearances. If he is remanded in custody, he can have daily visits from his wife. It is not unusual at this time for normal bills to go unpaid, because all resources both financial and emotional are being used for the husband. A wife usually comes to the day when her husband is to be sentenced completely drained of both financial and emotional energy.

Prisoner's wives don't always receive the necessary information to make a reasonable assessment of their situation. They rarely know the progress of their husband's case, his chances of acquittal and the possible length of sentence. The lawyer is often inaccessible and there is no one else to ask. At the time of the sentencing, there is no one to interpret the meaning of the sentence - where the husband is going to go - what she must do - and where she must go to get any of the information which is vital if she is going to cope with the new set of circumstances thrust upon her. As in any crisis, the wife must rely on the available supports particularly her family. She must often turn to her parents, but despite their desire to help their daughter - there is often great resentment of the imprisoned son-in-law. They feel that he is the person who has caused their child the grief she is now undergoing and often demand that she break with him. This same thought may have occurred to the wife herself. Her reaction to her parents' request however is almost always to come to her husband's defence.

The relationship of the wife to her in-laws is a reverse of that with her own parents. There may have been a good relationship with the husband's family during the time he was at home but after his imprisonment a feeling often develops that the wife is at least partially to blame for the man's return to crime. There may be an open split and an end to the relationship so not only does this deprive the wife of one possible avenue of support but it also creates another troubled relationship with which she must now deal.

When her husband goes into prison, the woman realises that she is alone in the house with children for whom she is entirely responsible. Although she may have made most of the child-rearing decisions - most wives feel that child-rearing is a two parent responsibility - the problem are made worse because the new single parent role comes at a time when the children are most in need of support and explanation - as they are confused and alarmed at what has happened. One of the woman's first problems is explaining to her children, the loss of their father and the reason for the loss. Because of her own feelings of shame and confusion - she is generally reluctant to tell them the whole truth about their father's arrest and conviction. Various cover-ups will be used such as 'Daddy is in Hospital' or 'working away from home " etc., or anything else that will explain his absence from home in a socially acceptable way - but there are difficulties for example of a mother taking a small boy on a visit to see Dad in hospital - he says "PRISON doesn't spell hospital."

So very many children know that it is a lie from the outset. They may have been present at their father's arrest and have heard snatches of conversation between their mother and other members of the family. If she decides to tell them the truth she treads the difficult path of telling them in such a way that it will not totally destroy their confidence and trust in their father.

In a neighbourhood where many fathers are in prison, mothers and children can allow themselves to be more truthful about the situation, but in a neighbourhood where few fathers, if any, are in prison, the family not only has to deal with their own feelings of guilt and shame but also have to make up a series of intricate lies to explain the absence of the husband and father.

The mother must now cope with all the normal reactions a child will exhibit in the loss of a father - he has his own anxieties and fears which are often made worse by the emotional upheaval being felt by the mother who may try to cope with the situation by withdrawing almost totally, sleeping most of the day and experiencing suicidal thoughts. The child may then show signs of uncontrollable behaviour, with eating or sleeping problems, fretting, clinging, bed-wetting and nerves but the mother often fails completely to see them as problems for the child or even from the child's point of view. They were essentially seen in terms of nuisance value for the mother.

The build-up of outside pressures, the absence of external support, her own irrational behaviour, and the needs of her children which she feels unable to cope with, often lead her to wonder if she is going to have a mental breakdown. Further strain is the visit itself. The prison is probably a very long way from home. It is by no means certain that a man will go to his local prison, so this means that the wife has the additional worry of transporting herself and her children on a long and tiring journey. She may have to leave home before breakfast - not returning until late at night - the journey itself will probably have been difficult, comprising numerous buses and trains - prisons not usually being centrally located. She will have had the financial problems of providing food for herself and children during the day and her husband will usually expect her to bring him cigarettes and papers etc.

When she reaches the prison, she may have to wait outside until the doors are opened. Inside while waiting to be called, there are often no facilities to get a cup of tea or to tidy up the children after the journey. In the morning they had all put on their best clothes but by now they are crumpled and grubby. The wife will be tired and anxious - the children may have become fretful and quarrelsome and all these factors contribute to a visit which has been anticipated with such hope and now degenerates into an awkward situation where the important things are left unsaid.

The wife feels afraid to display any emotion towards her husband in the very public setting of the prison visiting room. She feels everyone and in particular the prison officer is watching and listening to her. At the end of the visit both man and wife feel frustrated and dissatisfied. The wife after the ordeal of the visit, wishes she could have peace and quiet to get over her grief at yet another separation from her husband but instead she has to face the long return journey.

Letters are censored and therefore written with this in mind and may take several days to reach the man and all this tends to make the situation even more difficult. Therefore, if the prison sentence is long, it is very likely that the family will break up. For those wives who manage to keep going-until their husband is released, there is the very real fear and anxiety of how the whole family will adjust to their new circumstances.

Many women cannot cope with the sexual frustration they feel while their husband is in prison. They feel abnormal and frightened at having these feelings and are unable to talk about their problem to anyone else. They feel doubly guilty because they know the man has no normal outlet for his emotion at all. Because the outside world appears so hostile to these women, they are attracted to any man who shows the slightest sympathy towards them.

However they are frightened that if they do have an affair it will get back to their husbands who are always very jealous of their wives' lives outside. The wife hopes that an affair will not develop too far and will be over before her husband is released from prison. But for some women the reverse is true. They feel that no sexual demands will be made on them while their husbands are away and also that there will be no unwanted babies. It is these human problems which punish the wife whilst society punishes the husband.

At the time of the man's release, one might be forgiven for assuming his return home would be purely a matter for rejoicing but in fact there are special problems for both husband and wife in his return. If the wife is an inefficient muddler she may be very afraid of the husband's reaction to the chaos to which he is returning, she may even run out on him and not be there when he comes back or a wife may barely give him time to get home before she dumps the load of management on his lap and expects him to cope with it.

On the other hand if she has learned to manage the family's affairs, she may find it difficult to give up the dominant role and for a time being at least, the husband may find himself the odd one out at home. Then there are the children who sometime break down as the date of their father's discharge approaches, especially if he has been away for a long time perhaps serving a sentence for incest or sexual assault. Some of them particularly the older ones, had been helping their mother and showing a willingness and ability to accept added responsibility and doing better at school during their father's absence. However, when father returns, they can start truanting and their level of general behaviour may decline quite rapidly.

To conclude, the prisoner's family has not only to cope with all the practical problems of a one-parent family - but has the additional emotional problems of the second parent who is still part of the family, although no longer there. It is of great importance that more information should be made available about the children of these prisoners and the implication of having a 'criminal father'. We do know that few children are likely to escape the experience undamaged and even those who superficially remain unaffected may do so only at considerable cost to the future state of their mental health.

Now to be fair, I must add that I have visited many men in prison and it is only the most hardened and insensitive of men who can face separation from his wife and family without some form of emotional stress and there are very few of these. However much involved in crime a man is, with or without the knowledge of his family, there are many deep ties to be resolved and adjustments made. This is particularly so with men who are inside for the first time. They are understandably quite lost without the support of their loved ones.

'When a man is only serving a short sentence, he can get by without too much pain but with a man on a longer sentence if, for any reason, he loses his remission, there is often hell to pay with his family who do not always understand the pressures under which a man lives in a prison setting. In 1972, after a series of meetings with the Governor of Pentonville who was Alistair Miller at that time, with social workers, probation officers and voluntary workers, a Wives & Families Centre was opened in the clubroom, as it used to be, of a pub, the Balmoral Castle which was opposite the gate of Pentonville Prison. One of the first volunteers persuaded Allied Breweries to let us have the lease at a cut-price rate.

The Centre had direct communication with the Prison Gate Lodge, so that if a tired and worried wife arrived, she could wait in the Centre which was a bright and cheerful place equipped with lots of toys, games and books, facilities to make a variety of drinks, with sandwiches and biscuits available. It also had a small room for mothers where they could feed and change their babies in comfort and privacy. This very useful service was run voluntarily but the Welfare Staff at the prison were very much in on the act.

When the visit was over, the women would always be comforted, given tea or coffee, cigarettes offered and any necessary advice given. I had the good fortune to work there for over a year and enjoyed it very much, especially looking after the babies and younger children who were sometimes left with us if the mother wanted a quiet visit with her husband without the distraction of the little ones.

Dr Macdonald   *Mrs Macdonald*

George C. Macdonald, T.D. MD BSc MRCSA FRCGP

1958 Master of the Barber Surgeons' Company

WAYFARERS were most fortunate in having the interest and practical medical support and advice of this distinguished local General Practitioner who guided the fledging band of volunteer workers in this new field of forensic medicine.

His belief in the value of what was being attempted with the most difficult of men and women with alcohol problems all of whom had been in prison, was a constant encouragement to all engaged in this work of attempting rehabilitation in community with the barest of resources. It established a model of a medically based outreach group.

Mrs. Elaine Macdonald trained as a Nurse and Radiographer at the renowned London Guy's Hospital. The WAYFARER volunteers after two years of commitment were disbanded when the author was absorbed into the Probation Service and full-time prison appointments. A hostel however, had by this time come into existence with the particular support of the then Wood Green Council who had seen the value of the work. The volunteers were referred to the local Tottenham Probation Service as experienced members of the community, one becoming a J.P. Elaine Macdonald was introduced to Holloway Prison for women and served 25 years as a valued voluntary Associate. A particular duty was to convene a sewing group for the women prisoners (following in the steps of Elizabeth Fry, in this respect), combining home visiting to wives and families for the Lady Chancellor Prisoners' Wives organisation.

Mrs. Macdonald was invited to contribute the paper, 'The Tale of the Prisoner's Wife' arising out of her long experience in the prison field and also her involvement with a local Women's Refuge, then its infancy.

FRED'S STORY

MY MIND GOES back to the day when I was coming out of Pentonville. and it's a good many years ago and I'm putting me clothes on and in the top pocket was a card so I looked at this card and on it had "The Discharged Prisoners Aid Society. Mr. Preece would like to see you. Call around any time", so I just put this card away and thought no more about it and off I went back to the East End and back to the old haunts and got boozing again. Anyway, after a few days I was in a state again and was I wondering what to do. I put me hand in my pocket looking for something and I come across this card, so right away my first thought was "I might get something out of this" so I went across over to Stamford Street, to the D.P.A. (Discharged Prisoners Aid) Office and I met you and you made me welcome and had a good talk with me and you said to me "I'd like you to meet some friends of mine". So then you took me to this clinic and it turned out to be an out-patients alcoholic clinic and introduced me to this doctor who was a psychiatist and he had a talk with me for about an hour or so and then you says to me when I came out, "I'd like you to meet another friend of mine". So then you took me and we went over to meet this friend of yours and it turned out to be an alcoholics hostel run by a man called Mr. Smith and the hostel was called St. Luke's. Anyhow, we came out of there and by then, the time was rolling on and it was gone eight o'clock and you pulled up outside the Salvation Army at the Elephant and Castle and you gave me enough money and you said "Now book a bed there and come and see me in the morning".

So I thanked you very much and I couldn't get rid of you quick enough to be quite honest because all I was thinking of was getting to Penny's (a chemist's shop) before they shut, and in them times, they sometimes kept open until 9 o'clock (at night). But anyway, instead of going and booking me bed in the Salvation Army like you told me to, I went over to Penny's and I immediately got three bottles of surgical spirits and I was quite happy. "Anyhow," I thought to meself, "I won't see him again" but how wrong I was.

Anyhow, after a few days I'm in a bit of trouble again and this time I gets a month and I go into Wandsworth, just the usual month and as I'm coming out, there you are at the gates, eight o'clock in the morning and it was a terrible morning. It was cold, windy and snowing so you says to me "Well, why don't you have another try, and to be quite honest, I wasn't bothered and I thought "I'm just not interested. "So anyhow it passed off and time went on. I was back around the Elephant by this time. Started going over there (The South London Elephant and Castle area where homeless alcoholics congregated) and I formed up with a gang who called themselves the 'twilight division' - they were all mates of mine. and it was a matter of just coming out of Wandsworth and hanging about, not living anywhere 'cos no one would have you in anywhere, even if you had the money to pay you couldn't book a bed, you used to get yourself in such a state and the only time you ever got a bed was when you went back to jail and especially when it was cold weather and you didn't mind being in jail, you was better off in jail and you lost all interest in life. But what I couldn't understand was every time I came out you'd be there at the gates no matter what the weather was like so I thought one day "Well there must be something behind this chap. He seems as though he's determined and he's got something and I didn't know what it was but I've learnt since that it was the faith that you'd found and I was wondering if it would ever happen to me.

But you asked me to have another try, so I thought "Well I'm getting nowhere like I am, I will have a try this time". So I went with you and you took me back to Stamford Street and before the day was out, you took me over and got me a bed over in the Salvation Army in Middlesex Street and you gave me some money and you had already given me some clothes to make me look a little bit decent and you told me to come and see you next morning. Well that night I didn't have any drink. In the bedroom where I was in the Salvation Army there was a terrible fight started after the lights had gone out and all the drunks started to come in and I'm laying in this bed and wondering "I wonder if I'll ever make it - I'll not make it under these conditions", so anyway when I went to see you next day I told you that I didn't think that I would be able to carry on and still stay at the Salvation Army hostel in Middlesex Street.

So eventually, after doing a lot of phoning you run me around and you got me a bed in the other Salvation Army hostel over in Westminster which was a bit better and you told me to come and see you in the morning as usual, so I went with you I went to see you the next morning and I told you that it was a bit better there but I'd like to get out of that place as I had a feeling that I couldn't make it under those conditions so you eventually got me into the Church Army at Westminster and it was all right there as it was quiet and they wouldn't allow in anyone who was drunk or had had too much to drink. So I used to come over every morning to see you and you used to keep me a bit busy sending me messages and doing little odd jobs and at the end of the day you would give me a few bob and I'd go back to the Church Army and I thought "Well, this isn't such a bad life". I wasn't drinking and I was getting a bit stronger in health and I remember about that time, it was getting near to Christmas and you used to get me to go with you to collect these toys from different churches and these toys were for the children of people that was in jail and at the Office there was a lot of these W.R.V.S women parcelling these toys up and I used to help them to do this and then we'd go out at night time and you'd take me with you and we'd go round delivering these toys to diffeent homes and I used to realise then, I used to think, "There's something that this fella's got and I wish I had it because of the things you was doing and I realised what a genuine man that you was. Anyhow, I know that in the office where you worked there was a lot of people there, I don't know whether it was jealousy who didn't agree with what you was doing. Well anyhow as time moved on, I managed to get myself a job and I started work for the Savoy, well the Strand Power Company underneath the Savoy. It was a job that I did quite well and after a few weeks I was made a charge hand and everything was going great. And just about this time, you managed to get me a bed in St. Luke's so I went over to St. Luke's to this alcoholic hostel and everything was going fine. and it went on like that for three or four months and then it was getting near the end of the year again and was coming towards Christmas time and I decided to go to Manchester to try and see my daughter or to try and find where my daughter had got to. and what happened? Now I hadn't had a drink for well over six months by then and I felt quite confident.

Anyhow, I got myself down to Manchester, made a few enquiries and I couldn't get to know nothing, and whether I used that as an excuse or not, well anyhow I started drinking again and I was around Manchester for about six weeks until I eventually got back to London and I was in a terrible state and it always seemed to happen like that to me. I'd do a thing and get it well going and then all of a sudden something would happen, I'd go for a few drinks and then everything would be lost again. Well, I used to tell you. You would try to tell me that things would happen differently one day and I even sat down with you in the Salvation Army in Wood Green, at the Mercy Seat, I'll not forget that and asked the Lord to try and help me and seemingly I hadn't done enough to convince the Lord that I required help. Maybe he wanted to punish me in some way for the life that I'd led. That's how I used to look at things. But as usual, I was wrong as I've proved as time's gone on. But anyhow, I musn't go off the story, what I'm trying to say is it was people like you at that period that required help from other sources. You was getting help but not getting enough help. And then the Government decided to take over and help and at that time there was quite a lot of places sprung up. Some of them was genuine and some of them was not, some of them was in it just for what they could get out of it, seemingly and your office was moved from Stamford Steet, the old Discharged Prisoners' Aid Society and it was taken over to Borough High Street and it was given a new name. It was called the Probation and After-Care Service, and it seemed that it was run on different lines to the D.P.A. Anyhow, as I say, with me going to Manchester and making a mess of things, I lost everything and I lost all hope. I couldn't get in touch with my daughter and that was one of the main things I wanted to do and as usual, I'd lost my job at the Savoy and everything, I went drinking. They accepted me back at St. Luke's but that night I went out and had a drink again and Mr. Smith told me that I would have to go and I went and of course, as usual after a few days, I finished up back in Wandsworth, back to the old routine, everything gone once again.

Well, I came out of Wandsworth again, and you came to see me and asked me not to give up and to try again and you said, "Why don't you try over at Wood Green?" So I said "All right, I will do". So you gave me enough to get over to Wood Green and at that time you hadn't got an office in the prison, you were only allowed to meet prisoners by arrangement in the prison but as I say, with the Government taking over, things had altered later on and you was given an office inside of the jail where the time that I'm talking about, you had to meet everybody outside the jail in all sorts of weather and you was always there, 8 o'clock in the morning, you could guarantee it. Well anyhow, I went over to Wood Green and you'd got me fixed up in a kind of boarding house, a rough place it was, but anyhow, it was a bed and it was a start and while I was over there, I didn't have any drink, and I got a job. I went property repairing and things went fine. I moved out of this boarding house and I got my own room and I had a decent place and I wasn't drinking. Little by little, you got different lads who you was helping because you wasn't only helping me, you was helping dozens and dozens of lads and there was quite a few of us over at Wood Green. So then you decided that you'd try to form some kind of a club to try and help each other. At that period you used to go around selling War Crys for the Salvation Army and you got friendly with this publican in the Kings Arms who kindly let you have a room upstairs.

A funny place to hold meetings for the likes of us, all ex-drunks, anyhow, we had this room upstairs and we used to meet once a week so we decided to form this club and we called it the 'Wayfarers' and we formed a committee and I was elected chairman and anyhow, the next week I turned up and you was there and I think Lawrie Gardner was there and that was all, so

I said "Where's the committee?" and you says to me "Well, they are all in jail". Well, I'll not forget that". But instead of it putting you off it seemed as though it made you more determined and you was quite right because it wasn't long after that you got things organised again and you'd got a thing going at the Salvation Army in Wood Green again where after service you used to hold a kind of tea party on a Sunday afternoon where the lads that was over there could meet and talk and there was always tea and cakes and everybody seemed to enjoy it.

But it wasn't long before I went over to the Elephant and Castle one day and I started to have a drink and that was the beginning of the end. I finished up getting told to leave my room that I had. I lost all my clothes, got robbed and finished up eventually after a couple of days in jail again, back to Wandsworth, right back from where I started. By then, I thought "Well, I've tried, I've done this, I've done that and I thought well surely no one will be interested in me again but that wasn't to be, because by then you was given an office inside of Wandsworth and you used to send for me now and again or come and see me and have a talk with me. I think I'd just given up. I just didn't want to know and I used to say sometimes to you "Well, I'm sorry but you are only wasting your time with me, I just don't think that I'll ever be able to make it because I can go so far but seemingly I can't go the whole distance". And you did try and encourage me to take religion a bit more seriously than I did. I wasn't an atheist, I did used to believe but I think that it was only because I had been brought up that way. I didn't seem to be able to grasp the feeling that you must have and it used to puzzle me how you used to have so much faith in the thing that you was doing. Well, I have learnt since, Thank God, what faith can really mean to a person and how lucky I am to be able to say that I really and honestly believe that there is a Lord and he watches and looks after us in his own way because I've got proof of it and I only wish that I could explain myself a little better than I do and I know the feeling that you must have, now but I didn't at the time.

Well anyhow, as I say for quite a long time, I didn't want to know. I just used to go out go back to the Elephant and Castle. I was lucky if I'd be out for a week, maybe it would last for two or three days and it went on like that for months until one day I began to think, "Well, I wish I could finish and not have to go through all this suffering, because you was suffering while you were outside and you was suffering while you was inside. You just didn't know where you was. Well anyhow, it's funny how it happened to me, this faith. I know that I was on Waterloo where I used to go. I used to sit on the steps begging, and I had nowhere to go this night and it was the Simon Community which used to go around with tea and buns and a fella called

Anthony Wally Clifford said to me "Do you want a bed for the night?" and I thought "Well, it's a cold night" and he took me over to their place. So the next day, they decided to send all the people away from there that was called residents and just have that as an office and he asked me would I like to go to Oxford.

Well, I didn't care where I went, I just wanted to get out of London. I thought that there was that chance out of London, that I'd tried everything else, so I came to Oxford and I went into hospital at Oxford and I came from out of the hospital back to the hostel which was in 81, Cowley Road and met a fellow there called David Brown. But anyhow, Charlie, that's another story, I'm just telling you how I came to find my faith. Anyhow, I just decided to try and help David as much as I could so I became his assistant and I was virtually running the hostel at the finish. Well, anyhow, I got fed up with it all and I went out, back to Manchester one day and I came back and I was really out of me mind for about three weeks and they decided, did Dave to take me into the country into Somerset to a friend of his that had a house there and after a couple of days, I woke up and it was in the early hours of the morning and the room was just brilliantly lit up.

It was a marvellous experience and I only wish that I could describe what I actually seen and how I actually felt at that time. Anyhow I know that I got up next morning and I went down and I says to David and his friend, "Something happened to me during the early hours of this morning". I says "I feel a new man". I said "I just feel as though I want to go out and do as much good for people as I possibly can. It's a marvellous feeling". Anyhow, this feeling kept with me and we came back to Oxford and I just couldn't do enough for people. I didn't want to go to bed, I wanted to be up all the time, doing something, trying to help somebody and I was beginning to wonder how long this feeling would last. Well after about three or four weeks and during this time, I'd spoken to a lot of people about it, priests and a nun that used to come to the house and they all said that I'd had a vision. And from then on, everything seemed to go right for me because it wasn't long afterwards that we opened a new hostel to which I went.

One day, the bell rung and I went to answer the door, thinking it was someone tring to get in and there was a young fellow stood there, a big six foot lad and he said "Is your name Mr. Aldred?" I said "Yes". "Well" he said "I'm your son". I could have fell through the floor. I hadn't seen him since he was a little boy, three years old. Anyhow, I made him welcome of course and he stayed for a week and went back to Manchester and it wasn't long afterwards that I gets a letter from my daughter whom I hadn't seen for 18 years or heard of and she told me she was coming over from Canada to see me and as I say, everything just fitted into place and I know now how strong your faith is and that's why I've told you this little story so that it will make you understand that I understand now how you feel, but I didn't understand at the time. This isn't my life story. I'm just doing this or saying these things to try and help you to fill in some of the blanks as you've asked me to do.

Many years ago, the public used to think that an alcoholic was just something that wanted to be kept out of sight, kind of, that jail was the best place for him and there was very few people ever thought of trying to help those people and it was only people like you and a few more and I'm going back a long while, it's getting on for 20 years ago and now the average public, well, they do understand that it's a problem and it's a medical problem.

Well anyhow, my mind goes back to some of the lads that you did try and help and at that period, you took anybody, it didn't matter who it was, you'd try and help them in some way and give them a chance. It was up to them to take that chance when you gave it to them and another thing, you didn't used to go half way. If you decided to try and help this person you would go the full distance, you wouldn't go so far and then drop it. You kept carrying on until it was the person himself who gave up in the end because you never gave up and my mind goes back to some of the lads you did try to help that's not with us today as the most of them have died.

There's one thought that you must keep with you that for a short while if it was only a short while in some cases, you did give them a bit of happiness. Anyhow, my mind goes back to Jimmy Howlett. Now Jim was a lad - well you could write a book about some of the things that he used to get up to and I remember him once telling me a funny story, it was to me anyway, one of his many because, knowing Jimmy, in drink he was a terrible man, a violent man but underneath all that, when he was sober, he was just an ordinary fella, a kind-hearted fella because I've been in jail with him many, many times.

Anyway, this story is about Jim and one night he was coming off Waterloo station, late on and it was a terrible foggy night. You could hardly see your hand in front of you so Jim decided that he would go to jail for the night and get a bed so just outside of Waterloo station is a police box and there was a young policeman there so Jim goes up to him and starts acting the fool doing all sorts of things, making the policeman arrest him. As Jim was not really drunk, he was only half-drunk. Anyhow, this policeman arrested him and took him into the box and he could hear him ringing up on the telephone to the police station. And the policeman is saying "Will you bring the van around, I've got a person here that we'll have to put inside". Jim can hear the sergeant from the police station saying to the constable "Well can't you walk him around here, it's too bad to bring the van out, on a night like this." And Jimmy hears this, so Jummy immediately flops on the floor and he can hear the young policeman saying to the sergeant "I can't. I can't lift him up - he's on the floor! You'll have to get the van out. And of course, eventually, he did bring the van out after all the trouble. And Jim got into jail and he was happy. But that's only one of the many tales.

I remember another where he told me that he was in Walworth Road and he called in at the butchers to see if he could beg some meat. So Jim sees a big piece of steak on the counter so he does no more but grabs hold of this steak, stuffs it up his shirt and runs out of the shop and the butcher seeing him and there's the butcher chasing Jim down the Walworth Road. Well, needless to say, he caught Jim and Jim got another month for that. But that's only one of the tales. And some of the people, you remember. There was Moira and Ernie , they was a couple that you did everything to try and help, and many many more. Do you remember 'Larry the Lamb?' He died on Waterloo Station. And when you come to think back, most of the lads either died in tragic circumstances. Some got killed, some got run over, some were even murdered and it makes you think and wonder why these things had to happen. But you could only do what you did and as I've just said, you must feel a little bit of satisfaction that you did give everybody a chance.

Mickey Clark was another lad and still around today, seemingly. He was a good lad. Most of these chaps, all supposed to be hard nuts, hard cases, hindering, but when you met them all sober, talked to them sober and the mind was clear, you, yourself must have realised that they was all decent chaps but anyhow, I only wish that they could have grasped what I have today but when you first got to know these people they was past all caring, they just wanted to die as easily and quickly as they could because none of them seemed to have much to live for.

It must have been very hard for you at times and I know that you put some hours in. You was at it from morning til night, seven days a week, even on a Sunday, you'd have quite a lot to do in this field of helping people and I know that one time when I was staying at St. Luke's, I was asked to go to a big meeting in Camberwell where there was magistrates, quite a lot of doctors, all influential people and they had also invited a lot of people, well a few people who had been off drink for a certain period, to go to this meeting and they was allowed to take a friend with them and I asked you if you would like to come and you said you would. Well, we got to the meeting in Camberwell and it was quite packed with all these influential people and they decided to form some kind of a committee and you was elected on that committee.

That was adding yet another burden to your already overworked schedule but you took it on and I often wondered how you kept going with all the work that you had to do and I think that I remember once talking to you about this and telling you that you was going to make yourself ill with all this work, overwork. I saw that I was talking to you about people that you must have been disappointed in, myself included at times and you turned around to me and said, "If I can help only one peron, with all the effort and work that I try to put into this thing I'll be quite happy. I'll feel as though I've done something, and it will all have been worthwhile."

'Beery Docherty' was another lad that you tried to help and 'Beery' almost made it but unfortunately he died over the East side. 'Big Henry', he was a good fella, they were all good fellas and what you said hit me a bit mad at times, especially that time when the government decided to step in and help. These government officials. It must have been very worrying for you 'cos I remember one time that you must have been upset by these people because the problem with them was that they wanted instant things doing, they wanted numbers, they didn't seem interested in the type of person that you was dealing with, all that they was interested in was numbers and this must have upset you because I remember you coming to me when I was in Wandswoth and was doing the usual month and you came into my cell and says to me "Well, I have a bit of a problem and you said would I be willing to meet some people outside when I came out and to ask Mickey Clark who was in with me and as many people as was going out that morning to talk to some reporters. So you paid the remainder of our fine, Mickey's and myself and we came out that morning and you had some reporters who was there and we spoke to them and you had the van there and there was tea and buns going and I felt sorry for you that morning because I knew how hard you had been working and how hard it must have been for you to convince these government officials that you just couldn't do this thing in numbers.

Anyhow, you didn't give up, you persevered and you won through eventually but it's all right talking now, I mean, the public today, they understand, well, a lot of them understand the problem. Things seem to be run differently these days, I mean a person today is selected, is sent to a hospital and is even selected to go to a hostel and if the person running the hostel doesn't seem to fancy him, he just doesn't get in. Well, it's not the way that you would like to work things or that you ever did try to work things like that and it didn't matter what his circumstances was you was always there ready to help.

Do you remember Jimmy Campbell?1 He was a bit of a comedian. You know Jimmy, he used to be in the 'skipper' and he always used to be saying

'I'm Jimmy Campbell. I can drink and I can fight'. Anyway, we are all sitting there in the 'skipper' one morning and the police came in. A policeman said "Who's Jimmy Campbell?" and Jimmy Campbell jumps up "I'm Jimmy Cambell!" "Right" says the policeman "We've got a warrant for you" and of course they took Jimmy away and gave him a month. But that was someat, I mean, knocking around with the lads, even though it was rough at times, we used to get many a laugh. It wasn't all gloom especially when the beer was flowing, I'm saying 'beer', they didn't drink beer, it was always surgical spirits and wine but it was funny at times.

I remember being with a couple of blokes and we was just behind this hoarding, well, it was like a woodyard and we lit a little fire and it was no bigger, than, well it wouldn't have boiled a kettle of water and the next thing, the fire engines's there, breaking through the boards and hose pipes all over the place. It wasn't always serious like we seem to think, it's like anything else it's like when you was in the Army, you didn't think of the bad things, you always thought of the good things and the laughs that you used to have, I suppose that you felt like that at times when you was in the service.

Do you remember 'Tyrone'? He was another one. Every time you'd seen him, he had a black eye and then there was 'Pin-Head Murphy'. He unfortunately got stabbed on the steps of the Union Jack Club and he died on the steps at Waterloo and there was another one called Mickey Clarke and I believe he's still around, but talking about Mickey I remember that one time we was sleeping in the graveyard right facing Waterloo Station and I lay at one side of the place and Mickey and this other lad lay on the other side. Anyhow, during the night, I thought that I'd imagined this, I seen like a big white cloud floating about and well, to me it seemed like a ghost but it didn't worry me. Anyhow , I'm talking to Mickey about this the next morning and he says to me "Well, you know last night, this lad, he had 'the rats' during the night, the D.T.s and they was both pretty strong Catholics and Mickey and him was saying a prayer and I've often wondered since if this cloud that was floating about or this ghost as I thought had anything to do with it because he said that after they'd said the prayer together to try and bring this lad back and think a bit more normal, he seemed to settle down and sleep peacefully. So thinking back along these lines it makes me think that there was somebody watching us all the time and that's why I think that Mickey will eventually come through this and overcome the problem. I hope so anyhow.

Author's note [1]:- I had been sent about this time, in 1964 by the Officer in charge of the Salvation Army Harbour Light Centre, Chicago, what I felt was a classic study SKID ROW IN AMERICAN CITIES, by Dr. Donald J. Bogue.

Published by The Community and Family Study Centre, University of Chicago, 1963. This substantial and authoritative work provided me with, what, I felt, was the academic and medical background for my own very basic model of what had been evaluated and proven in the United States of America. It gave me the confidence, when little else was on offer, 37 years' ago, to persevere with our own WAYFARER project in particular. This later in the Crown Court setting was an alternative to imprisonment in the case of alcoholics before the courts for more serious offences and facing long sentences.

Mother Shepherd the Salvationist. From a watercolour by Goronwy Owen, 1999.

"She always had a nice piece of lace about her neck, and a red shawl, looking like a soldier" recalled the young woman who had described her as "Mawreddog' ('Noble") when she walked around Aberdare on her continual visits.

It was the need for information and photographs of Mother Shepherd that provided the introduction to Aberdare Spinners, the makers of the book and the Cynon Valley Millennium Tapestries, through our old friends the Cynon Valley History Society. We might otherwise not have met and this book not seen the light of day in its present form.

Just another instance of how the influence of Mother Shepherd has reached out and continued to create an extended family to the present day. I feel often that no one ever came into a sense of personal contact with her and her story, even though simply reading or hearing about her without their lives being touched and enriched to the point of spiritual kinship. "My Mother too!' as Phoebe Paxford declared.

Sadly Goronwy, or 'Ron' as he was known, former RAF and veteran jungle survival instructor and Senior NCO died suddenly while the book was being completed. 'Ron' was due to exhibit his acclaimed work as a local painter and Cynon Valley Millenium Tapestry artist at the new Aberdare Museum and as a tribute to this delightful man, his friends Joan and Bourke Le Carpentier are ensuring that this still takes place as he had planned. "Well done Ron."

GORONWY OWEN

The Cynon Valley Millennium Tapestry Project and Travels With Alice
A personal salute from the Author, Charles A Preece.

It was Goronwy's research for detail in his work on the Cynon Valley Millennium Tapestries that strangely brought Alice and I, in 1999 into friendship with both Ron as he was known, and Bourke Le Carpentier at Joan and Bourke's home in Abernant.

Ron was working on a portrait of Mother Shepherd for a tapestry panel to compliment one depicting Gwen Obern as two of the Valley's outstanding women and was wanting any photographs which might help in his portrait.

Through our mutual friends, at the Cynon Valley History Society, I was asked to contact Aberdare Spinners and found myself and Alice, one day in the spacious studio at Cartref where I was amazed to see the work in progress on the tapestries. Little did I know that the publication of TRAVELS WITH ALICE was also to come, providentially, in large part from this home.

It was a thrilling experience and I warmed to the company of Ron, Joan and Bourke, their several skills and commitment. It led to providing photographs from the archives which Aberdare residents had kindly given me over the years and for deep ranging conversations about my great-grandmother, Mother Shepherd. I am sure that she and Gwen Obern would have been great friends too.

Ron managed to capture something beyond what was in the photographs, true as these were. That wonderful look of compassion, love, and care in her deep-seeing eyes, came through in an amazing way. Ron has bequeathed us something very special. He was going to contribute more of his art to the book. One was to be a watercolour of a pathway, which led to the painting on the front cover,

During our very real travels, Alice and I found our lives greatly enriched by many people. Ron was one of them. A deeply spiritual man, expressing his faith through his artistry and gracious personality. We were glad that we were able to see him in Prince Charles Hospital and share a prayer, before he shortly set off to climb his own pathway to meet the greatest Artist of all.

172

Appendix III

From the Daily Telegraph Colour Supplement, Friday 25th February 1966

One Man's campaign to help
BOMB SITE ALCOHOLICS

CALLED "THE RAMP", this bomb site in Whitechapel is a regular haunt of meths drinkers. Ironically, a police station is to be built on it

In an old ironmonger's shop due for demolition, a Billy Graham convert has set up a centre for homeless alcoholics, especially ex-prisoners and the raw-spirit addicts living on London's bomb-sites. To get help, an alcoholic has to prove he really wants it.

REPORT BY KENNETH MARTIN
PHOTOGRAPHS BY MICHAEL HARDY

WAYFARER HOUSE IS two rooms on the ground floor of a house in Wood Green High Road, North London, due for demolition in four years' time. It used to be an ironmonger's shop. Now it is the first centre in Britain dedicated to curing the homeless, hopeless alcoholics whom other centres regard as unsuitable for treatment.

The men who come here are mainly the alcoholics who have just been released from prison, particularly the raw-spirit drinkers.

IN LONDON THERE are at least 1,000 of these "jake drinkers".

The windows at Wayfarer House are hung with anti-drink posters and typewritten lists giving instructions on what to do if you have no place to sleep, no money or shoes or food - information, for instance, on the one place in London where a man can turn up and expect a bed for nothing: The National Assistance Board Reception Centre, Consort Road, London, SE15.

Wayfarer House was started on January 1 last year and is open six nights a week from 7.30 to 9.30. So far 200 alcoholics have passed through its doors, six of them women.

CHARLES PREECE, right, meets prisoners as they are released and tries to persuade those he thinks he can help to come to Wayfarer House. One-third of men in jail, he says, are there because of drink

Now Charles Preece, a welfare officer from Wandsworth Prison who runs the centre, has also been given a whole house in Wood Green High Road by the Haringey Borough Council. It too is due for demolition in four years, and it has a hole in the roof. But soon it will be ready as a hostel to sleep 12 men while they are rehabilitated. The Home Office has promised to refer all the alcoholic prisoners released from Springhill open prison to the Wayfarers Hostel.

Preece is 45, a miner's son born in Glamorganshire. He moved to London when he left school in, 1937 and served an engineering apprenticeship. After the war he ran his own small business for seven years. In 1945 he married a girl he met in a cycling club. They have three daughters.

Preece was converted to Christianity at a Billy Graham meeting in Glasgow in March 1955. He still goes to a Salvation Army meeting on Sunday mornings and evenings.

After he was converted, he went to night classes at Bible colleges for four years and began to do voluntary prison visiting because "I wanted to do something which was more help to my fellow men than being in business". In 1960 he became a full-time welfare officer for the Royal London Prisoners' Aid Society.

His day begins at 7.30 a.m. when he meets released prisoners at Wandsworth Prison. He is often accompanied by a voluntary helper from Wayfarer House. They give the ex-prisoners a cup of tea and a roll and a list of accommodation.

If the prisoner is an alcoholic it is not easy for him to find work. But a proven desire to help himself is the essential requirement Wayfarer House demands from a man before it will help him. Preece will then try to find him a job. The most readily available is kitchen work.

Meanwhile, Wayfarer House provides clothes, meal vouchers, an appointment with a local doctor to discuss prescribing Antabuse or Disulfiram. Most of all, Wayfarer House is somewhere to go at night, every night for months on end if necessary. It doesn't push religion. What it really offers is friendship.

The grim battle against drink began in a room over a pub

That phrase, and the amateur cosiness of some of its manifestations at Wayfarer House and other voluntary social work centres, makes me cringe. But I have never been an alcoholic.

Preece's manner, is permanently tired but very patient, with a great reserve of energy to draw on!

"When I started work with the Royal London Prisoners' Aid Society, the worse part was dealing with the begging of the people we simply called drunks. They smelt sickeningly of surgical spirit, their faces were often black from the smoke of camp fires. They were so foul we had to open the windows and spray the room after they left

We gave them half a crown to get rid of them so we could get on with more rewarding cases. We knew we weren't helping but there seemed nothing else to do."

He began the Wayfarer House plan in June 1963 in a little room over a pub near his home at Wood Green. When he suggested it the landlord thought he was joking.

"For the first meeting at the pub Laurie Gardner, an electrical contractor, and I turned up with a dozen ham rolls and a primus stove to make the tea. We'd written to half a dozen men I'd met at Wandsworth. That day 12 men turned up. We just sat and talked. We were very much feeling our way. We didn't know what facilities there were available to help the men."

In fact the facilities were almost non-existent, and still are.

After a year the Kings Arms changed landlords. One night a drunk went berserk.

For six months Preece held his meetings in a hall run by a mission which calls itself The Brethren and whose members had helped him at the pub. In October 1964 Mrs Joyce Butler, MP for Wood Green, arranged a meeting with the Town Clerk. A month later Preece was promised Wayfarer House - in a road due for demolition. The rent is free. Rates are £50 a year.

The first caller on January 1 was Big Fred, a bricklayer who had also been the first caller at the Kings Arms.

He was the first man whose alcoholism Preece believed he had arrested. During the first year at the Kings Arms Big Fred got a good job, saved money and stayed sober. Last year he stopped coming to the new centre, began drinking again through loneliness and is now in prison.

Wayfarer House has 12 regular helpers - a doctor's wife, a lorry driver, sweet salesman, clerk, accountant, cook, company secretary, typists, housewives.

Some nights two alcoholics will turn up and there will be seven or eight helpers. Other nights there have been two helpers and 30 alcoholics.

WAYFARER HOUSE began its fight against alcoholism in a room over a pub. It moved to its present quarters, above, in 1965. Preece was given the shop rent-free, but it will be demolished in 1970

To put a newcomer at ease, the helper first offers him a tin of tobacco to roll himself a cigarette, which seemed to me, a non-smoker, a little out of date. If possible, the first time a man comes the helper tries to fill in a form with details of his circumstances and what kind of help should have priority. If an alcoholic turns up really drunk, he may be fed and allowed to sit down while he sobers up. Then he is told that if he wants help he had better come back sober another night.

Andy, resplendent in a Fair-Isle pullover, hands round cups of coffee and tea and plates of biscuits, looking thoroughly ill at ease. He is big and rough and seems ashamed of looking soft. He is 35. He has been stinking drunk most of his life from the age of 17, when he was in the RAF. Until he met Preece the longest he had been out of prison since 1947 was seven months.

"I just got sick of it," he said. "I looked at the meths drinkers in the prison. Here you are, I said, you have no friends, nobody wants to know you, another ten or 15 years and you'll be like one of them.

In 12 months, six cures

PREECE TALKS to three men who visit Wayfarer House regularly from a hospital in Tooting Bec. Preece, who became a Christian during Billy Graham's 1955 crusade, is a full-time prison welfare officer

The Wandsworth doctor introduced me to Mr Preece. I went on a course of the tablets in the prison to see the effect they had. I'm on Disulfiram. Antabuse makes me groggy. Then before I came out they gave me a couple of bottles of beer to show me what would happen if I ever drank on top of the pills. I was as sick as a dog.

I spend all my time here now, helping the other lads."

The problem confronting everyone dealing with alcoholism is that when the disease has been arrested the alcoholic has to survive alone in the same world which previously defeated him. The answer is probably that it is better for most alcoholics not even to try.

During the first year at Wayfarer House, Preece has probably cured only six men, three of them off the bomb sites. All six spend most of their free time working at the centre.

I seems that the surest way most ex-alcoholics can stay sober is to go on helping alcoholics, which is why centres like Wayfarer House could snowball from small beginnings, why they are probably the most practical means of treatment and why Preece, would like to see a Wayfarer House in every town in the country.

He claims that drink is the precipitating factor causing at least one-third of prison sentences (the prison population is 30,000).

"Say it costs £500 year to keep each man or woman," says Preece. 'If they were put on probation under medical supervision the country would save, £5 million a year." The figure, like the man, is optimistic. "A whole army of social workers would be needed to supervise the men on probation," he goes on. "This is where centres like Wayfarer House come in.

The average caseload of probation officer is 50. In my year at Wayfarer House, working only two hours a night, I've managed to multiply that number by four, using the help of unpaid, untrained volunteers, many of them ex-alcoholics.

All you have to do is put up a sign in every court and prison in the country: Come to Warfarer House. But first there has to be a Wayfarer House. Just a room like this."

The idea of using voluntary, help under the guidance of trained workers is in line with the most modern thinking in the social services.

Even if Preece's scheme achieved a small fraction of what he claims for it the results would be far-reaching. ***No one has thought of anything cheaper.***

Words & pictures by courtesy of the Daily Telegraph

Alice at Pengellifach Farm, Vaynor, near Merthyr Tydfil.* The Brecon Beacons in the background. Pen-y-fan, the highest point in South Wales, being just visible.

* *Our base for much of the field work in the Rhondda and Cynon Valleys.*

Appendix IV

THE ELEMENT OF COMPLIANCE IN TREATING ALCHOLIC OFFENDERS

Reprinted from *THE ALLIANCE NEWS* July/August 1981

A N ARTICLE DEALING with Compliance in the Treatment of Alcohol-Dependent Individuals1 from the Conservation of Manpower Unit in London, is not only timely but of considerable importance to legal practitioners, probation officers, social workers and the public at large who may not in the ordinary way be familiar with the journal in which the article was published, nor the work of this Unit or the implications in the world of reality that its work has in the rising tide of alcoholism.

As a liaison court probation officer, I would like to deal with some of the reservations which have been expressed as to the use of court orders in an endeavour to secure compliance. This may genuinely trouble those who are sensitive to what appears to be enforcement of treatment by the courts for alcohol-related offenders who are alcohol-dependent while those who show such concern may also question the ethical aspects of such action.

REFUSE

The fact that a man or woman has at all times the right to refuse the offer of treatment should surely allay any fears of those who may question this line of approach. The making of a traditional form of probation order itself requires in law the acceptance in open court of its terms which may already include the willingness to submit to medically prescribed treatment. It is the sheer practical matter of providing such treatment effectively and not its legality or even its hitherto unquestioned natural justice, that has prevented probation orders in particular from proving the effective instruments of management and control of alcohol-dependent offenders in the community which the courts might wish them to be.

Community Service, which is frequently one of the Probation Service's recommendations as an alternative to imprisonment, has developed a robust and firm attitude, requiring compliance in attendance and application from those clients who would otherwise be appropriately serving a prison